T0318787

Etienne Balibar

London: NLB

Atlantic Highlands: HUMANITIES PRESS

On the Dictatorship
of the Proletariat

Introduction by Grahame Lock

Afterword by Louis Althusser

Translated by Grahame Lock

Library of Congress Cataloging in Publication Data
  Balibar, Etienne.
    On the dictatorship of the proletariat.
    Translation of Sur la dictature du prolétariat.
    Includes index.
    1. Dictatorship of the proletariat. I. Title.
  JC474.B3413   1977   321.9'4   77-4068

  ISBN: 978-0-902308-59-6

First published as *Sur La Dictature du Prolétariat*
by François Maspero, 1976

© François Maspero, 1976

This edition first published 1977

© NLB, 1977

Filmset in Monophoto Plantin by
Servis Filmsetting Ltd, Manchester

Printed in Great Britain by
Unwin Brothers Ltd, The Gresham Press, Old Woking, Surrey

NLB, 7 Carlisle Street, London W1

ISBN: 978-0-902-30859-6

Contents

Introduction to the English Edition by Grahame Lock   7

Foreword   34

I. Paris (1976)–Moscow (1936)   38
'Dictatorship or Democracy'   38
Three Simple and False Ideas   42
A Precedent: 1936   49

II. Lenin's Three Theoretical Arguments about the Dictatorship of the Proletariat   58

III. What is State Power?   64
Marxism and Bourgeois Legal Ideology   66
Has the Proletariat Disappeared?   77

IV. The Destruction of the State Apparatus   88
The Opportunist Deviation   88
The Organization of Class Rule   93
What Has to be 'Destroyed'   99
The Main Aspect of the Dictatorship of the Proletariat   111

V. Socialism and Communism   124
The Historical Tendency to the Dictatorship of the Proletariat   133
What is Socialism?   139
The Real 'Problems of Leninism'   146

A Few Words in Conclusion   154

**Dossier – Extracts from the Pre-Congress Debate
and the Proceedings of the 22nd Congress of the
French Communist Party (January–February 1976)**   157

Georges Haddad   *On the Question of the Dictatorship of
the Proletariat*   159

Georges Marchais   *Liberty and Socialism*   161

Georges Marchais   *Ten Questions, Ten Answers to
Convince the Listener*   165

Etienne Balibar   *On the Dictatorship of the Proletariat*   168

Guy Besse   *On the Dictatorship of the Proletariat
(Reply to Etienne Balibar)*   175

Georges Marchais   *In Order to Take Democracy Forward
to Socialism, Two Questions are Decisive*   182

**Louis Althusser: The Historic Significance
of the 22nd Congress**   193

**Etienne Balibar: Postscript to the
English Edition**   212

Index   235

Introduction to the English Edition

'I think that it is out of place to go around shouting that this or that is real Leninism. I was recently re-reading the first chapters of *The State and Revolution* [. . .] Lenin wrote: "What is now happening to Marx's theory has, in the course of history, happened repeatedly to the theories of great revolutionary thinkers [. . .] Attempts are made to convert them into harmless icons, to canonize them, so to say, and to hallow their *names* [...] while at the same time robbing the revolutionary theory of its *substance*." I think that this bitter quotation obliges us not to hide such-and-such of our conceptions behind the label of Leninism, but to get to the root of all questions. [. . .] For us, as Marxists, truth is what corresponds to reality. Vladimir Ilyich used to say: Marx's teaching is all-powerful because it is true. [. . .] The task of our Congress must be to seek for and to find the correct line. [. . .] Bukharin has declared here with great emphasis that what the Congress decides will be correct. Every Bolshevik accepts the decisions of the Congress as binding, but we must not adopt the viewpoint of the English constitutional expert who took literally the popular English saying to the effect that Parliament can decide anything, even to change a man into a woman.'

N. Krupskaya-Lenin, *Speech to the 14th All-Union Communist Party Congress*, 1925.[1]

No-one and nothing, not even the Congress of a Communist Party, can abolish the dictatorship of the proletariat. That is the

[1] Quoted by J.-M. Gayman, 'Les Débats au sein du parti bolchevik (1925–1928)', in *Cahiers de l'Institut Maurice Thorez*, 1976, p. 311.

most important conclusion of Etienne Balibar's book. The reason
is that the dictatorship of the proletariat is not a *policy* or a
strategy involving the establishment of a particular *form of government or institutions* but, on the contrary, an *historical reality*. More
exactly, it is a reality which has its roots in capitalism itself, and
which covers the whole of the transition period to communism,
'the reality of a historical tendency', a tendency which begins to
develop *within capitalism itself*, in struggle against it (ch. 5). It is
not 'one possible path of transition to socialism', a path which can
or must be 'chosen' under certain historical conditions (e.g., in the
'backward' Russia of 1917) but can be rejected for another, different 'choice', for the 'democratic' path, in politically and indus-
trially 'advanced' Western Europe. It is not a matter of choice, a
matter of policy: and it therefore cannot be 'abandoned', any more
than the class struggle can be 'abandoned', except in words and at
the cost of enormous confusion.

Balibar spells out the reasons for this conclusion against the
background of the 22nd Congress of the French Communist Party,
which decided to 'drop' the aim of the dictatorship of the proletariat
and to substitute the objective of a 'democratic' road to socialism.
His concrete references are therefore usually to arguments put
forward within the French Party. But it is quite obvious that the
significance of the book is much wider, not least because, in spite
of the important political and economic differences separating the
nations of Western Europe, many of their Communist Parties are
evolving in an apparently similar ideological direction, and indeed
appear to be borrowing arguments from one another in support
of their new positions.

Yet in spite of these remarks, it is likely that the very idea of a
debate on the 'dictatorship of the proletariat' may appear to many
outlandish in the British situation. A book that argues, against the
current, *for the necessity of the dictatorship of the proletariat* might
therefore at first sight appear to border on the bizarre. For is it not
at best a sign of eccentricity to invoke such an argument in a
country without even a powerful Marxist presence in the labour
movement, let alone a mighty revolutionary Party, and where the
traditions of parliamentary government and so-called political
moderation are so overwhelmingly strong? And if – as the French,
Italian, Spanish, Portuguese and Japanese Communist Parties,
among others, believe – there are in any case good reasons from a

Marxist point of view for *abandoning* the dictatorship of the proletariat, then what possible reason could any British Communist have for disagreeing?

But not only is the term *dictatorship of the proletariat* apparently old-fashioned and out-of-date; it is also *distasteful*. For how can the Left condemn the 'dictatorships' in Chile or Argentina, Iran or South Korea, etc., while proposing to instal its own dictatorship? And if the term *dictatorship* is unpleasant, its partner – *proletariat* – is seemingly plainly absurd (just try suggesting to a British factory worker that he is a 'proletarian' . . .). It is therefore easy to imagine the relief with which Communists in Britain, perhaps even more than elsewhere, have learned that the abandonment of the dictatorship of the proletariat is on the agenda here, too (in the land where Karl Marx 'invented' it).

If only things were so simple! But, unfortunately, they are not; and this book indicates at least some of the reasons why. It is not intended to resolve all the questions which it raises, but to contribute towards a *genuine debate* on these questions. This theoretical debate must take place, and it will necessarily be international in character, though of course it cannot and must not be regarded as an opportunity for any side to interfere in the decisions of another, foreign Communist Party.

In spite of the major differences distinguishing the States of Western Europe, it is impossible, as I pointed out, not to have noticed that their Communist Parties have in many cases recently come to similar conclusions about the need to modify certain practical and theoretical positions which they have previously defended. This phenomenon has been dubbed as the birth of 'Euro-communism', for reasons which are perhaps not as transparent as they might seem. In any case, these Parties have in general now taken up positions which have brought them into conflict with the Soviet Union on a number of important points, some concerning questions of 'freedom' and 'human rights', etc. It has therefore been possible for commentators to conclude that there are now two different brands of communism in Europe: the 'Western' and 'Eastern' varieties.[2] In consequence it has been widely assumed that any debate on fundamental questions like

---

[2] The actual situation is rather more complicated, since e.g. the West German and Portuguese Communist Parties are generally regarded, correctly or not, as belonging from the doctrinal standpoint to the 'Eastern' group.

that of the *dictatorship of the proletariat* is basically a debate *between parties* of the two types – e.g. between the French and British Parties (etc.) on the one side and the Soviet and Hungarian Parties (etc.) on the other. Two remarks are called for in this connexion.

First, this way of presenting the question suggests, wrongly, that there exist only two alternatives: *either* the rejection of the concept of the dictatorship of the proletariat and the adoption of a 'democratic interpretation' of socialism *or* uncritical acceptance of the Soviet position and of its own brand of the concept; and

Second, it raises the question: if the time is past when there was one single model of socialism – the Soviet model – accepted by all Communist Parties, then must the time not also be past when there can be one, single 'Western' model of socialism – e.g. the so-called 'Euro-communist' model – to be not only automatically adopted by all West European Communist Parties but also, without further debate, by every single one of their members? Is the old dogmatism to be rejected simply in order to be replaced by a new one?

Of course, the reader might, in leafing through this book and noting the frequency of the references to and quotes from Lenin, conclude that, in any case, the author is himself actually imprisoned in a form of the old dogmatism, since he is unable to break with the nostalgic past of the Russian Revolution. He might even conclude that the book is simply an attempt to draw a direct and therefore mechanical comparison between Lenin on the one hand and present-day 'official' Communist theory on the other, to the detriment of the latter. But that is by no means the intention, for two very important reasons:

(1) It is absolutely true, as the opponents of the dictatorship of the proletariat claim, that the world has 'moved on' since Lenin's day. It would certainly be absurd to try to find all the answers to present-day problems in Lenin. The question is, however: *how* has it moved? *What* has changed? And in this connexion what is remarkable is the extent to which the 'new' arguments deployed by these opponents of the dictatorship of the proletariat are actually *very old*, dating from the beginning of this century or even from the last century, and that they were already, sixty years ago, subjected to withering criticism by Lenin. That being so, it would be foolish *not* to refer back to Lenin's arguments.

(2) The second reason is that Lenin was not always right, *even in his own time*. It is rather bizarre, in fact, to see how those very same Marxists who assure us that Lenin's arguments are now out-of-date (or, to use that special philosophical language which has got Marxists out of so many tight corners, that they have been 'transcended by history') at the same time so often assume or insist that, *for his own epoch*, his positions were always entirely correct – which is of course, paradoxically, actually a way[3] of attacking Leninism by explaining that, though not false, it is of 'historically limited' relevance. Lenin is canonized, his name is hallowed in order to make it all the easier to 'rob his revolutionary theory of its substance'.

In one of the best books published on the subject for a long time,[4] Robert Linhart has shown that Lenin never considered that he had found the final answer to every problem, was sure that on many fundamental matters he had not,[5] and changed his position on certain very important questions over a relatively short period of time. Balibar himself also gives an example (ch. 4, below): Lenin's rectification of his position on the *trade unions*, between 1919 and 1921. In spite of the fact that these changes of mind were obviously provoked by a study of the particular problems facing the Russian Revolution, they also bore on very general aspects of the struggle for communism, in particular the crucial problem of the definition and realization of *mass democracy* – including the problem of the control of production – that would avoid falling either into bureaucratism or into any form of anarcho-syndicalism (like the 'workers' control' advocated in 1920–21 by the so-called Workers' Opposition).[6] It is absurd to imagine that Lenin could have or would have spent so much time trying to work out answers

[3] There is another, connected but slightly different way, as we shall see.
[4] *Lénine, les paysans, Taylor* (Editions du Seuil, Paris, 1976).
[5] *Cf.* the *Journal of Lenin's Duty Secretaries*, XLII, 490–91: 'I was with Vladimir Ilyich at about 12.30. [. . .] Dictated on the subject of (1) how Party and administrative bodies could be merged, and (2) whether it was convenient to combine educational activities with official activities.
'At the words "And the more abrupt the revolution . . ." he stopped, repeated them several times, obviously struggling with them; asked me to help him, re-read the preceding passages, laughed and said "Here I've got completely stuck, I'm afraid, make a note of that – stuck on this very spot!"'
[6] See for example the article 'Once again on the Trade Unions, the Current Situation and the Mistakes of Trotsky and Bukharin', *Collected Works*, XXXII, 70–107; and the 'Preliminary Draft Resolution of the Tenth Congress of the RCP on the Syndicalist and Anarchist Deviation in our Party', XXXII, 245–248.

to these questions without considering their *general significance*, beyond the immediate circumstances of the new Soviet Republic. The importance of this point is obvious: for if (1) Lenin's efforts were directed not simply to resolving immediate problems but also to clarifying general questions concerning the transition to communism, and if (2) he was very unsure about the answers to some of these questions, and often changed his mind and plainly contradicted himself, then it becomes impossible to conclude without further ado *either* that his 'successes' (his 'correct answers' – including his insistence on the need for the dictatorship of the proletariat) are of relevance only to the special difficulties faced by 'backward' Russia *or* – the same argument in another, alternative variant, which has recently revived in popularity, but this time among Communists – that his 'failures', and in particular his supposed tendency to 'underestimate the importance of democracy' can and must be 'corrected' now by those Western European Communists lucky enough (the argument has been applied to France, and would presumably also apply, by the same title, to Britain) to live in countries 'with an old democratic tradition' (*cf.* ch. 4).

The impression which this line of reasoning tries to create is that we can now speak very generally of two 'models of socialism': *on the one hand* the Russian model, based historically, for certain (regrettable) reasons, and in particular because of the primitive circumstances with which it had to contend, on the dictatorship of the proletariat, *and on the other hand* the Western model, which owing to the democratic conditions and/or possibilities existing in France, Italy and Britain, but also in Spain and Japan, etc., will be able to avoid *every form of dictatorship*, including the dictatorship of the proletariat. This general thesis also allows Western Communists to re-assess their attitude to the USSR, which is now considered to be still suffering from the heritage of its primitive origins. It also 'explains', on the same basis, the Soviet government's recalcitrance on the question of the dictatorship of the proletariat itself.

Now what is astonishing about this whole approach to the problem is that, in spite of its 'modern' appearance, its two basic elements – (1) the use of the abstract contrast between 'dictatorship' and 'democracy', in order to sing the praises of the latter and to condemn the former (and what could be more 'obvious'?), and

(2) the treatment of Leninism as the theory and practice of socialism *in the specific form determined by the Russian conditions of 1917*
– already, long ago, formed the basis of the Social-Democratic
Parties' attacks on Bolshevism and the Bolshevik Revolution. They
are for example the two pillars of Karl Kautsky's book on *The
Dictatorship of the Proletariat* (1918), to which Lenin replied in
the pamphlet *The Proletarian Revolution and the Renegade Kautsky*.
Thus the present-day relevance of Lenin's writings is once again
reinforced.

Kautsky uses the identification of Leninism with contemporary
Russian conditions in order to *condemn* it (remember that the
whole of Social-Democracy, following the Russian Mensheviks,
was at this time insisting that the Bolshevik Party had tried to 'take
a short cut' to socialism by attempting to establish it in a backward
country, i.e. in a land which was not yet sufficiently 'mature',
either economically or politically, for socialist revolution), but the
same approach can also be used, as it is today by certain Communist theoreticians, to 'excuse' Lenin's shortcomings and to
'explain' his failings and the limits of his teachings – which must
consequently be 'transcended'.

Turning his attention to the question of 'dictatorship', Kautsky
argues that since 'the exploiters have always formed only a small
minority of the population', the rule of the proletariat need not
assume a form 'incompatible with democracy'. Lenin comments:
the 'pure' and 'simple' democracy which Kautsky talks about 'is
sheer nonsense. Kautsky, with the learned air of a most learned
armchair fool, or with the innocent air of a ten-year-old schoolgirl,
asks: Why do we need a dictatorship when we have a majority?'[7]

An 'innocent' question, because it relies on what seems to be an
'obvious' idea. I should like to ask the reader himself to decide
whether it is not the same 'obvious' idea which lies behind the
argument now commonly met with in many Western Communist
Parties, including the British Party, to the effect that the dictatorship of the proletariat is now out-of-date and the 'democratic road
to socialism' now a real possibility because it is nowadays possible
to win not just a minority but the 'vast majority' of the people in a
broad 'anti-monopoly alliance'. Now I am not denying the need
to fight for the broadest possible alliance of the people, nor that

[7] XXVIII, 252.

monopoly (= imperialist) capital constitutes the dominant fraction of the ruling capitalist class and therefore, in an important
sense, the principal enemy of the people. But this kind of general
consideration is useless if it is not used to draw attention to the
urgent need for a concrete analysis of the precise relations of
contradiction (antagonistic or non-antagonistic) and of common
interest between the working class and the various other social
strata and groups among the people, if instead it is employed
precisely in order to 'demonstrate', on the basis of the old Social-
Democratic (= bourgeois) opposition between democracy and
dictatorship,[8] that whereas Lenin, in the conditions faced by the
Bolshevik Revolution – with a small working class isolated in a sea
of peasants, and so on – correctly insisted on the need for a dictatorship (of the proletariat), Western Europe will be able to take the
democratic road to socialism. Thus democracy and dictatorship
are interpreted as *forms of government* (parliament *versus* the one-
party system, and so on) or as *political or institutional forms*
(consent *versus* coercion). Yet on this point Lenin's argument is
perfectly clear:

'Bourgeois States are *most varied in form*, but their essence is the
same: *all* these States, *whatever their form*, in the final analysis are
inevitably *the dictatorship of the bourgeoisie*. The transition from
capitalism to communism is certainly bound to yield a tremendous
abundance and variety of *political forms*, but the essence will
inevitably be the same: *the dictatorship of the proletariat*' (my
emphasis – G.L.).[9]

Of course a simple reference to Lenin can never be a proof. But
we can at least ask those theorists who have abandoned and rejected
Lenin's position on this matter to admit as much.

I should like, in order better to illustrate the relevance of the
present book to the debate which must take place in Britain, to
make reference to a recent article by Jack Woddis (member of the
Political Committee of the British Communist Party) in *Marxism*

[8] *Cf.* Lenin, *The Proletarian Revolution and the Renegade Kautsky* (XXVIII,
232): 'Kautsky's great discovery of the "fundamental contrast" between "democratic and dictatorial methods" [. . .] is the crux of the matter; that is the essence of
Kautsky's pamphlet. And that is such an awful theoretical muddle, such a complete
renunciation of Marxism, that Kautsky, it must be confessed, has far excelled
Bernstein.'
[9] In *The State and Revolution*, ch. 2; XXV, 418.

Today, November 1976, entitled 'The State – Some Problems'. I do so not in order to engage in a personal polemic, but to make it possible for a serious discussion to take place around the question of the dictatorship of the proletariat (which, by the way, can certainly not be reduced to the simple question of whether or not the term itself figures in the Party Programme or in other publications). Woddis's article has the merit – so far a rare merit – that it attempts to take account, not pragmatically but in theoretical terms, of the recent development of capitalism (imperialism) and to consider what changes are correspondingly required in the positions and activity of British Marxists. However, I think that it is not possible to agree with all the points which he makes, and I shall try briefly to show why.

First of all, Woddis suggests that *the reason why Lenin insisted on the need to 'smash the State'* was that he realized the impossibility – in the conditions inherited from 'old Russia' – of winning a majority of the people for socialism. It follows that, in cases where it is indeed possible to win such a majority, it would be *unnecessary* to smash the State, or at least that to talk in such terms would 'serve to hide the essence of the question' (p. 341). *But this was not Lenin's reason.* It is clear that his argument is not intended to apply only to the particular conditions of the Russian Revolution but to *all revolutions* against capitalist rule, because it is *directly implied by his general conception of the State.* For example, in ridiculing Kautsky's position ('Workers, fight! – our philistine "agrees" to this [. . .] Fight, but *don't dare win!* Don't destroy the State machine of the bourgeoisie . . .') he comments that: 'Whoever sincerely shared the Marxist view that the State is nothing but a machine for the suppression of one class by another, and who has at all reflected upon this truth, could never have reached the absurd conclusion that the proletarian organizations capable of defeating finance capital must not transform themselves into State organizations. It was this point that betrayed the petty bourgeois who believed that "after all is said and done" the State is something outside classes or above classes.'[10]

This is the crux of the whole question: the idea that the State or any part of it is or might be *above classes, above the class struggle.* This is, however, the position adopted in effect by Woddis, when

[10] XXVIII, 261.

he argues in the following terms: 'The non-coercive sides of the
State in Britain today are far more comprehensive, more diverse,
and have a far larger personnel than the State in old Russia. Our
State institutions embrace extensive economic functions and the
nationalized industries, as well as education, the health services,
social services, and so on. In essence what is required in these
State sectors is a democratic transformation and forms of democratic control, not any "smashing" of such bodies which, under
socialism, can really serve the people's interests once the essential
democratic changes have been made.'[11]

If you turn to Appendix II of Lenin's *The Proletarian Revolution
and the Renegade Kautsky* you will find that he refutes precisely
this argument, as put forward on that occasion by the Belgian
Socialist Emile Vandervelde. Like Woddis, Vandervelde distinguished between the coercive side of the State, 'the State as
the organ of authority', *the State 'in the narrow sense'*, and the non-
coercive sides, the State 'as a representative of the general interests
of society', *the State 'in the broad sense'*. His programme was
therefore 'the transformation of the present State as the organ of
the rule of one class over another into [. . .] a people's labour State,
by the conquest of political power by the proletariat'.[12] What does
Lenin say about this programme, about the idea that the aim of the
conquest of State power is to put an end to the capitalists' use of
the State as a means of coercion, the State 'in the narrow sense',
but at the same time to develop and expand the non-coercive sides
of the State, the State 'in the broad sense'? He remarks, precisely
in reply to this idea: 'The Kautskys and Vanderveldes say nothing
about the fact that the transitional stage between the State as an
organ of the rule of the capitalist class and the State as an organ of
the rule of the proletariat is *revolution*, which means *overthrowing*
the bourgeoisie and *breaking up*, smashing, their State machine'.
The reason is that they 'obscure the fact that the dictatorship of
the bourgeoisie must be replaced by the dictatorship of *one* class,
the proletariat'. Thus, their denial of the need to 'smash' the
capitalist State (for the sense of this expression, see below) follows
directly from their general conception of the State, from their
attitude to the dictatorship of the proletariat. Lenin concludes:

[11] p. 341.
[12] Quoted by Lenin, XXVIII, 324.

'Like Kautsky, Vandervelde quotes Marx and Engels with great zeal, and like Kautsky, he quotes from Marx and Engels anything you like *except* what is absolutely unacceptable to the bourgeoisie and what distinguishes a revolutionary from a reformist. He speaks volubly about the conquest of political power by the proletariat, since practice has already confined this within strictly parliamentary limits. But as regards the fact that after the experience of the Paris Commune, Marx and Engels found it necessary to supplement the partially obsolete *Communist Manifesto* with an elucidation of the truth that the working class cannot simply lay hold of the ready-made State machinery, but must *smash* it – *not a single word* has he to say about that! Vandervelde and Kautsky, as if by agreement, pass over in complete silence what is most essential in the *experience* of the proletarian revolution, precisely that which distinguishes proletarian revolution from bourgeois reforms. Like Kautsky, Vandervelde talks about the dictatorship of the proletariat only to dissociate himself from it.'[13]

It is therefore quite clear that Lenin's insistence on what he calls 'the main point, namely, the *smashing* of the old, bourgeois-democratic State machine' is directly linked to his insistence on the need for the dictatorship of the proletariat. But since this latter insistence applies, as he says, to *all* bourgeois States – not just Russia in 1917! – because '*all* these States, *whatever their form*, are inevitably the dictatorship of the bourgeoisie', and because the transition from capitalism to communism will always, in essence, '*inevitably be the same: the dictatorship of the proletariat*', it follows that from Lenin's viewpoint the need to 'smash' the capitalist State *also* holds for *all* such States, however developed their 'non-coercive sides' may be.

It is true that there are in Britain, as elsewhere, small 'Marxist' groups, whose positions are characterized by a kind of 'anti-parliamentary cretinism', and which constantly confuse and discredit the issue by associating it with the idea of the masses storming parliament in a repeat of the attack on the Winter Palace in Petrograd. *But that is not its meaning.* Far from it! In a moment we shall see why.

The whole problem of Woddis's position lies, if I may say so, precisely in his conception of the dictatorship of the proletariat,

---

[13] XXVIII, 320. (*Cf.* pp. 74–77, below.)

even though the term itself hardly figures in his article. The
reason is that he associates Lenin's notion of this dictatorship
exclusively with the use of *coercion*, with the *violent* smashing of the
existing State machine, and thus with the installation of another,
equally coercive machine (now directed against other classes, of
course, and especially but not only against the old exploiting
classes). Thus the dictatorship of the proletariat is once again
identified with a particular 'form of government' – a dictatorial,
coercive form, lacking a 'democratic parliament', 'free elections',
freedom of speech and association, universal and constitutionally
guaranteed civil rights, and so on. But Lenin explicitly points out
(1) that 'the form of government has absolutely nothing to do with
it'[14] and (2) more specifically that in examining the question of the
dictatorship of the proletariat we are not dealing with 'a special
question, such as the franchise', but with a much more general
problem (how in general can the proletariat exercize its dictatorship *over* the old exploiting classes?). Thus he remarks that in the
pamphlet *The State and Revolution* '*I did not say anything at all*
about restricting the franchise. And it must be said now that the
question of restricting the franchise is a nationally specific and not
a general question of the dictatorship' (XXVIII, 255–56); and a
little later: 'The disenfranchisement of the bourgeoisie is not a
necessary and indispensable feature of the dictatorship of the
proletariat'. But Kautsky, against whom Lenin is arguing here, 'is
exclusively interested in the formal, legal aspect of the question'
(273). This is the crucial point: the dictatorship of the proletariat
is not to be defined in terms of a particular *system of institutions*
(= in formal, legal or *constitutional* terms – i.e. as a *non-constitu-
tional*, basically *coercive* system) but as *genuine mass democracy*,
whatever the institutional forms in which this democracy is realized
and developed.[15]
  But in that case, it might be asked, what is the meaning of

---

[14] XXVIII, 238.
[15] Though it is not *any kind of institution* which can, at a particular moment, play
the role demanded by the development of mass democracy. There is no doubt, for
example, that at a certain moment, in any given revolutionary process, parliamentary
institutions (to the extent that they already exist) will become hindrances to this
development, even if at an earlier moment they have played a very necessary role.
The particular moment at which this occurs can only be decided by reference to the
specific circumstances. But in any case the problem of institutions, though enormously important, *is not the main problem*.

Lenin's insistence on the need to 'smash' the capitalist State as a first step in the establishment of this dictatorship? We already have the key to the answer. Just as it is wrong to identify the dictatorship of the proletariat with a form of government based exclusively on violence and coercion, so it is wrong to identify the process of breaking up the capitalist State with a series of violent blows directed against particular institutions. The need, the vital necessity of 'smashing' or 'breaking up' the State machine can only be understood in terms of the need to break up 'the system of social relations which provides the bourgeois State apparatus with its astonishing capacity for resistance' (Balibar, ch. 4), to break up the *division of manual and intellectual labour* which has *not only* *survived* the contemporary development of the capitalist State and in particular of what Jack Woddis calls its 'non-coercive sides' (which 'in Britain today are far more comprehensive, more diverse, and have a far larger personnel than the State in old Russia',) but has actually been *deepened and extended* by that development. The need to 'smash' or 'break up' the capitalist State – i.e., the need to destroy this division of labour, itself both the source and the reflection of deep-rooted class contradictions – is therefore, if anything, *greater than ever* in our own day, greater than it was in Lenin's own time.

But this brings me to another, related point. To abandon the idea of 'breaking up the old State'[16] – provided that this idea is properly understood, and not confused with the notion of brute force – is to close one's eyes to the real, material contradictions deriving from and expressed in this division of labour, and thus to blind oneself and others to the grave problems which must arise from the continued existence of this division of labour and its accompanying contradictions *after the revolution* (even when this revolution is based on the 'consent' of the people as 'expressed in

---

[16] Jack Woddis: 'The "rare exception" [winning a majority of the people] has now become the real alternative for the people in Western Europe [. . .] Talking in terms of "smashing" the State can, I believe, serve to hide the essence of the question [. . .] What is required in these State sectors [the "non-coercive sectors" – G.L.] is a democratic transformation and forms of democratic control, not any "smashing" of such bodies . . .' (pp. 340–41). *Cf.* Lenin, XXV, 489–90: 'Kautsky abandons Marxism for the opportunist camp, for this destruction of the State machine, which is utterly unacceptable to the opportunists, completely disappears from his argument, and he leaves a loophole for them in that "conquest" may be interpreted as the simple acquisition of a majority.'

an electoral majority').[17] Consequently, it helps to create the impression that any contradictions which happen to surface in this period must actually have not so much a *material* as an *ideological* cause, and are therefore to be treated as problems of (a lack of) political consciousness, hang-overs from the bad, old capitalist days, when the monopolists controlled the 'mass media', etc. (Jack Woddis: 'Years of propaganda by the ruling class . . . have deceived the majority of working people . . .').[18] The consequence: the principal means of struggle under socialism would also be ideological, in order to correct or straighten out false ideas. In this connexion I ought, in parenthesis, to mention the fact that this curiously idealist picture of socialism, coupled with its accompanying idealist notion of *ideology* (ideology = *deception*), is nowadays sometimes 'legitimated' by the (mis)use of a term drawn from the writings of Antonio Gramsci, the term *hegemony*. Thus it is argued that Gramsci, in drawing attention to the important role played by the propaganda, educational and cultural system in the maintenance of the State power of the ruling class, made it possible to 'correct' Lenin's 'one-sided' emphasis on the coercive function of the State, *including the proletarian State*, and thus opened the way to the 'modern' non-coercive and democratic conception of socialism now being developed in the Western European Communist Parties. Jack Woddis too presents something like this argument (pp. 333–34). Its force derives however only from the attribution to Gramsci of an equally idealist notion of ideology, i.e. from an idealist 'interpretation' of his concept of hegemony and therefore of his whole work.

Why do I talk about an *idealist* conception of ideology? Because in effect this conception is completely isolated from the Marxist theory of class struggle in the economy, in politics and in ideology, and misrepresents or even destroys the relations between these forms of the class struggle. We have already seen an example: for if you avoid, ignore and thus effectively deny the contradictions involved in the division of manual and intellectual labour, in the socialist State apparatus but also outside it, you make it impossible to understand the symptoms and expressions of these contradictions except as ideological remnants of an earlier historical

[17] Woddis, p. 342.
[18] p. 331.

epoch, i.e. *they hang in the air* without any material support: they become nothing more than 'ideas', to be fought and replaced by other ideas, by means of propaganda (given that the propaganda, educational and cultural system is now in the hands of the working class – or rather, given that it has now been 'democratized'). That is why the conception in question is an idealist one.

In fact it is a very old idealist conception, for the identification of ideology or 'false consciousness' – it used to go by other names – with the end result of a process of *deception*[19] is a typically eighteenth-century procedure (it can be found, for example, in the writings of Jean-Jacques Rousseau). This however is only logical, for a very important reason which I shall outline in the following pages, but which I can sum up here, schematically, in a few words: namely, because certain theoretical positions today defended by some members of the British and other Communist Parties – in particular in connexion with the development of the theory of 'State Monopoly Capitalism' – remind one of *another* typically eighteenth-century (and therefore of course pre-Marxist) conception: I am talking about their presentation and definition of classes not in terms of a fundamental relation of antagonism between the capitalist class on the one side and the proletariat on the other but as groups (in this case the working class, middle strata, small and middle bourgeoisie, etc. and of course monopoly capital) each with its own *'particular interest'* (this general notion can also be found in Jean-Jacques Rousseau). I shall try to outline the content and implications of my argument.

Jack Woddis treats in detail the question of *what it is* to hold State power, thereby however distracting attention from another, equally important question, namely: *who holds* State power? He assumes throughout his article that the answer is obvious: the *'monopoly capitalists'*. But this is less obvious than it seems. Whereas Woddis himself speaks of the 'monopoly capitalists' (or of the 'big monopolies', 'monopoly capitalism', etc.), Lenin, in the

[19] Jack Woddis: '"Force" or "coercion" or "compulsion" is an essential element of political power but [. . .] "consent" or acceptance by a substantial part of the population, even when gained by *deception*, is also essential' (p. 332); 'The power of ideas [. . .] partly by people's force of habit in their thoughts and actions, and partly by *deception* [. . .] wins or *seduces* the majority into accepting the *status quo*' (*ibid.*). The emphases are mine – G.L.

passage quoted by Woddis himself on page 331, speaks of 'the bourgeoisie', and in the passage quoted by Mr Woddis himself on p. 341, of 'the capitalists'. Why the difference? Perhaps, of course, because the world has changed in the relevant respect. But let us look at this problem a little more closely.

It concerns, in particular, as I said, the theory of 'State Monopoly Capitalism', which is today almost an official theory among Communist Parties. We can therefore assume that Woddis subscribes to it.[20] There are various versions of this theory to be found in Britain and elsewhere, but I think that they are not essentially different, and I shall therefore treat it as a single (but not homogeneous) theory.[21] Now, according to this theory, State power is indeed assumed to be held not by the bourgeoisie or by the capitalist class as a whole, but by monopoly capital alone. There may sometimes be a reference to 'the dictatorship of the bourgeoisie' or something similar, but to all intents and purposes it is, for the theory in question, the monopolies (or monopolists), and sometimes even the *big* monopolies alone, which hold State power. But this argument – this is what is immediately striking and curious about it, as soon as you think about the problem – actually appears to violate the Marxist thesis that State power is always held by a 'single' class – i.e., a *whole* class, and not simply by one of its fractions, *even if* a given fraction of that class can be said to play a *dominant role* in the State. The difference between the two theses is however much greater than this mere formal statement would suggest. For example the theory of State Monopoly Capitalism suggests that only monopoly capital has an ('objective') interest in defending capitalism, because while the monopolies are making 'super-profits', the profits of the middle-sized and small enterprises are being correspondingly forced down, so that, 'objec-

---

[20] *Cf.* Jack Woddis, p. 332: 'Political power [is] in the hands of the most powerful monopolies.' This is an extreme representation of the idea essential to the theory of State Monopoly Capitalism that it is *monopoly capital* (and therefore *one particular fraction* of the capitalist class) which holds State power; for Woddis (here) it is only 'the *most powerful* monopolies'. See below for a discussion of the consequences of this general position.

[21] *Cf.* for example the collectively written *Traité marxiste d'économie politique* (Editions sociales, 1971) for what is perhaps the most sophisticated exposition of this theory. Lenin himself used the term 'State-monopoly capitalism' – e.g. in his contribution to the 7th Bolshevik Party Congress (1917), in *The Impending Catastrophe and How to Combat It* and in *The State and Revolution* – but *not in the same sense.*

tively', their owners are being drawn into the anti-monopoly alliance.

Marx and Lenin however argued that it is the bourgeoisie as a whole that holds State power, and not simply one or another of its fractions. Note that this was not because, *in their own time*, monopoly capital had not yet emerged or won the dominant position which it enjoys in our own day; their argument does not in the first place concern the question of the existence or non-existence, or the domination or non-domination of any *particular fraction* of capital at any *particular historical moment* – it is a general argument concerning the definition of the State, whereby they claim that the State is and always must be an instrument of class rule (i.e. of the rule of a given class), and that capitalist society contains, tendentially, only two classes, bourgeoisie and pro-letariat,[22] the consequence being that every modern State is either a dictatorship of the bourgeoisie or a dictatorship of the pro-letariat. At any moment in the development of the bourgeoisie this class does of course contain a dominant fraction (this was also the case in Marx's own time, and in that of Lenin), but neither con-cluded that State power was held by *that fraction* of the bour-geoisie; on the contrary, they spoke, as we have seen, about the State power of the *capitalist class* as a whole. Now in the present day, monopoly capital has clearly emerged as the dominant frac-tion within the capitalist class; but that would nevertheless not seem, if we follow Marx and Lenin, to be a good reason for con-cluding that it now, alone, holds State power.

Why did Marx and Lenin insist that it is the capitalist class as a whole which holds State power? Because (1) the State is defined as a product and an instrument of the antagonism between the classes; (2) this antagonism is never purely political ('following on from' the existence of economic and cultural inequality, poverty, etc.) but essential to the definition of the capitalist production relation; (3) this production relation is defined first of all in terms

---

[22] A point which is not invalidated by the development, transformation (and disintegration) of other so-called 'intermediate' social strata. *Classes*, in Marxist theory, are defined in the epoch of capitalism first of all by the fundamental antagon-ism, rooted in the capitalist production relation, between the bourgeoisie on the one hand and the proletariat on the other. Naturally, however, if you abandon Marxism for a sociological definition of classes, you will be faced with the enormous (and insoluble) problem of that apparently ever-expanding 'new middle class'!

of exploitation (the extraction of surplus-value); but (4) the production relation is one whose terms are (whole) classes; the exploiting class is the bourgeoisie as a whole. The general process of capitalist accumulation must therefore be defined as a single (though complex) process in which all the fractions of the bourgeoisie are united in and by their exploitation of the working class. This remains true *even if* (which is today quite obviously the case) the process of the *distribution* of surplus-value heavily favours monopoly capital, and therefore even if certain important new contradictions are arising within the bourgeoisie, between its various fractions, of which the working class and its political leadership certainly *must make use*.

This argument is not an exercise in logic-chopping; it has material political consequences. I shall outline three of them.

(1) There is no suggestion here that the middle and small (petty) bourgeoisie form a single reactionary bloc; that does not follow from the argument. On the contrary. What is implied, however, is that there are good material reasons for the empirically observable fact that it is extremely difficult to pry these groups away from the big bourgeoisie, at least on any substantial political basis and for any substantial length of time. Certain consequences thus follow with respect to what might be called the political strategy and tactics of the Marxist Labour Movement, not least because *the divisions inside the bourgeoisie are intimately linked with the divisions inside the proletariat*. It is this connexion, and this latter set of divisions which make things so much more complicated than is suggested by the picture drawn by the theory of State Monopoly Capitalism.

(2) In this theory, as we have seen, the bourgeoisie as a class tends to disappear, to be replaced by monopoly capital, etc. It is therefore no surprise that, analogously, *the proletariat as a class should tend to disappear too*, either entirely, or to become simply the 'core' of the working class or of the working people, and so on. In consequence it is similarly no surprise that theorists of State Monopoly Capitalism should conclude that, for this same reason, the idea of the dictatorship *of the proletariat* also has to be abandoned.

(3) Once the dictatorship of the proletariat has been abandoned, it becomes possible to develop more consistently than before the particular notion of socialism and of the transition from capitalism

to communism *originally introduced by Stalin.* This is not a slip of the pen: the conception of the transition from capitalism to communism now held and defended by those Communists who favour the abandonment of the dictatorship of the proletariat on the basis of general theoretical considerations like those recently invoked, *really does derive, in the last instance, from Stalin,* who revised Lenin's position in this respect. The differences can – very schematically, it must be pointed out[23] – be illustrated in the following diagrams:

Diagram 1: Lenin's conception

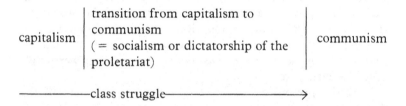

| capitalism | transition from capitalism to communism (= socialism or dictatorship of the proletariat) | communism |

————————class struggle————————————→

This conception was abandoned by Stalin, who introduced another, crucially different idea:

Diagram 2: Stalin's conception

| capitalism | transition from capitalism to socialism (= dictatorship of the proletariat) | socialism (friendly relations between classes) | communism |

————class struggle————————→

For Stalin, socialism was not essentially a period of class struggle but of 'friendly collaboration between classes' (see the 1936 Constitution in particular, and the debate around it); yet there remained a 'socialist State'. A very curious thing, given that Marx and Lenin had always argued that the existence of the State

---

[23] Particularly because in Lenin's conception the various 'stages' are not rigidly separated from one another as they are in Stalin's evolutionist model (*cf.* pp. 52–3).

was and could only be understood as an instrument of class struggle, and indeed given that Marxism defines classes themselves precisely in terms of class struggle. The dictatorship of the proletariat, which was necessarily bound up with the existence of class struggle, therefore had to be historically restricted in Stalin's theory to the period of transition *not to communism* but *to socialism*. At the cost of introducing an extra stage, Stalin therefore also introduced some logic into his scheme. But he had to do more: since he could not admit what Lenin insisted on – namely, the *contradictory nature of the proletarian State*, which at one and the same time both defended the proletariat against its enemies and yet constituted a threat *against which* the proletariat had to defend itself[24] – he had to transform the dictatorship of the proletariat from an historical tendency, describing the growing power of the proletariat both *within and where necessary against* the 'proletarian State' *into a simple set of State institutions* – even if they were (still) called 'Soviets', etc.

Now the present-day advocates of the abandonment of the dictatorship of the proletariat only take Stalin's scheme one step further. They want to abolish the dictatorship of the proletariat (in Stalin's sense of this term – Lenin's sense is not mentioned! N.B.), and they can do so just because they have already, with respect to the period not just of socialism but of capitalism itself, effectively *'abolished'* classes, however amazing this claim may seem. Of course the term 'class' is still used, but *no longer in the Marxist sense*[25] for in the Marxist sense classes are defined not in sociological terms, as a form of *classification* of a given population – which is only a modern, 'scientific' version of the eighteenth-century notion of 'particular interests' to which I referred earlier – but exclusively in terms of the *antagonism* between *the two classes* of capitalist society, bourgeoisie and proletariat, *and* – this is crucial – because it is impossible to analyze this antagonism except with reference to the essential role played in the process of exploitation (in which the relation of antagonism takes material form) by the State, and its use as an instrument of the rule of one

---

[24] Lenin: The workers' organizations must 'protect the workers from their State'; XXXII, 25.

[25] Or, if it is sometimes still used in the Marxist sense, this shows only that the 'theory' of State Monopoly Capitalism is, as I pointed out, not homogeneous, but an internally contradictory combination of Marxist and non-Marxist 'elements'.

of these two classes, namely the bourgeoisie. Therefore, once you abandon the notion, basic to Marxism and Leninism, that State power always lies in the hands of a single class, i.e. that every State is the dictatorship of a class, you are naturally led to drop the idea that present-day capitalism is a dictatorship of the bourgeoisie; but since you have ceased to define the bourgeoisie in a Marxist sense, and therefore the proletariat too, you will naturally conclude that the conception of the dictatorship of the proletariat is *also* quite superfluous and indeed wrong, because the proletariat does not really exist any more, except as a sociological category ('core of the working class', etc.). It is for all these reasons that there is a close connexion between the emergence of the theory of State Monopoly Capitalism and the abandonment of the dictatorship of the proletariat, and that this abandonment cannot be considered (as some sections of the bourgeois press have maliciously but stupidly contended) as a tactical electoral manoeuvre.

But at the same time we cannot therefore identify the abandonment of the dictatorship of the proletariat unequivocally with a process of 'de-Stalinization'. On the contrary, it is rather a question of ironing out discrepancies in Stalin's picture, for Stalin, following immediately upon Lenin, could not at once abandon all the aspects of the latter's position (and certainly not all of the words: in particular, the term 'dictatorship of the proletariat' was retained for certain purposes). It is worth remembering (see ch. 1 below) that the trials, purges, labour camps, etc. for which the Stalin period is renowned *for the most part followed* the introduction of the 1936 Constitution, i.e. followed the effective *abandonment by Stalin* of the dictatorship of the proletariat as applied to the Soviet Union.

It is of course quite obvious that, in abandoning the dictatorship of the proletariat in their turn, Western European Communists do *want* and *intend* to break with (the remnants of) 'Stalinism', not to reproduce or to reinforce them. In a certain sense, it must be admitted that they have done so. Their new positions are certainly not, in spite of what has been said above, identical with those defended by Stalin, and the practical consequences of these new positions, in what are in any case different historical conditions, will certainly not be the same. Yet their positions remain in another important sense structurally equivalent to Stalin's. *In what sense?* In the sense, as I said, that they defend an analogous conception of socialism. This may sound like an astonishing claim, given that so much attention has been paid (e.g. in the French Communist Party's 22nd Congress) to defining a form of socialism apparently as different as you can possibly imagine from the Soviet variety, and especially from the pre-1956 Soviet variety. But the point here is not that the contents of the two packages are different; it is that both conceptions picture socialism as a form of society *in its own right*, which can be defined in terms of public ownership of the means of production, planned growth, economic justice, etc. The fact that individual and collective liberty is now added to the list as an essential element changes nothing of the fact that in both cases you find a conception of the *socialist State* (N.B.) not as a contradictory phenomenon, both a vital necessity and yet a mortal danger to the struggle of the working class for communism, but as a simple instrument for the administration of a society without antagonistic contradictions (except with regard to the remnants of the old ruling classes, destined in any case to die out), an instrument for the 'satisfaction of the people's needs'. Yet this is not only Stalin's but – strangely – exactly the typical Social-Democratic conception of socialism! Since it is a Social-Democratic conception, it should be no surprise to discover that it is also a typically bourgeois conception.

Bourgeois ideology can imagine (a fact which is reflected in its classic contrast between democracy and dictatorship) two forms of the exercise of State power: the democratic form (parliamentary institutions, multi-party system, freedom of speech and assembly, etc.) and the dictatorial form (single-party system, fusion of party and state, refusal to tolerate opposition, and so on). It can imagine these two forms of the exercise of State power, and it classifies existing States accordingly. *What it cannot imagine* is a State of the kind portrayed by Lenin, a genuinely proletarian State, a State whose function is to exercize power *only and precisely* in order to prepare the conditions for its own disappearance, a State whose very existence is based on a contradiction, a State which itself recognizes that it must finally 'wither away', a State which accepts that it cannot achieve its goal unless it ceases to exist – and all this not in any formal or merely verbal sense, but in the material practice of the class struggle. Such a State would have to recognize that it *can never be 'universal'*, for if, *impossibiliter*, it were ever to become universal, its material reason for existence would have been eliminated. It can only exist as long as society is divided by the class struggle. But bourgeois ideology cannot imagine such a thing. For bourgeois ideology the State is, on the contrary, essentially universal, serving the whole of the people. Marxism says: such a State cannot exist; it is literally a *nonsense*. But our old (Stalin-type) and brand-new 'Marxists' say, turning bourgeois ideology to their own ends: such a State as you, the bourgeoisie, dream of can be realized – under socialism. It is our (projected) socialist State! The socialist State is thus represented as the first truly universal State, the first genuine 'State of the whole people'. What separates our old, Stalin-type Marxists from the brand-new variety is that the latter have swallowed a little bit more of the bourgeois line: they have swallowed the whole story about democracy *versus* dictatorship, too, which Stalin – and the Communist Parties, up until recently – for their own (different) reasons always refused. So, applying this contrast, they assure the world: we no longer want a *dictatorial* socialist State but a *democratic* socialist State.

Of course this process of ideological evolution must not be exaggerated. There is all the world of difference between a Communist Party and any bourgeois political formation. What we are talking about is an ideological and political tendency (what lies behind it?) and the resulting *contradictory* forms of theory and practice. Our task is however not to congratulate any Communist Party on the fact that its theory and practice are in part Marxist, but to draw attention to the respects in which *they are not*. For in a number of important respects, in particular in their conception of socialism, the Communists of whom we spoke are, consciously or unconsciously, still following Stalin in his departure from Marxism.

The struggle of the Communist Parties cannot be a struggle for *socialism*, in its own right, but must be a struggle for *communism* (see ch. 5, below). To suppose, as Stalin did and as many present-day Communists do, that there is a particular *form of society* called socialism naturally leads you to try and *define* it – e.g. in terms of a so-called 'socialist mode of production',[26] in terms of the replacement of the *anarchy* of capitalist production by the *planned* expansion of socialist production, in terms of the transformation

[26] *Cf.* e.g. M. Decaillot, *Le Mode de production socialiste*, Editions sociales, 1973.

of the State from an instrument of class rule into an instrument for
the satisfaction of the needs of the people, etc. Thus the contradictory nature of the socialist State tends to be lost from view. This
in turn opens the way to bourgeois propaganda, which accuses the
Communists precisely of fighting for a form of society in which the
State will be allowed to crush the individual, to destroy his creative
talents and initiative and steal his freedom. What do our up-to-the-
minute comrades answer? Accepting the false bourgeois theory of
the State and of its *potential* function in the *universal satisfaction*
of the people's needs (while disagreeing of course as to *which* or
whose State can realize this potential) they now simply answer: but
our State, the socialist State, will actually provide the individual
and the community with an unprecedented 'liberty'! What is
astonishing is that the bourgeoisie and its propagandists should
thus be allowed to get away so easily with their conjuring trick.
They of course accuse communism of elevating the *State* to an
unprecedentedly powerful position *vis-à-vis* the *individual* (thus
the constant reference to Police States, 'dictatorships', totalitarian-
ism, etc.). The 'modern' (or new-fangled) Communists reply: *our*
socialist State, unlike the USSR, *will meet all your demands* – there
will be a genuine parliament (unlike those in Eastern Europe), a
multi-party system, all the freedom of speech and association that
you could imagine, and so on. But this is a very curious answer, not
so much in the detail of its proposals – and we are not suggesting
instead the 'other alternative' within the same framework, a
'model' of socialism based on the single-party system! – but in its
basic assumptions, including its assumption that these proposals
satisfactorily deal with the main point at issue. It is certainly not
Lenin's answer.

Lenin says: parliamentary democracy is one form of the State,
and therefore a form of dictatorship – of a given class. There is no
'pure democracy', no 'democracy in general'. The struggle of the
Communists is not in the end to establish a 'democratic State' but
to *abolish the State*. Their tactics and their strategy must be adapted
to this end. *The aim of the Communists* is thus *infinitely more radical*
than that of the most radical Social-Democrat or liberal, and their
struggles must be directed *to this aim*. But since the road to this
end *is not necessarily a direct or straight one*, since it may involve the
most difficult detours, it cannot be conceived of simply in terms of
the ever-expanding development of 'liberty'. There can be no

easy answer to the question of what strategy a Communist Party ought to follow in any concrete set of national and historical conditions, and this book certainly cannot provide one. But it is possible, under certain circumstances, to try and establish a little theoretical clarity with respect to the basic problems of socialism and communism.

It would for instance certainly be false and even absurd to claim that the struggle to establish (in Spain) or maintain (in France, Britain, etc.) a functioning parliamentary system is unimportant. It may even be crucial at certain moments. But it does not follow that the State power of the bourgeoisie is *any less absolute* in such a system than in what is popularly called a 'dictatorship', or that in such a system, even when it succeeds in electing 'representatives' to the national parliament (Socialists or even Communists), the working class thereby gains the *slightest grasp* of State power, that it thereby holds the *slightest scrap* of State power. It does not! The struggle to establish or defend parliamentary democracy is for the Communists a struggle to strengthen the forces of democracy, in the Marxist sense of the term, to give them room and opportunities in the fight and a greater chance of one day seizing State power – i.e. of establishing a dictatorship of the proletariat, whatever *governmental forms* this may take. The reason for seizing State power is that, one day, it may thereby be possible to cause State power to disappear, and with it class struggle and exploitation. The fight for socialism makes no sense if it is interpreted as a fight to establish a 'universal' State, satisfying the interests of the whole people; it only makes sense as a fight to establish a State – a dictatorship of the proletariat – which will itself pave the way to the abolition of every State. Such an idea, as I already pointed out, is incomprehensible to bourgeois ideology, which has classified communism as an ideology of unlimited State power; but that is no reason why it should be incomprehensible to a Communist.[27]

I said earlier that a debate on the dictatorship of the proletariat might appear to be outlandish in present-day Britain. But there is a very good material reason for this. Every such debate, which touches on questions of real importance to the struggle of the working class *is bound to appear 'unreal'*, because it has to take place

[27] Nor therefore any reason why he should now classify it instead as a doctrine of *limited* State power!

outside the boundaries set by the dominant ideology, the ideology of the capitalist State, therefore outside the boundaries of 'common sense'. Since these boundaries are rather narrower in Britain than in France, because of the past and present history of the labour movement in the two countries, and in particular of the relative weakness of a Marxist tradition in Britain, the effect produced by such a debate may appear correspondingly more disconcerting. *That is no reason to refuse the debate*, and even less is it a good reason to throw overboard the concept of the dictatorship of the proletariat. No-one suggests that the explanation, defence and development of this concept does not have its 'difficult' side, that it does not involve serious contradictions, that it cannot be exploited by the propagandists of the ruling class for their own purposes. No-one is suggesting that Marxists should play into their hands by plastering the *term* 'dictatorship of the proletariat' over all their pamphlets and leaflets, in conditions where its real meaning cannot.be explained and where, in consequence, it is bound to be misunderstood. But that does not mean that all efforts should cease to explain its meaning to the masses and to *develop the reality of that meaning* by learning from the experience of the masses, so that this concept can finally become *their own*. To insist on the concept of the dictatorship of the proletariat does not mean to condemn or to abandon hope of all other social groups than the proletariat; *on the contrary*, it means to insist on the development of the only concept which can provide the foundation of a *materialist analysis* of the concrete possibilities of alliances between the proletariat and other groups and social strata (see ch. 4), which can do more than refer us to some abstract notion of the convergence of 'objective interests' uniting all sections of the population outside of monopoly capital (*cf.* p. 230).

I already pointed out that the concept of the dictatorship of the proletariat (together with its accompanying theory of the 'socialist State') *is infinitely more radical* than *the most radical* liberal or Social-Democratic theory of the State, since it insists not on the 'widest possible liberty' for the individual and community *in the face of the State* but on the *disappearance of the State itself*, of every State, precisely *through* the establishment of a dictatorship of the proletariat, which must itself develop the contradiction which will lead to its own disappearance. I would add: it also provides for an infinitely more genuine, an infinitely deeper form of *democracy* than the most radical liberal or Social-Democratic theory, *precisely because* it works to 'overcome democracy'.[28] And therefore we are obliged to conclude with Etienne Balibar that those who want to *abandon* the dictatorship of the proletariat are – consciously *or unconsciously* – motivated not by a desire to preserve and extend democracy but by a *fear of what genuine mass democracy might mean*, unless it be that they have simply given up hope, under the constant pressures and problems which every Marxist must face, that such a form of democracy, therefore communism, could ever really be on the agenda in Britain. But that is not a reason for accepting the abandonment of the dictatorship of the proletariat – on the contrary, it is a reason for continuing the fight not simply to defend it, but to develop it and thereby finally to bring about *real freedom* (Lenin: 'So long as the State exists there is no freedom. When there is freedom, there will be no State'),[29] however impossible that may now seem. Because if the arguments contained in this book are well-founded, then the dictatorship of the proletariat is indeed an historical reality *which no-one and nothing can abolish*.

Grahame Lock

---

[28] *Cf.* Lenin, *The State and Revolution*, ch. V, 4 (XXV, 479): 'The more complete the democracy, the nearer the moment when it becomes unnecessary.'
[29] *Op. cit.*, XXV, 473.

Foreword

What is the 'dictatorship of the proletariat'?

In the following study I should like to suggest the first elements of
a reply to this question, a question whose topical nature has
brought it to the attention of all Communists. I hope thus to
contribute to opening and to advancing a now unavoidable
theoretical discussion in the Party and around it.

The decisions of the 22nd Congress of the French Communist
Party on this point, in spite of their apparently abstract character,
have produced what might be considered a paradoxical result – in
any case, a result which has surprised certain Communists.

The theoretical question of the dictatorship of the proletariat
was not explicitly mentioned in the Preparatory Document. It
arose in the course of the discussion, when the General Secretary
of the Party, Georges Marchais, took up the suggestion of abandoning the notion of the dictatorship of the proletariat and of
removing it as soon as possible from the Party statutes. From that
moment on, this question dominated the pre-Congress debate:
its solution seemed to be the necessary consequence and the concentrated expression of the political line approved by the Congress. The Central Committee's report, presented by Georges
Marchais, made the point at great length: in order to establish a
foundation for the democratic road to socialism for which the
Communists are fighting, a new way must be found of posing and
assessing the theoretical question of the dictatorship of the proletariat. The Congress in fact unanimously decided to abandon the
perspective of the dictatorship of the proletariat, considered
out-of-date and in contradiction with what the Communists want
for France.

34

But this decision settled nothing, at root. No-one can seriously claim that the question was subjected to a profound examination during the preparatory debates, and even less during the Congress itself.[1] So it is not surprising, under these circumstances, that Communists are asking questions about the exact meaning of this decision. They are asking how far it implies a rectification or a revision of the principles of Marxism. They are wondering how it helps us to analyze the past and present experience of the Communist Movement. They are wondering what light it sheds on the present situation of the International Communist Movement, faced with an imperialism which, in spite of the crisis, is as aggressive as ever. They are wondering what changes will have to take place in their daily activity and struggles.

They are asking: what precisely is the 'dictatorship of the proletariat'? How is it to be defined? And, consequently, if the 'dictatorship of the proletariat' is being rejected, then what exactly is it that is being rejected? This common-sense question is very simple, and it ought not to be difficult to resolve – but it is clearly decisive. To anyone who thinks about the problem it will become quite clear that the expressions 'rejecting the dictatorship of the proletariat' and 'renouncing the dictatorship of the proletariat' can have no precise meaning as long as this question has not been answered. It is quite clear that there is a very close link between the abandonment of a political line or of a theoretical concept and the content and the objective meaning of the alternative which is adopted.

But since not all Communists are agreed on the meaning of the dictatorship of the proletariat, the result is precisely that the discussion which apparently took place did not go to the roots of the matter. And since the concept or concepts of the dictatorship of the proletariat, as they figured in the discussion, do not correspond to its objective reality; since, in spite of appearances, the discussion was not really about the dictatorship of the proletariat but

---

[1] In a press conference preceding the opening of the 22nd Congress, Georges Marchais appealed to the Communists for a new type of Congress, whose debates would go to the roots of the questions at issue and of the contradictions which they involve. But this did not happen. Why not? It is not enough to cite the weight of old ways of working, of old deformations of democratic centralism. There are also reasons connected with the object of the debate itself: the dictatorship of the proletariat. How should a public discussion on this principle be 'opened'? This is the problem which, for the time being, has not been resolved.

about something else, it happened that the unanimity in the Congress only disguised what are, tendentially, divergent interpretations and practices. Not unity, but division. At the same time it happened that, although the dictatorship of the proletariat – the word and the thing – appeared to have been completely abandoned, the problems which had led to its being brought into question nevertheless remained, and were even aggravated. Such are the ironies and upsets of real history.

If you want an example, just look at the reaction of the French bourgeoisie, which did not miss the opportunity of fishing in troubled waters and of exploiting our weakness, even at the theoretical level. Its most illustrious ideologists (Raymond Aron) and political chiefs (Giscard d'Estaing), newly qualified as Experts in Marxism, are making full use of their positions in order to trap the Communists in a dilemma: either give up the theory and practice of the class struggle, or return to the one-way street of the Stalin deviation, which of course had such a lasting effect in weakening the Party. Their tactic: to jump onto the Communist Party's own separation of the Leninist principle of the dictatorship of the proletariat from the politics of popular union – and popular union really is a condition of victory over big capital – in order to take the argument one (logical) stage further: by demanding that the Party should abandon class struggle too, since the dictatorship of the proletariat is nothing but the consequent development of this class struggle.[2] In addition, they claim that the decision made by the 22nd Congress, thus by the Communists themselves, amounts to an admission that these same Communists have up to the present indeed been opposed to democracy, that they have been fighting against it, and against freedom, in fighting for socialist revolution.

---

[2] *V. Giscard d'Estaing*, Press Conference, April 22, 1976: 'These changes seem to be related to an electoral tactic. The French C.P., for the first time in a long period, has the idea that it will soon be taking on governmental responsibilities, and at present it is directing all its activity to that end. Which means that it makes whatever announcements and public statements that it thinks might help it to enter the government. This is a matter of electoral tactics.

'What is the significance of the suppression of the dictatorship of the proletariat, as long as this Party continues to affirm the class struggle? The truth is that the French Communists cannot renounce the class struggle, because once they do so they will become Social-Democrats [. . . .] The only elements of disagreement with Soviet policy concern questions like those of liberties and individual rights which, since the French public is sensitive to these matters, have to be taken account of

It is important that Communists should realize that there is no way out of these paradoxes, out of these real difficulties, except through a broad collective discussion. They should not be frightened that this might weaken them. On the contrary, if it goes to the root of things, it can only strengthen their influence. Every Communist has the duty to help the whole Party in this respect, as far as he is able. And with respect to the dictatorship of the proletariat, the Congress does at least have a good side: it can free Communists, in their theoretical work, from a dogmatic conception and use of Marxist theory, in which formulae like 'dictatorship of the proletariat' are taken out of their context and separated from the lines of argument and proof which underlie them, becoming blanket solutions, formal ready-made answers to every question. Emptied of their objective historical content, they are then ritually invoked in order to justify the most diverse and even the most contradictory kinds of politics. *This use* of the principles of Marxism and of the concept of the dictatorship of the proletariat not only ought to be but urgently must be rejected.

---

when the French Communist Party works out its electoral tactics.' *Raymond Aron*, in *Le Figaro*, May 17, 1976: 'Georges Marchais suddenly proclaimed the abandonment of the formula of the dictatorship of the proletariat amidst a quasi-general scepticism. He was not the first to carry out the operation: Gottwald and Cunhal too made similar announcements. Yet the former eliminated his allies, or at least brought them to heel, on the first possible occasion, and the latter led his party in a bid for the seizure of power, unsuccessfully it is true, but without hesitation. In the esoteric language of Marxism-Leninism, the dictatorship of the proletariat remains a necessary transition between capitalism and socialism, whatever the form taken by this dictatorship. You can therefore interpret Georges Marchais' declarations in a limited, banal sense, similar to that implied by the words of Alvaro Cunhal, or in a doctrinal sense; in the latter case, the French Communist Party would have taken a first step in the direction of revisionism.'

Paris (1976)–
Moscow (1936)

In order for a discussion to get to the bottom of a question, it needs clear starting-points. A correct, Marxist definition of the dictatorship of the proletariat is the first of these starting-points, in the theoretical field. It is not sufficient in itself: you cannot settle political questions by invoking definitions. But it is necessary. If you do not pay explicit attention to it, you run the risk of implicitly adopting not the Marxist definition of the dictatorship of the proletariat but a definition imposed by the constant pressure of the dominant bourgeois ideology. That is what happened at the 22nd Congress, whatever is said to the contrary. I am not going to quote or sum up the details of the debates: everyone remembers them, or can look them up. I shall be as brief as possible, in order to direct attention to what seems to me most important, namely the way in which the problem was posed; this more or less, leaving aside details, underlay the reasoning presented at the Congress. To many comrades it seems to be the only possible way of posing the problem, it seems 'obvious' to them today. We shall therefore begin by examining it.

'Dictatorship or democracy'
The question was first of all posed within the framework of a simple alternative: *either* 'dictatorship of the proletariat' *or* the 'democratic road to socialism'. The choice was between these two terms: no third solution, no other alternative. Given the definitions used, this choice is imposed more by 'logic' than by history. The historical arguments in fact are only introduced after the event, they only ornament and illustrate a logical schema so simple

that it seems unavoidable. We are told that the choice is not between a revolutionary path and a reformist path, but between two revolutionary paths, both based on mass struggle, a choice between two kinds of means to make revolution. There are 'dictatorial' means of struggle and 'democratic' means: they are suited to different circumstances of place and time, and they produce different results. The Congress thus had to demonstrate what distinguishes the democratic from the dictatorial means, and did so by borrowing three common contrasts.

(a) First, the contrast between 'peaceful' political means and 'violent' means. A democratic road to socialism, it is said, excludes on principle armed insurrection against the State as a means of taking power. It excludes civil war between the classes and their organizations. It therefore excludes both white terror, exercised by the bourgeoisie, and 'red' counter-terror, exercised by the proletariat. It excludes police repression: for the workers' revolution does not tend to restrict liberties but to extend them. In order to maintain themselves in power democratically, the workers must not primarily use constraint, the police and 'administrative methods', but political struggle – i.e., in the event, ideological propaganda, the struggle of ideas.

(b) Secondly, the contrast between 'legal' and 'illegal' means. A democratic road to socialism would allow the existing system of law to regulate its own transformation, without recourse to illegality. The transformation of the existing system of law – for example, in the form of the nationalization of enterprises – is only to be carried out according to the forms and norms contained in (bourgeois) law itself, according to the possibilities which it opens up. Such a revolution would therefore not contradict the law; on the contrary, it would simply realize in practice the principle of popular sovereignty to which it constantly refers. Conversely it is the legality – therefore the legitimacy – of this revolutionary process which is supposed to authorize and strictly to limit the use of violence. For every society and every State, so the argument goes, have the right (and the duty) forcibly to repress 'crimes', the illegal attempts of minorities to oppose by force and by subversion the abolition of their privileges. Thus, if the need for constraint arises, this will be considered no fault of the new régime itself. And this use of violence will not be a form of class violence, but a constraint on particular *individuals*, just as bourgeois law itself now provides.

(c) Finally, the contrast between union and division, which is linked to the contrast between majority and minority. In the dictatorship of the proletariat, it is said, political power is exercized by the working class alone, which itself is still only a minority. Such a minority is and remains isolated: its power is clearly fragile, it can only maintain itself by violence. The situation, so the argument goes, is exactly opposite when, in the new historical conditions, the socialist State represents the democratic power of a majority. The existence of the union of the majority of the people, the 'majority will', expressed by universal suffrage and by the legal government of the majoritarian political parties, is therefore supposed to guarantee the possibility of peaceful transition to socialism – a revolutionary socialism, certainly, with respect to its social content, but gradual and progressive with respect to its means and forms.

Once you accept and reason according to these contrasts (I have only mentioned the most important ones), contrasts which become more and more closely linked to and dependent on one another, then at each stage you are forced to choose one of the two poles: civil war or civil peace; legality or illegality; union of the majority or the isolation of the minority and the division of the people. At each step you have to work out which choice is 'possible' and which is not; which is the one that you 'want' and which is the one that you 'do not want'. A simple choice between two historical roads for the transition to socialism, a choice between two conceptions of socialism, two systematically opposed 'models'. On the basis of these choices, the dictatorship of the proletariat, it is implied, must be defined as the *violent political power* (in both senses of the term 'violent': repression and recourse to illegality) of a *minoritarian working class*, bringing about the transition to socialism by a *non-peaceful road* (civil war). To this, one last argument – and it is not the least important – may be added, since it is a natural consequence: that such a road would lead to the political domination of a *single party* and end by institutionalizing its monopoly. Many comrades demand of us: if you do not want to abandon the notion of the dictatorship of the proletariat, at least admit frankly that you are for a one-party system, against the plurality of parties. . . .

But what are we to think of these pairs of alternatives?

Their first characteristic is that they do not make a real analysis possible, because they contain the answer to every question ready-made. Posed in these terms, the problem of the dictatorship of the proletariat already implies its solution. It is an academic exercise. To define the dictatorship of the proletariat becomes a simple matter of listing its disadvantages, compared with the democratic road. To analyze the concrete conditions of the transition to socialism in France becomes a simple matter of self-congratulation on the fact that the evolution of history now (finally) allows us to take the good road, that of democracy, and not the bad road, that of dictatorship. You can be very optimistic about socialism when you know that history itself is looking after the job of creating the conditions which will impose precisely the choice preferred in the first place. It only requires one more step in order to draw the conclusion: when a capitalist country has a non-democratic State (as in the case of Tsarist Russia), it cannot make the transition to socialism except in a non-democratic manner, with all the risks attached. But when a capitalist country is *also* (as in the case of France) a country of an 'old democratic tradition', it can make the transition to socialism in a manner which is itself democratic. Better: the transition to socialism will slowly appear to the immense majority as the only means of preserving democracy, which is under attack by big capital. Better still: the socialism which can be established in this case will be right from the first a superior form, rid of the contradictions and dangers represented by dictatorship (of the proletariat).

This line of argument is indeed seductive, but that does not explain how Communist militants, involved for years in the class struggle, have nevertheless allowed themselves to be taken in by it and to adopt its 'common sense' language. To understand why they have done so, we must look into the question of what – in the history of the Communist movement itself and in the interpretation of Marxist theory which has prevailed in the movement for many years – could have produced this kind of 'common sense'. In this connexion, the arguments of the 22nd Congress are dominated by three ideas which are by no means new, and which are clearly present. First: the idea that the dictatorship of the proletariat is, in its essential characteristics, identical to the road followed in the Soviet Union. Secondly, the idea that the dictatorship of the proletariat represents a particular 'political régime', a set of

political institutions which guarantee – or fail to guarantee – the
political power of the working class. Finally – and this is the decisive point at the theoretical level – the idea that the dictatorship of
the proletariat is a means or a 'path of transition' *to socialism*. It
must now be shown why these three simple ideas, though they are
the product of real historical causes, are nevertheless incorrect.

Three simple and false ideas
A few words on these three ideas.

It is enough to read the reports of the debates of the 22nd Congress,
and earlier contributions,[3] in order to recognize that behind the
question of the dictatorship of the proletariat there lies first of all
the problem posed by the historical evolution of the Soviet Union.
It is no accident if, at the very same time that the Party is claiming
that socialism is on the agenda in France, its leaders are also
publicly raising their voices to pose the question of its 'differences'
with the policy of the Soviet Communists, in terms such that it is
clear that a real contradiction is involved. Look at the facts, which
the careful selection of words cannot hide: disagreements on
'socialist democracy' (therefore on the structures of the Party and
State); disagreements on 'peaceful co-existence' (which our Party
refuses to accept as implying the status quo for capitalist countries
like France, as overshadowing the class struggle, or – even worse –
as requiring the socialist countries to give political support to the
power of the French big bourgeoisie); disagreements on 'proletarian internationalism' (which our Party refuses to interpret in
terms of 'socialist internationalism', an interpretation dramatically
illustrated by the military invasion of Czechoslovakia). Such
contradictions demand a thoroughgoing explanation. This question clearly lay behind the deliberations of the Congress. And it is
this question, and no other, which underlies the argument several
times advanced by Georges Marchais: 'The phrase "dictatorship
of the proletariat" today has an unacceptable connotation for the
workers and for the masses.' This is the vital question, and not the
example of the fascist dictatorships which have appeared since the

[3] *Cf.* the series of articles published by Jean Elleinstein in *France Nouvelle*
(September 22, 1975, and following issues) on 'Democracy and the Advance to
Socialism'. With admirable foresight Elleinstein was already advancing arguments
used a few weeks later to oppose the principle of the dictatorship of the proletariat.

time of Marx and Lenin. The workers and the masses obviously expect nothing from fascism but increased oppression and exploitation. The existence of fascist dictatorships only gives increased weight to Marx's and Lenin's thesis: that the proletariat must oppose the class dictatorship of the bourgeoisie with its own class dictatorship.

What the Communists are concerned with above all is the old idea which expressed their hopes during decades of difficult struggles: that the dictatorship of the proletariat is possible, since it is simply the historical road taken, the road taken in history, by the socialist countries making up the present 'socialist world' or 'socialist system', and above all by the USSR. Which implies something very simple and concrete: 'If you want to understand the dictatorship of the proletariat, its conditions, why it is necessary, then look at the example of the USSR!' So it turns out that something which for so long has served as a guarantee and as an inspiration must now, without changing its character, serve as a warning and as an example to be avoided. Which means that the same idea is shared by many comrades, though they draw different conclusions: the idea that *the essence, the fundamental characteristics of the dictatorship of the proletariat are directly realized and manifested in the history of the USSR*, therefore in the role played by the State in the USSR and in the kind of institutions which exist or have existed in the USSR.

I have presented this idea in schematic form, but I think that no-one will seriously deny that many of our comrades did see things in this way. That does not mean that they would not, if necessary, add a number of nuances and corrections. Many would say that the dictatorship of the proletariat, as it existed in the USSR, had its 'peculiar' side (very peculiar, indeed . . .): its imperfections, its faults, its deviations, its crimes; and that in consequence you have to be able to 'extract' from this imperfect reality the essential characteristics of the dictatorship of the proletariat. What does not occur to them is the idea that the history of the USSR, before, during and after the Stalin period, might represent *a process and a tendency in contradiction with the dictatorship of the proletariat*. It does not occur to them that the history of the Soviet Union might demonstrate not just the possibility of the dictatorship of the proletariat and its emergence in history but also and perhaps above all the obstacles faced by the dictatorship of the proletariat, the very real and very present power (not just a power inherited from the 'feudal' past . . .) of historical tendencies *opposed* to the development of the dictatorship of the proletariat. Now their representation of Soviet history, in spite of its lack of any dialectical materialist and therefore of any Marxist quality, is today shared by comrades, some of whom use it to argue for the dictatorship of the proletariat, others to argue against. Which means, to put it clearly: both by comrades who still, even if with qualifications, believe in the universal validity of the Soviet 'model' of politics and society, and by others who reject this claim to validity (either absolutely, or because of their view of the evolution of historical conditions). But this idea is an obstacle both to any critical and scientific analysis of Soviet history and to any treatment of the theoretical problem of the dictatorship of the proletariat, while nevertheless providing 'historical' arguments to justify, after the event, a hasty decision.

Of course, there are powerful historical reasons for the direct identification of the concept of the dictatorship of the proletariat with Soviet history. They are related to the determinant place of the Soviet revolution and to its objective role in the history of the international labour movement. In a certain sense this identification is a fact, an irreversible fact, which binds us, for there is no theory whose meaning is independent of the conditions of its practical utilization. But if it is an irreversible fact, that does not mean that it is immutable.

To this first idea, a second is closely linked – an idea which also underlies the arguments of the 22nd Congress – according to which *the dictatorship of the proletariat is only a particular 'political régime'*. In Marxist (or apparently Marxist) terminology, the word 'politics' refers to the State, to its nature and its forms. But the State does not exist in a vacuum: everyone knows that it is a 'superstructure', i.e. that it is connected to an economic base on which it depends, to which it reacts. Yet it is precisely not that base and must not be confused with it. 'Democracy' and 'dictatorship' are terms which can apparently only designate political systems. Did not Lenin go so far one day as to say that 'Democracy is a category proper only to the political sphere. . . . Industry is indispensable, democracy is not'?[4] Why not, with even better reason,

[4] In the rest of the book, the references to Lenin's works will be given in the following way: XXXII, 19, means volume 32, page 19 of the *Collected Works*,

extend this formulation to the symmetrical opposite, in everyday language, of democracy: i.e., dictatorship? The State, the level of political action and institutions, is quite distinct from the other levels, in particular from the economic level, is it not?

I want to concentrate on this idea, even though I have had to present it schematically, because it plays a crucial role in the thinking of many Communists. And here again the question of the Soviet Union arises. It is this idea for example which might lead us to say: from the 'economic' point of view, essentially, socialism is the same everywhere, its 'laws' are universal; but from the 'political' point of view, it can and must be very different, since Marxism teaches the relativity of the superstructures, the relative independence of the political superstructures and of the State vis-à-vis the economic base. And it is this idea too which might lead us to say: the dictatorship of the proletariat in the Soviet Union resulted in catastrophic consequences from the point of view of the political régime, it resulted in the establishment of a political régime which is not really socialist, which contradicts socialism, because, from the political point of view, socialism implies the widest possible liberty and democracy. But, it will be argued, this did not prevent the development of socialism as an 'economic system', or at least it only held it back a little, hindered it, made it more difficult, without affecting its 'nature', its essence. The proof: in the Soviet Union there is no exploiting bourgeoisie, monopolizing property in the means of production, no anarchy in production; there is social, collective appropriation of the means of production, and social planning of the economy. Thus the anti-democratic political régime has, it is argued, nothing to do with the 'nature' of socialism; it is only a historical 'accident'. To which it is added, with an apparently very materialist air, that there is nothing astonishing about the fact that the superstructure is 'lagging behind' the base – such is the law of the history of human societies, which guarantees that, sooner or later, the political régime will come into line with the mode of production, will come to 'correspond' with the mode of production.

But it has to be pointed out that we are dealing here with an extraordinarily mechanistic caricature of Marxism, linking a mechanistic separation between State and means of production with a mechanistic dependency of politics on the economic base

English edition, published by Lawrence and Wishart, London, and Progress Publishers, Moscow.

(in the form of the talk about the 'nature' of socialism, about 'accidents', about things which are 'in advance' of others which are 'lagging behind'). In such a perspective it is already impossible to explain the history of the capitalist State. It is *a fortiori* impossible to pose the problem of *what changes*, in the relation of politics and of the State to the economic base, when a transition is made from capitalism to socialism and to the dictatorship of the proletariat.[5]

Now this idea of the dictatorship of the proletariat as a simple 'political régime' directly determines the terms in which the problem of the political power of the working class, or of the working people, is posed. The dictatorship of the proletariat becomes *a special form of the political power of the working people*, and a narrow form at that (since not all working people are proletarians). In fact, this amounts to saying that the dictatorship of the proletariat is *a form of government* (in the legal, constitutional sense), that it represents a particular *system of institutions*. To choose between a number of paths of transition to socialism, for or against the dictatorship of the proletariat, is – according to this idea – to choose between a number of systems of institutions, notably between institutions of a parliamentary or so-called 'pluralist' type (containing several political parties) and institutions of a non-parliamentary type, in which the power of the working people is exercized through a single party. Socialist democracy differs from the dictatorship of the proletariat, in this view, as one political régime differs from another; it is conceived of as another form of the political power of the working people, in which other institutions organize in a different way the choice of the 'representatives' of the working people who run the government, and the 'participation' of individuals in the functioning of the State.

According to this picture the transition to socialism could be conceived, in theory at least, either in terms of a dictatorial form of politics or in terms of a democratic form. It would depend on the circumstances. It would depend in particular on the degree of development, on the level of 'maturity' of capitalism: in a country where capitalism is particularly developed, where it has reached the stage of State Monopoly Capitalism, big capital would already be practically isolated, the development of economic relations

---

[5] I am not making all this up. This caricature of Marxism can be found throughout the book by Jean Ellenstein, *The Stalin Phenomenon*, Lawrence and Wishart, London, 1976.

would itself provide the outline for a broad union of all working people and non-monopoly social strata, and the dictatorial road would become impossible and futile, while the democratic road would become possible and necessary.

But this way of posing the problem supposes that there exist in history very general forms of the State, régimes of different kinds like 'dictatorship' or 'democracy', which pre-date the choice of a society, the choice of a path of transition to socialism and of a political form for socialism. To put it bluntly: the alternative dictatorship/democracy would be *exterior* to the field of class struggle and its history, it would simply be 'applied' after the event, from the standpoint of the bourgeoisie or from that of the proletariat. Which means that revolutionary Marxism would be subordinated to the abstract categories of bourgeois 'political science'.

But here we touch on the most deeply rooted of the theoretical ideas which dominated the arguments of the 22nd Congress – and yet the least controversial idea in appearance, since the terms of our ordinary language directly express it, since these terms have entered everyday usage to such a degree that no-one any longer asks whether they are correct or not. I am referring to *the idea that the dictatorship of the proletariat is only a 'path of transition to socialism'*, whether or not it is considered a good one, whether or not it is considered as the only possible road or as a particular (political) road among others. It is only by bringing this idea into question that we can understand the way in which the other ideas force themselves on us, the power of ideological 'obviousness' from which they benefit.

But someone will ask me: if the dictatorship of the proletariat cannot be defined in this way, then how can it be defined? I will reply to this question later, at least in principle. But we have to understand what the first definition implies. If the dictatorship of the proletariat is a 'path of transition to socialism', this means that the key concept of proletarian politics is the concept of 'socialism'. This means that it is enough to refer to socialism in order to study these politics and put them into practice. The transition to socialism and the so-called construction of socialism – these are the key notions. But what now becomes of the problem of the dictatorship of the proletariat? It becomes the problem of the *means* necessary for this transition and for this construction, in the different senses of this term: intermediate 'period' or 'stage' between capitalism and socialism, therefore the whole of the strategic and tactical, economic and political means capable of bringing about the transition from capitalism to socialism – of 'guaranteeing' it, according to the expression which spontaneously occurs to certain comrades. And how are these means to be defined, how are they to be organized into a coherent strategy, objectively based in history? Quite naturally, by confronting present and past, the point of departure and the point of arrival (i.e. the point where one *wants*, where one hopes to arrive . . .). By defining, on the one hand, the decisive, universal 'conditions' of socialism – classically: the collective appropriation of the means of production, coupled with the political power of the working people – and by examining the way in which these conditions can be fulfilled, given the existing situation and the national history of each country. Good old Kant would have called it a 'hypothetical imperative'.

This would mean that proletarian politics is dependent on the definition of a 'model' of socialism by which it is inspired – even when (indeed, above all when) this 'model' is not borrowed from other, foreign experiences, but worked out independently as a national 'model'. Even when (indeed, above all when) this model is not a sentimental vision of a future golden age of society, but is presented as a coherent, 'scientific plan' for the reorganization of social relations, coupled with a meticulous computation of the means and stages of its realization.

And it would mean, more fundamentally, that the question of the dictatorship of the proletariat can no longer be posed, nor can the dictatorship of the proletariat be defined, except *from the point of view of socialism*, according to a certain definition of socialism and with a view to its practical realization. On this point everyone apparently is agreed: if, up to very recently, Communists used to insist on the need for the dictatorship of the proletariat, it was in order to make the transition to socialism, in one country after the other; if they have now decided to abandon the dictatorship of the proletariat, and to set out a different strategy, it is nevertheless still in order to make the transition to socialism.

But when Marx discovered the historical necessity of the dictatorship of the proletariat, he did not refer simply to socialism: he referred to the process which, within the very heart of the existing class struggles, leads towards the *society without classes, towards communism.* Socialism, alone, is a half-way dream house, where everyone can choose his own menu, where the demarcation line between proletarian politics and bourgeois or petty-bourgeois politics cannot be drawn in a clear way. The classless society is the real objective whose recognition characterizes proletarian politics. This 'shade of meaning' changes everything, as we shall see. By defining the dictatorship of the proletariat in terms of 'socialism', one is *already* trapped within a bourgeois framework.

A Precedent: 1936

Let us stop there for a moment. Before undertaking the study of the Marxist concept of the dictatorship of the proletariat for its own sake, we must briefly look at the historical antecedents of the situation which I have just described. Such a situation does not just drop out of the sky. It is not so much that the decision of the 22nd Congress was the logical consequence, or the recognition after the event, of a long political evolution which had led the Party towards an original revolutionary strategy; it is rather that *the particular* conception of the dictatorship of the proletariat to which it referred had *already*, in all essentials, been for a long time accepted and even dominant in the International Communist Movement. The decision of the 22nd Congress does have an historical precedent, without which it would remain in part incomprehensible.

We ought at this point to recall a fact of which most young Communists are unaware, or whose importance with regard to the present debate is not clear to them. It was the Soviet Communists themselves, under Stalin's direction, who first historically 'abandoned' the concept of the dictatorship of the proletariat, in a quite explicit and reasoned way. They did so *in 1936*, on the occasion of the introduction of the new Soviet Constitution. The 1936 Constitution solemnly proclaimed, less than twenty years after the October Revolution, the *end of the class struggle in the USSR.* According to Stalin, who inspired and laid the foundations of what is even today the official theory of the State in the USSR, distinct classes still existed in the Soviet Union: working class, peasantry of the State farms and collective farms, intellectuals, industrial managers and State administrators.[6] But these classes were no longer antagonistic, they were equal members of a union, of an alliance of classes, which constituted the foundation of the Soviet State. From that moment on, the Soviet State was no longer concerned with classes as such, but, beyond the differences which separate them, with the *individuals*, with all the citizens, with all the working people. It became *the State of the whole people*.

Even then it was possible – and it is still possible in retrospect – to ask questions about the validity (and even about the good faith) of the statement: 'Class antagonisms have disappeared'. This statement came for example only a few years after the collectivization of agriculture, which witnessed an outbreak of class conflict as acute as the conflicts of the revolutionary period, in which the socialist State had to break the resistance of the capitalist peasantry (the kulaks) and also, no doubt, of whole masses of the poor and middle peasantry, by using every available means, both propaganda and force. Above all, the statement came at the very moment when there began to develop in the whole country, and among all classes, what we now know to have been a bloody mass repression, of which the great 'Moscow trials' were only the visible and spectacular façade. How are we to explain this repression (which was then only in its first phase!) in a materialist way, unless we relate it to the persistence and development of a class struggle which, though it was perhaps unforeseen and uncontrolled, was nevertheless quite real? How are we to interpret the proclamation of the 'end' of the class struggle, and the administrative decision to finish with the dictatorship of the proletariat, except as an amazing refusal to look the existing state of things in the face, that in turn, by the mystifying effects which it produced, then reinforced and crystallized a tragic theoretical and practical deviation? This example, if there was need of it, would already be sufficient to warn us that the abandonment of the dictatorship of the proletariat is no historical guarantee against violence; in fact it might even suggest that, in this case, such violence only becomes more cruel and damaging to the people and to the revolution.

Stalin did not of course retrospectively reject the past applic-

[6] The question whether the basic 'classes' are two or three in number has never been clearly settled. An inexhaustible field of studies was thereby provided for 'Marxist sociology'.

ability of the dictatorship of the proletariat (he even used the concept in order to justify and idealize *en bloc* the whole history of the preceding years): he simply argued that the Soviet Union had no more use for it. And so, he insisted, it remained absolutely necessary . . . for everyone else, for all other countries which still had to make their revolutions. The particular way in which he proclaimed the end of the dictatorship of the proletariat thus allowed him, at the same time, to develop the idea that the Soviet Union constituted a 'model' for all socialist revolutions, present or future.

If Stalin's justification of the notion of the 'State of the whole people' ignored – and for a good reason – the existence of acute forms of class struggle in the USSR, it nevertheless did recognize, formally, the importance of the *theoretical* problems raised by such a decision, from a Marxist point of view. Now Marx, Engels and Lenin had shown that *the existence of the State is linked precisely to class antagonism*, and they spoke of the disappearance of class divisions and of the 'withering away of the State' as of two inseparable aspects of a single historical process. From their standpoint, the dictatorship of the proletariat – the necessary transition to the disappearance of classes – could only come to an end when classes really had disappeared; it could not be followed by the *strengthening* and eternalization of the State apparatus, but on the contrary only by its disappearance, even if this process would necessarily take a long time.

In order to counter this objection, Stalin advanced two arguments.

The first tackled the problem obliquely. Stalin made use of the correct thesis of 'socialism in one country', verified by the October Revolution and by the foundation of the USSR. But instead of inferring from it the possibility for socialist revolution to develop in one country after another, as 'breaks' occurred in the imperialist chain, depending on the conditions existing in each country, he argued that the socialist revolution could achieve final victory in the USSR *independently* of the evolution of the rest of the capitalist world. Thus a socialist country (and later the 'socialist camp') was considered to constitute a closed world, which however was at the same time threatened from outside – but only from outside. The State had no reason for existence as an instrument of class struggle *inside* the country, since this class struggle no longer existed; but it remained absolutely necessary as an instrument of class struggle directed *to the exterior*, as a means of protection for socialism against the threat and the attacks of imperialism. Neither Marx, nor Engels, nor Lenin himself (though on this point Stalin was more prudent) could, it was argued, have foreseen such a situation: and what better opportunity could there have been, in passing, to issue a wise reminder that Marxism is not a fixed dogma, but a science in the course of development and a guide to action?

However, this first argument could not do the whole job. Even admitting its validity (that is, even leaving completely aside the question of what *type of State* is suitable for defending the country against external enemies – and it is true that Stalin used the opportunity to condemn every opponent of his policies as a 'foreign agent'), it presupposes *another argument: that of the complete victory of socialism in the USSR*.

Stalin claimed in his Report on the Draft Constitution of the USSR:

'The total victory of the socialist system in all the spheres of the national economy is now an established fact. This means that the exploitation of man by man has been suppressed, abolished, and that the socialist property of the instruments and means of production has developed into the unassailable foundation of our Soviet society. [. . .] Is it still possible to call our working class a proletariat? Obviously not [. . .] The proletariat of the USSR has become an absolutely new class, the working class of the USSR, which has destroyed the capitalist economic system and reinforced socialist property in the instruments and means of production, and is steering Soviet society on the road to communism.'

This second thesis is the most important aspect of the argument developed by Stalin, because it brings to light the theoretical deviation underlying the 1936 decision. It is a deviation of an evolutionist type, in which the different aspects of the revolutionary process are isolated from one another, and presented as moments which simply follow one another, distinct historical 'stages'. Revolution, as Stalin presents it, begins by overthrowing the power of the bourgeoisie, by eliminating capitalist property, by replacing the old State apparatus by a new one: this is the first transitory stage, the stage of the dictatorship of the proletariat. Once this period has been *completed*, a new stage is entered, that of socialism: socialism is based on a particular 'mode of production', and brings with it a stable State, the socialist State, which is no longer a class State, but a State of the whole people, a people made up of different classes of working people collaborating peacefully together. And it is within socialism, under the direction of the socialist State, that the 'foundations' of a future society, communism, are being laid, more or less quickly according to the rhythm of the development of the productive forces; under communism, the State will become superfluous, just as classes themselves will disappear. In all, therefore, three successive stages, each one of which can only begin when the preceding stage has run its course; and the links between them, according to Stalin's theory, can be explained by the great historical necessity of the development of the productive forces, to which Stalin's mechanical materialism attributes the role of the motor of history.

As a consequence, two essential factors were eliminated, or at least pushed to one side: the dialectic of historical contradictions, and class struggle.

The dialectic disappeared, because Stalin, in his theory of successive stages, purely and simply suppressed the tendential contradiction brought to light by Marx and Lenin: the proletarian revolution is *both* the 'constitution of the proletariat as a ruling class', the development of a State power which makes this a reality, *and* the revolution which undertakes, on the material foundations created by capitalism, the abolition of all forms of class domination, and therefore the suppression of every State. What Marx and Lenin had analyzed as a real contradiction, Stalin dissolved in a scholastic manner (in the strict sense of the term), by *distinguishing* mechanically between separate aspects and stages: *first* the abolition of antagonism, *then* the abolition of classes; *first* the construction of a 'new type' of State, a socialist State, *then* the disappearance of every State (Stalin did not answer the legitimate question: why should the State now disappear, since the 'socialist State' already represents the power and the interests of the whole people? Or, at least, he was content to point out that 'Marx had foreseen' its disappearance). One more example can be added to this list of mechanical distinctions: the idea that *first* comes dictatorship (dictatorship of the proletariat, transition to socialism), *then* comes democracy (socialism).

The class struggle ceased, at the same time, to represent in Stalin's theory the motor of historical transformations, and in particular of revolutionary transformations. It represented no more than a particular aspect of certain stages. There is thus a necessary connexion between Stalin's general argument (*cf.*

Dialectical and Historical Materialism, 1938), according to which the motor of history is the development of the productive forces, the class struggle being only an effect or a manifestation of this, and his theory of socialism: socialism is the transition to the classless society, which takes place not as an effect of the class struggle itself, but *after* the completion of the class struggle, as an effect of a different kind of necessity, a technical-economic necessity directed by the State. And there is a necessary connexion between this conception of socialism, the proclamation of the 'total victory of socialism' in the USSR, and the abandonment of the dictatorship of the proletariat, which coincided with a strengthening of the bureaucratic and repressive State apparatus. In the same way there is a necessary connexion, in Marxist theory, between the opposite theses: the recognition of real contradictions in the historical relation of the proletariat to the State, and the demonstration that it is impossible to abolish class divisions except through the development of the class struggle itself, since classes are, historically, nothing but the effects of antagonistic class relations, effects which appear, are transformed and disappear together with these relations. The 1936 decision (and it was no accident that it took the *Statist* form of a constitutional decision, and thus bore the profound imprint of bourgeois ideology) therefore put the seal on the link, then the intimate fusion, between a particular practice and a particular theory. Anyone who is surprised that the 'freest', most democratic (restoring universal suffrage) constitution in the world should have been accompanied by the establishment of the most anti-democratic bureaucratic and police apparatus, and *a fortiori* anyone who reassures himself by interpreting all this as a proof that, 'at the level of principles at least', socialism maintained its links with democracy, thereby permanently blinds himself with regard to the real history of socialism, with its contradictions and retreats. You must take account of this paradox: that the tendential fusion of Marxist theory and the Labour Movement, which is the great revolutionary event of modern history, also extends to their deviations. The misunderstanding or underestimation of the class struggle in theory does not prevent it from unleashing itself in practice: for the precise reason, one which deserves to be recalled today for the benefit of all those who seem to doubt it, that the class struggle is not an idea but an unavoidable reality. Yet the theoretical misunderstanding of the class struggle is not simply a theoretical event: its result is that the proletariat can lose the practical initiative bought at a high price, it can become the pawn of social relations of exploitation and oppression instead of the force capable of transforming them.[7]

There can of course be no question here of making a direct comparison between the decision taken by Stalin and the Soviet Communists in 1936 and that just taken by the 22nd Congress of the French Communist Party. Neither the intentions (which however count for little in history), nor especially the historical conditions, and therefore the anticipated effects, are the same. However, the decision of the 22nd Congress can neither be understood nor seriously discussed independently of this precedent.

The first reason is that it does in fact constitute one of the remote consequences of the decision of 1936. To restrict ourselves to the theoretical level, it is this decision, and more generally the whole of the ideological output which prepared for it and surrounded it, that imposed on the whole International Communist Movement a dominant mechanistic and evolutionist conception of Marxism, based on the primacy of the development of the productive forces, within which the dictatorship of the proletariat only functioned as a means, or even as a political 'technique' for the establishment of the socialist State (in spite of the fact that the Guardians of the Dogma insistently repeated and even hammered in the fact that it was a necessary means). For this decision provided – at the cost of a gigantic effort of idealization and thus of misinterpretation of Soviet reality, for which millions of Communists in every land were enrolled, willingly or unwillingly – the means

---

[7] It is certain that the mechanistic deformation of Marxism which occurred *after* Lenin was not invented by Stalin, nor did it suddenly appear in 1936. As far as the concept of the dictatorship of the proletariat is concerned, it can be shown that this deformation is *already* present in the famous texts of 1924 and 1926 on the 'principles of Leninism': in particular, in the very significant form consisting of the *transposition onto legal terrain* of Lenin's analyses concerning the role of the Soviets and of the Party in the Russian Revolution, and of the definition of their 'historical superiority' over the bourgeois parliamentary system as the effect of a certain *system of institutions*. But it is not my purpose here to study the problems raised by these texts. It is also interesting to examine the *Manual of Political Economy* published by the Academy of Sciences of the USSR.

for its own immediate 'verification'. The proof that Marxism, in its evolutionist and technicist Stalinian version, was 'true' and 'scientific' was precisely that the dictatorship of the proletariat had come to an end, that a 'definitive' victory had been won over capitalism, that a socialist society and State had been constructed which were now confronting other tasks – fundamentally peaceful, technical, cultural and economic tasks. In other words, this proof on the omni-historical scale was in reality nothing more than an imaginary projection, onto the 'facts', of the very theory which it was supposed to verify.

We are therefore obliged to state that the French Communist Party – at the very moment when, in order to respond to the demands made by its own revolutionary struggle, it is trying to fight its way out of this mystification and at last to take a critical look at socialist history – is nevertheless trapped more firmly than ever in the *theory* on whose basis the critique is being developed: it is posing, *in the same general form, the same question* of the 'transition to socialism', even if it has tried to provide a *different answer*. Unfortunately, it is the question itself which is wrong, and it is this question which has to be rejected.

But the decision of the 22nd Congress is not therefore simply a remote consequence of its 1936 precedent: it also constitutes, in the changed conditions, its *repetition*. It is simply that what Stalin and the Soviet Communists applied to socialism in the period *following* the seizure of power by the workers, the 22nd Congress applied to the period *before* the seizure of power, to the very process of the 'transition to socialism'. But the procedure is the same: having argued that economic and social conditions have now 'matured' in this respect, the Party declares that the moment has come to renounce the use of dictatorship, which was always irregular, and adopt democratic means, espousing legality and popular sovereignty. The same rectification (or revision) of the Marxist conception of the State is therefore necessary: the State, it is said, is *not only* and *not always* an instrument of class struggle; it also has 'another' aspect, one which is repressed under capitalism, but which allows it to become an instrument for the management of public affairs in the common interest of all citizens. The same restriction of the concept of the dictatorship of the proletariat to its repressive aspect is involved, together with its immediate identification with the institutional peculiarities of the Russian

Revolution (the single party, the limits on universal suffrage and on individual liberties for representatives of the bourgeoisie). The same restriction is placed on the role of the class struggle and of the antagonism between capital and the proletariat in the historical process of the disappearance of classes. It is therefore impossible to avoid asking the question: can you really hope, when you repeat the precedent of 1936 in this way, to rectify the deviation which it represents? Is it not more likely that this deviation will be retrospectively reinforced, within the framework of a nowadays untenable compromise? And above all: are you not exposing yourself once more to the nasty surprises reserved by the class struggle for those who do not take full account of the contradictions which it involves and of the antagonisms which lie hidden within it during the historical period of the socialist revolutions?

These questions must be asked, and will become more and more urgent. Only through practice will satisfying answers be found. But this will only happen if we succeed in 'settling accounts' with the theory of the dictatorship of the proletariat, which has been passed on to us in its Stalinian form in a truncated and deformed image that is today being in all innocence reproduced. And because fifty years of the history of the Communist Parties and of revolutionary struggles, marked with victories and with defeats, have brought their own objective and contradictory sanction to Leninism, which the same Stalin was not wrong to define, formally, as 'Marxism in the epoch of imperialism and proletarian revolution', it is also and necessarily a question of settling accounts with Leninism. Therefore, in order to begin, we must re-establish what it is and study it, so that we can discover the real questions which it raises.

Lenin's Three Theoretical Arguments about The Dictatorship of the Proletariat

Everyone knows that Lenin never wrote a 'treatise' on the dictatorship of the proletariat (which has since been done), and neither did Marx and Engels. As far as Marx and Engels are concerned, the reason is obvious: apart from the brief and fragmentary experiences of the 1848 revolutions and of the Paris Commune, whose main tendency they were able to discover and to analyze, they were never able to study 'real examples' of the problems of the dictatorship of the proletariat. As far as Lenin is concerned, the reason is different: *for the first time, Lenin was confronted with the real experience of the dictatorship of the proletariat.* Now this experience was extraordinarily difficult and contradictory. It is *the contradictions of the dictatorship of the proletariat*, as it was beginning to develop in Russia, that form the object of Lenin's analysis and of his arguments. If you forget this fact, you can easily fall into dogmatism and formalism: Leninism can be represented as a finished theory, a closed system – which it has been, for too long, by Communist parties. But if on the other hand you remain content with a superficial view of these contradictions and of their historical causes, if you remain content with the simplistic and false idea according to which you have to 'choose' between the standpoint of theory and that of history, real life and practice, if you interpret Lenin's arguments simply as a reflection of ever changing circumstances, less applicable the further away they are in history, then the real causes of these historical contradictions become unintelligible, and our own relation to them becomes invisible. You fall into the domain of subjective fantasy. In Lenin's concrete analyses, in his tactical slogans is expressed a permanent effort to grasp general historical tendencies and to formulate the corresponding theoretical concept. If you do not grasp this concept, you will not be able to study, in a critical and scientific manner, the historical experience of the dictatorship of the proletariat.

In order to be as clear as possible, I shall first of all set out *en bloc* what seems to me to constitute the basis of the theory as you find it in Lenin.

The theory of the dictatorship of the proletariat can be summed up in outline in *three arguments*, or three groups of arguments, which are ceaselessly repeated and put to the test by Lenin. They can be found in identical form, explicitly or implicitly, in every page of the texts of Lenin covering the period of the Russian revolution, and in particular they appear every time that a critical situation, a dramatic turning-point in the revolution necessitates a rectification of tactics, on the basis of the principles of Marxism, in order to realize the unity of theory and practice. What are these three arguments?

The first of them deals with State power.

You can sum it up by saying that, historically speaking, *State power is always the political power of a single class*, which holds it in its capacity as the ruling class in society. That is what Marx and Lenin mean when they say that all State power is 'class dictatorship'. Bourgeois democracy is a class dictatorship (the dictatorship of the bourgeoisie); the proletarian democracy of the working masses is also a class dictatorship. Let us be more precise: this argument implies that, in modern society, which is based on the antagonism between capitalist bourgeoisie and proletariat, State power is held in an absolute way by the bourgeoisie, which does not share it with any other class, nor does it divide it up among its own fractions. And this is true whatever the particular historical forms in which the political domination of the bourgeoisie is realized, whatever the particular forms which the bourgeoisie has to make use of in the history of each capitalist social formation in order to preserve its State power, which is constantly menaced by the development of the class struggle.

The first thesis has the following consequence: the only possible historical 'alternative' to the State power of the bourgeoisie is an equally absolute hold on State power by the proletariat, the class of wage-labourers exploited by capital. Just as the bourgeoisie cannot share State power, so the proletariat cannot share it with other classes. And this absolute hold on State power is the essence of all the forms of the dictatorship of the proletariat, whatever their transformations and historical variety. To talk about an alternative, however, is really imprecise: we ought rather to say that the class struggle leads inevitably to the State power of the proletariat. But it is impossible to predict in advance, in any certain way, either the moment at which the proletariat will be able to seize State power or the particular forms in which it will do so. Even less can we 'guarantee' the success of the proletarian revolution, as if it was 'automatic'. The development of the class struggle can neither be planned nor programmed.

The second argument deals with the State apparatus.

You can sum it up by saying that the State power of the ruling class cannot exist in history, nor can it be realized and maintained, without taking material form in the development and functioning of the State apparatus – or, to use one of Marx's metaphors which Lenin is always borrowing, in the functioning of the 'State machine', whose core (the principal aspect: but not the only aspect – Lenin never said that) is constituted by the State *repressive* apparatus or apparatuses. These are: on the one hand, the standing army, as well as the police and the legal apparatus; and on the other hand, the State administration or 'bureaucracy' (Lenin uses these two terms more or less synonymously). This thesis has the following consequence, with which it is absolutely bound up: the proletarian revolution, that is, the overthrow of the State power of the bourgeoisie, is impossible without *the destruction of the existing State apparatus* in which the State power of the bourgeoisie takes material form. Unless this apparatus is destroyed – which is a complex and difficult task – the dictatorship of the proletariat cannot develop and fulfil its historical task, the overthrow of relations of exploitation and the creation of a society without exploitation or classes. Unless this apparatus is destroyed, the proletarian revolution will inevitably be overcome, and exploitation will be maintained, whatever the historical forms in which this takes place.

It is clear that Lenin's arguments have immediate bearing *both on the State and on the dictatorship of the proletariat.* The two problems are inseparable. In Marxism you do not have on one side a general theory of the State, and on the other side a (particular) theory of the dictatorship of the proletariat. *There is one single theory only.*

The first two arguments, which I have just set out, are already contained explicitly in Marx and Engels. They were not discovered by Lenin, though Lenin did have to rescue them from the deformation and censorship to which they had been subjected in the version of Marxist theory officially taught by the Social-Democratic parties. Which does not mean that, on this point, Lenin's role and that of the Russian revolution were not decisive. But if we restrict our attention to that core of theory which I have been talking about, it is true that this role consisted above all of inserting the theory of Marx and Engels for the first time in an effective way into the field of practice. It allowed a fusion to take place between the revolutionary practice of the proletariat and masses on the one hand and the Marxist theory of the State and of the dictatorship of the proletariat on the other – a fusion which had never, or never really taken place before. Which means that although important progress in organization took place in the Labour Movement after Marx's time, this was accompanied by a considerable reduction in its autonomy, in its theoretical and practical independence from the bourgeoisie, and thus in its real political force. It is the transformation of Marxism into Leninism which enabled it to overcome this historical regression by taking a new step forward.

This brings us to the third argument which I mentioned. *This third argument deals with socialism and communism.*

It is not without its precedents, without preparatory elements in the work of Marx and Engels. It is obviously no accident that Marx and Engels always presented their position as a *communist* position, and only explicitly adopted the term 'socialist' (and even more so the term 'social-democrat') as a concession. We can in fact say that in the absence of this position (and of the thesis which it implies) the theory of Marx and Engels would be unintelligible. But they were not in a position to develop it at length. This task fell to Lenin, and in carrying it out he based his work on the development of the class struggles of the period of the Russian revolution, of which his work is therefore the *product*, in the strong sense of the term. This argument is now meeting the fate which the first two arguments suffered before the time of Lenin and the Russian revolution: it has been 'forgotten', deformed (with dramatic consequences) in the history of the Communist movement and of Leninism, just as the first two arguments were forgotten in the history of Marxism.

A first, very abstract formulation is sketched out by Marx in the *Communist Manifesto* and in the *Critique of the Gotha Programme*: it is that *only communism is a classless society*, a society from which all forms of exploitation have disappeared. And since capitalist relations constitute the last possible historical form of exploitation, this means that only communist social relations, in production and in the whole of social life, are really in antagonistic contradiction with capitalist relations, only they are really incompatible, irreconcilable with capitalist relations. Which implies a series of immensely important consequences, both from the theoretical and especially from the practical point of view. It implies that *socialism is nothing other than the dictatorship of the proletariat*. The dictatorship of the proletariat is not simply a form of 'transition to socialism', it is not a 'road of transition to socialism' – it is identical with socialism itself. Which means that there are not two different objectives, to be attained separately, by 'putting the problems into an order': first of all socialism, and then – once socialism has been constructed, completed, once it has been 'developed' (or 'developed to a high level'), i.e. perfected, once it has, as they say, created the 'foundations of communism' – secondly a new objective, the transition to communism, the construction of communism. There is in fact only one objective, whose achievement stretches over a very long historical period (much longer and more contradictory, no doubt, than was imagined by the workers and their theoreticians). But this objective determines, right from the start, the struggle, strategy and tactics of the proletariat.

The proletariat, the proletarian masses and the whole of the masses of the people whom the proletariat draws with it are not fighting for socialism as an independent aim. They are fighting for communism, to which socialism is only the means, of which it is an initial form. No other perspective can *interest* them, in the materialist sense of this term. They are fighting for socialism just because this is the way to arrive at communism. And they are fighting for socialism with the means already provided by communist ideas, by the communist organization (in fact by communist *organisations*, because the Party can never be more than *one* of them, even if its role is obviously decisive). In the last analysis, the masses are fighting to develop the *tendency to com-*

munism which is objectively present *in capitalist society*, and which the development of capitalism reinforces and strengthens.

A very important consequence follows, which I will state in abstract form: the theory of socialism is only possible when developed from the standpoint of communism, and the effective realization of socialism is only possible from the standpoint of communism, on the basis of a communist position in practice. If this position is lost, if it drops out of sight, if the extraordinary difficulties of achieving it lead us to ignore or to abandon it in practice, even if it still has a place in our theory, or rather is still talked about as a distant ideal, then socialism and the construction of socialism become impossible, at least in so far as socialism represents a revolutionary break with capitalism.

It is now a question, not of working out all the implications of these arguments, but simply of preparing a more complete analysis, of explaining the way in which it is formulated, and of countering certain false interpretations and unfounded objections.

3

What is State Power?

The question of power is the first one which must be examined. It is the most general question: it is in the historical possession of power by such-and-such a class that you find in concentrated form the conditions either of the reproduction of the existing social relations (relations of production and exploitation) or of their revolutionary transformation. It is also the most immediate question, the one which the workers face in their daily struggle for liberation, one which can be very quickly settled in one way or the other as soon as a revolutionary situation leads them into an open confrontation with the ruling class on the political terrain.

Lenin, following Marx, constantly pointed out that the basic question of revolution is that of power: who holds power? and on behalf of which class? It was the question posed in the weeks immediately preceding the October Revolution (the question of the 'two revolutions', bourgeois and proletarian): will the Bolsheviks seize power? That is to say: will the Bolsheviks be the instrument of the seizure of power by the masses of the working people, who have become conscious of the irreconcilable antagonism between their own interests and those of the bourgeoisie? Or will the bourgeoisie, rallying to itself the remnants of Tsarism, imposing by terror and by mystification its hegemony over the peasant masses and even over a fraction of the proletariat, and supported financially and militarily by its imperialist allies, succeed in crushing the revolution and re-establishing the bourgeois State, thanks to which, in spite of the change in political form, the essential factor (exploitation) can persist? All the revolutions and all the counter-revolutions which have taken place since, however diverse their conditions, their forms and their duration, only provide massive confirmation of this point. Which means that it is valid for the whole of modern history: and what is modern history but the history of revolutions and counter-revolutions, their head-on clash being felt even inside those countries which, temporarily, 'benefit' from an apparent tranquillity? That is why you will never find a revolutionary who does not recognize, at least in words, the decisive character of the question of power.

But there is more. You only have to follow the course of any socialist revolution (especially the Russian Revolution) in order to convince yourself that this question, which has to be immediately decided, nevertheless cannot be settled once and for all. It remains – or better, it reproduces itself – throughout the whole revolutionary process, which provides it in the forms imposed by each new conjuncture with a determinate answer. Will State power be held or lost? That is the question with which the historical period of the dictatorship of the proletariat begins. But it is also a question which continually reappears, just as long as a reason for its appearance persists in the form of the existence of class relations in production and in the whole of society. As long as this basis exists, the dictatorship of the proletariat remains necessary in order to develop the revolutionary forces and to defeat the counter-revolutionary forces whose contradictory unity is not destroyed until long after the seizure of power.

This shows that the problem of power can absolutely not be reduced to a *tactical* question. The forms in which this seizure of power is carried out *in the first place* (armed uprising, prolonged people's war, peaceful political victory, other perhaps unprecedented forms) depend strictly on the conjuncture and on national particularities. We know that, even in the Russian conditions of the period between April and October 1917, Lenin did for a short time believe that the conditions existed for a peaceful (but not 'parliamentary') victory of the revolution, when he launched for the first time the slogan: 'All power to the Soviets!' In fact, there exists no historical example of a revolution which can be reduced to a *single one* of these forms, which does not represent an original combination of several forms. But in any case this diversity does not affect the nature of the general problem of State power, or rather it represents only one aspect of this problem, which must not be taken for the whole. *The concept of the dictatorship of the proletariat has nothing essentially to do with the conditions and forms of the 'seizure of power'. But it is ultimately linked with the question of holding power*, which in practice determines the whole course of the revolution.

If this is how things are, it is because, in the last analysis, State power is not the power of an individual, of a group of individuals, of a particular stratum of society (like the 'bureaucracy' or 'technocracy') or of a simple, more or less extensive fraction of a class. State power is always *the power of a class*. State power, which is produced in the class struggle, can only be the instrument of the ruling class: what Marx and Engels called the *dictatorship* of the ruling class.[1]

Why the term 'dictatorship'? Lenin answered this question absolutely clearly in a ceaselessly repeated phrase, whose terms only have to be properly explained:

'Dictatorship is rule based directly upon force and unrestricted by any laws.

The revolutionary dictatorship of the proletariat is rule won and maintained by the use of violence by the proletariat against the bourgeoisie, rule that is unrestricted by any laws.

This [is a] simple truth, a truth that is as plain as a pikestaff to every class-conscious worker [. . .] which is obvious to every representative of the exploited classes fighting for their emancipation [. . .] which is beyond dispute for every Marxist.' (*The Proletarian Revolution and the Renegade Kautsky*, C.W., XXVIII, 236.)

Elsewhere, Lenin uses an equivalent and very illuminating expression (I am quoting from memory): Dictatorship is the *absolute* power, standing above all law, *either* of the bourgeoisie *or* of the proletariat. State power cannot be shared.

Marxism and bourgeois legal ideology

'As plain as a pikestaff to every class-conscious worker', says Lenin. He is right, because this argument is only the logical

[1] Kautsky produced a host of arguments to prove that the term 'class dictatorship' cannot be understood 'in the strict sense', because a class as such cannot *govern*. Only individuals or parties can govern . . . Consequence: 'by definition' every dictatorship is the rule of a minority, and the idea of the dictatorship of a majority is a contradiction in terms. Lenin, refusing to confuse government, which is only one of its instruments, with State power, showed in 1903 (in 'To the Rural Poor') that in the Tsarist autocracy it is not the Tsar nor the 'omnipotent' functionaries who hold State power, but *the class of great landowners*. There is no 'personal

development of the recognition of the class struggle, and this recognition is part of the daily experience of the exploited workers, in their struggle against exploitation. Which does not mean that this logical development does not have to overcome any obstacles. On the contrary, it never stops coming up against the power (i.e. the operation) of *bourgeois legal State ideology*, which the bourgeoisie has a vital interest in maintaining. Bourgeois legal ideology inevitably influences the workers themselves. They are not 'vaccinated' against it: indeed, it is inculcated in them by all the practices of the bourgeois ideological State apparatuses, from their childhood in the primary school to their adult participation as citizens in the political institutions of the country. To develop the analysis of the State from the proletarian standpoint of the class struggle is therefore at the same time to criticize its constantly resurgent bourgeois legal representation.

The whole question of 'democracy' versus 'dictatorship' is profoundly rooted in legal ideology, which then reappears within the labour movement itself in the form of opportunism: it is striking to note the degree to which the terms in which this opportunism is formulated remain constant from one period to another. It is impossible to understand the reason unless you go back to its cause, the reproduction of legal ideology by the bourgeois State apparatuses.

Legal ideology is related to the law; but although it is indispensable to the functioning of the law, it is not the same thing. The law is only a system of rules, i.e. of material constraints, to which individuals are subjected. Legal ideology interprets and legitimates this constraint, presenting it as a natural necessity inscribed in human nature and in the needs of society in general. The law, in practice, does not 'recognize' classes, which is to say that it guarantees the perpetuation of *class relations* by codifying and enforcing rules addressed only to 'free' and 'equal' *individuals*. Legal ideology on the other hand 'proves' that the social order is not based on the existence of classes but precisely on that of the individuals to which the law addresses itself. Its highest point is the legal representation of the State.

---

power': neither that of Giscard or of Jacques Chirac nor that of the Company Presidents of the 25 greatest capitalist monopolies! For this 'personal power' is only the political expression of the power of the bourgeoisie, i.e. of its dictatorship.

Bourgeois legal ideology tries (successfully) to make believe
that the State itself is above classes, that it only has to do with
individuals. That these individuals are 'unequal' in no way em-
barrasses it, since, seeing that they are 'equal' in the sight of the
law, any State worthy of the name will naturally set about dealing
with these inequalities . . . So it would follow that State power
cannot be described as the exclusive domination of a single class,
because this expression, from a legal point of view, *actually does
not make sense.* Instead of the idea of the domination of a class you
find in legal ideology, to be precise, the notion of the State as the
sphere and the organization of *public* interests and of *public* power,
as against the *private* interests of individuals or groups of individuals and their *private* power. It is essential to grasp this fundamental aspect of bourgeois legal ideology if you do not want to
find yourself, voluntarily or otherwise, trapped within its im-
placable 'logic'.

I said that the law is not the same thing as legal ideology, though
the latter sticks to it like a limpet; and here is the direct proof: the
distinction between the 'public' and the 'private' spheres is a very
real legal relation, constitutive of all law, whose material effects are
unavoidable as long as law exists. But the idea that the State (and
State power) must be defined *in terms of* this distinction, as the
'public' sector or sphere, as the organ of 'public' service, of 'public'
security and order, of 'public' administration, of 'public' office,
etc., represents a gigantic ideological mystification. The legal distinction 'public'/'private' is the *means* by which the State is able
to subordinate every individual to the interests of the class which
it represents, while leaving him – in the bourgeois epoch – the full
'private' liberty to trade and to undertake 'business' . . . or to sell
his labour power on the market. This distinction is however not
the historical cause of the existence of the State. Otherwise one
would have to admit that, like the omnipotent God of our priests
and philosophers, the State is its own cause and its own end.

The same circle is in operation in the manner in which bourgeois legal ideology presents the opposition between 'dictatorship'
and 'democracy': as a general and absolute opposition between
two kinds of institutions or of forms of State organization, in
particular of two types of government. A democratic State *cannot,*
from its own point of view, be a dictatorship, because it is a
'constitutional State' in which the source of power is popular

sovereignty, in which the government expresses the will of the majority of the people, etc. Bourgeois legal ideology thus performs a clever conjuring trick: it ceaselessly explains, convincing itself and especially convincing the masses (it is only the experience of their own struggles which teaches them the contrary) that the law is its own source, or, what comes to the same thing, that the opposition between democracy (in general) and dictatorship (in general) is an absolute opposition. This really is the case, it says, because democracy is the affirmation of the law and of its legitimacy (and 'democracy taken to the limit' is the affirmation of and respect for the law taken to the limit), while dictatorship is the negation of this same legality. For bourgeois ideology, in short, *where does law come from? – from democracy. And where does democracy come from? – from the law.* To the notion of the State as the 'public' sphere, as 'public' service, is now added, to complete the circle, the idea of the 'popular will' (and of 'popular sovereignty'): the idea that 'the people' is a *unified whole* (collectivity, nation), unified beneath its divisions, linking together the 'will' of all the individuals and transforming it into a single will represented in the legitimate majority government.

You must therefore make a choice: either the system of notions of bourgeois legal ideology, which *rules out* any analysis of the State in terms of class struggle, but which precisely for this reason *serves* the class struggle of the bourgeoisie of which the existing State is the instrument; or the proletarian point of view, which denounces this mystification in order to struggle against the class domination of the bourgeoisie. Between these two positions there is no possible compromise: it is impossible to 'make room' for the standpoint of the class struggle inside the bourgeois legal conception of the State. As Lenin said, with reference to Kautsky:

'Kautsky argues as follows: "The exploiters have always formed only a small minority of the population".

This is indisputably true. Taking this as the starting point, what should be the argument? One may argue in a Marxist, a socialist way. In which case one would proceed from the relation between the exploited and the exploiters. Or one may argue in a liberal, a bourgeois-democratic way. And in that case one would proceed from the relation between the majority and the minority.

If we argue in a Marxist way, we must say: the exploiters inevitably transform the State (and we are speaking of democracy,

i.e., one of the forms of the State) into an instrument of the rule of
their class, the exploiters, over the exploited. Hence, as long as
there are e ploiters who rule the majority, the exploited, the
democratic State must inevitably be a democracy for the exploiters. A State of the exploited must fundamentally differ from
such a State; it must be a democracy for the exploited, and a means
of *suppressing the exploiters*; and the suppression of a class means
inequality for that class, its exclusion from "democracy".
If we argue in a liberal way, we must say: the majority decides,
the minority submits. Those who do not submit are punished. That
is all.' (C.W., XXVIII, 250.)
For the Marxist theory of the State, which involves a class
standpoint diametrically opposed to that of bourgeois legal
ideology, *every democracy is a class dictatorship*. Bourgeois democracy is a class dictatorship, the dictatorship of the minority of
exploiters; proletarian democracy is also a class dictatorship, the
dictatorship of the immense majority of working and exploited
people. By holding on to the direct relation between the State and
the class struggle, we preserve the only key to its materialist
analysis.

Let us return to Lenin's phrase, which I quoted above: 'A power
standing above the law'. Does this definition mean that a State
power might exist without any law, without any organized legal
system – and here we must include the dictatorship of the proletariat, since the dictatorship of the proletariat is once again
always a State power, *as is* the dictatorship of the bourgeoisie?
Absolutely not. It means on the contrary that every State imposes
its power on society through the mediation of a system of law, and
thus that the law cannot be the basis of this power. The real basis
can only be a relation of forces between classes. It can only be *a
relation of historical forces*, which extends to all the spheres of
action and intervention of the State, i.e. to the whole of social life,
since there is no sphere of social life (especially not the sphere of
the 'private' interests defined by law) which escapes State intervention; for the sphere of action of the State is by definition universal.
We might here deal with a current 'objection', which is of course
in no way innocently meant, which creates confusion by surrep-
titiously reintroducing the point of view of legal ideology.

According to this objection, *Lenin's definition of the State is 'too narrow'*, since it identifies State power with the repressive function, with the brutal violation by the ruling class of its own law. Apart from the fact that this objection is not at all new – contrary to what one might think, given that, though it is in fact a theoretical revision of Leninism, it is presented as an example of theoretical progress and as 'transcending' Lenin's position – it is particularly absurd from a Marxist or even quite simply from a materialist point of view.

In Lenin's definition the essential factor is not repression or repressive violence, as exercized by the State apparatus about which we were just speaking, and by its specialized organs – police, army, law courts, etc. He does not claim that the State operates *only* by violence, but that *the State rests on a relation of forces between classes*, and not on the public interest and the general will. This relation is itself indeed violent in the sense that it is in effect unlimited by any law, since it is only on the basis of the relation of social forces, and in the course of its evolution, that laws and a system of legislation can come to exist – a form of legality which, far from calling this violent relation into question, only legitimates it.

I said that this current objection is particularly absurd, because if there is anything true about repression, for example police repression, it is precisely the fact that *it does not stand* 'above the law'. On the contrary, in the vast majority of cases it is provided for and organized by the law itself (a law which can, in case of need, be specially constructed to this end by the ruling class with the aid of its legislative and judicial State apparatus). It is worth recalling in this connexion that the closure of factories put into 'judicial liquidation' or their simple 'transfer' elsewhere, the sacking of workers, the seizure by the bailiffs of debtors' property, the attacks on 'illegal' popular demonstrations are all perfectly legal practices, at least in most cases, while the use of strike pickets attempting to prevent non-striking workers or blacklegs from entering a factory, the occupation of factories, organized opposition to evictions from workers' homes, and political demonstrations dangerous to the government constitute, in the official language, 'interference with the right to work', 'attacks on the property right', or 'threats to public order', and are quite illegal. You only have to think a little about the significance of these everyday

examples in order to understand Lenin's formula: 'Class dictatorship is a power above the law'. It is therefore not a question of
forgetting about the law, of reducing State power to its repressive
functions, but of recognizing the true material relation between
State power, law and repression.

You will see at the same time how absurd it is to present the
bourgeoisie, and in particular the imperialist bourgeoisie of the
present day, as a class driven by history, by the crisis of its own
system, to 'violate its own legality'! It may of course happen, in
fact it certainly does sometimes happen, that the working people,
defending themselves step by step against exploitation and making
use in this struggle of all the means at their disposal, including legal
means, succeed in exploiting, in the fight against a particular
employer or a given administrative decision, the 'gaps' in the
existing system of legislation and the contradictions which even
the unceasing activity of the jurists has been unable to eliminate,
and even certain favourable legal provisions which they have been
able to force through by their struggles. No trade union or Communist militant is however unaware of the extraordinary difficulties of such an enterprise and of its necessary limits, and
especially of the fact that it can in any case never succeed except
on the basis of a certain relation of forces, and with the support of
mass pressure. But, above all, what this ceaselessly repeated struggle teaches the working people is precisely the fact that the ruling
class, *because it holds State power*, remains in control of the game:
from the standpoint of the ruling class – as long as you do not confuse this standpoint with the moral conscience of its jurists and its
petty-bourgeois ideologists – law is not an intangible absolute. In
applying the law, or in getting it applied, it may be necessary to
find a way round it; it certainly always has to be transformed and
adapted to the needs of the struggles of the capitalist class and of
the accumulation of capital. And if this process of adaptation
cannot be carried out without calling into question the constitutional *form* (the public institutions – parliamentary, legal and
administrative) in which the power of the ruling class is exercized –
then, in that case, the bourgeoisie is not averse to making a political
'revolution': the history of France, from 1830 to 1958, provides
enough examples of the fact.

No relation of forces between the classes can be maintained
without institutionalized repression. But no relation of forces can

be maintained by or rest on or be identified with repression *alone*. That would be a completely idealist notion. An historical relation of forces between the classes can only be founded on the *whole* of the forms of the class struggle, and it is perpetuated or transformed in function of the evolution of all the forms of the class struggle. In particular, it rests on the relation of *economic* forces, in which the bourgeoisie possesses the advantage of the monopoly of the means of production, and therefore of permanent control and pressure on the conditions of life and work of the masses. And it rests on the relation of *ideological* forces, in which the bourgeoisie possesses the advantage of legal ideology (including what Lenin called 'constitutional illusions' and the 'superstitious religion of the State', which are supported by bourgeois law), the advantage of the whole of bourgeois ideology materialized in the daily operation of the ideological State apparatuses, in which the exploited workers themselves are held.

Lenin's definition cannot therefore be 'too narrow', in the sense that it might be supposed to take account of only one aspect of State power (the repressive aspect). On the contrary, it aims precisely to show that *all* the aspects of State power (repressive and non-repressive, which actually cannot be separated) are determined by the relation of class domination and contribute to the reproduction of its political conditions. In this sense, all the functions of the State are through and through political: including of course, the 'economic' and 'ideological' functions. But Lenin's definition is *just 'narrow' enough* to exclude the possibility that, in a class society, any aspect whatever of the State might escape the field of class antagonism.

In reality the distinction between a 'narrow' and a 'broad' definition of the State is an old theme, which can be traced a long way back in the history of the labour movement. It was already invoked by the theoreticians of Social-Democracy against the Marxist theses on the State and the dictatorship of the proletariat: 'Marx and Engels regard the State not as the State in the broad sense, not as an organ of guidance, as the representative of the general interests of society. It is the State as the power, the State as the organ of authority, the State as the instrument of the rule of one class over another', wrote the Belgian Socialist Vandervelde in 1918, quoted by Lenin. (C.W., XXVIII, 322.) The need, stressed by Marx, to overthrow the State power of the bourgeoisie *by destroying* the bourgeois State apparatus would in this perspective obviously only concern 'the State in the narrow sense'. . . As far as 'the State in the broad sense' is concerned, the organ of guidance and public service, it would have to be not destroyed but developed: the point would be to make 'the transition from the State in the narrow sense to the State in the broad sense', to organize 'the separation of the State as an organ of authority from the State as an organ of guidance, or, to use Saint-Simon's expression, of the government of men from the administration of things' (Vandervelde; in *op. cit.*, pp. 323–24). The reference to Saint-Simon's humanist technocratism is illuminating.

Those of our comrades who, after the event, are hurriedly seeking 'theoretical' foundations for the abandonment of the concept of the dictatorship of the proletariat are being driven into exactly the same position. Here is a typical example. François Hincker, immediately after the 22nd Congress of the French Party, published a series of three articles in which he wrote:

'Throughout the whole history of the Marxist-Leninist labour movement, two appreciations [*sic*] of the concept of the State have circulated and intersected. [. . .] A "narrow" appreciation: the State is a repressive apparatus which has been produced by the governing class [*sic*], which is separated from the social base (relations of production), and intervenes on it from the outside [. . .] A "broad" appreciation: [. . .] the essence of the State is the organization of the functioning of *class* society *in the direction* of the reproduction of the existing relations of production, *in the direction* of the reproduction of the domination of the ruling class. [. . .] Everything suggests that, precisely, to "do politics", for the political personnel of the ruling class, is to surpass the immediate and competing interests of the individual members of the bourgeoisie. This domination, this hegemony, is exercised by means of repression, by means of ideology, but also by *means of organization*, to the point that, and just because, it renders *services which, taken separately, have a universal use-value*. This last aspect has not been sufficiently attended to by the old and new classics of Marxism.[2] [. . .] The ruling class has to represent its interests in universal terms, [. . .] to construct roads, schools, hospitals, to assure the

[2] Note the elegance with which the author constructs, to measure, a 'narrow' conception of the classics which he needs in order then triumphantly to introduce his argument for 'broadening' it.

function of *arbitration* in the form of a system of justice, which in general works in favour of the ruling class [*sic*], but which also, willy nilly, *guarantees a certain security, a certain order, a certain state of peace,* etc.'[3]

Thus he finally comes up with this pearl of Statist ideology: '*To smash the State is to develop the democratic State* with the aim of causing it to take on its full social function'.[4]

In fact, if the State 'in the broad sense' could not be reduced to class domination, if this domination only affected its operation after the event, pulling it and deforming it 'in the direction' of the reproduction of such domination, and sooner or later coming into contradiction with the 'needs of society', then the revolutionary struggle would not be a struggle against the existing State, but more fundamentally a struggle *for* that State, for the development of its universal functions, a struggle to rescue it from the abusive 'stranglehold' maintained on it by the ruling class . . . It is not surprising, then, that this definition of the State quite simply adopts the traditional image provided for it by bourgeois legal ideology. The Marxist thesis says: it is *because* the social relations of production are relations of exploitation and antagonism that a special organ, the State, is necessary for their reproduction; that is why the maintenance of the working population, *which capitalism needs* and the conditions of the development of the productive forces, *which capitalism needs* – including the construction of roads, schools, hospitals – must *inevitably take the form of the State.* But what we are now being offered, on the contrary, is the bourgeois thesis (whose value has, it seems, not been 'sufficiently attended to' by the classics of Marxism) that the State is *something other* than the class struggle; that it is partly (for the essential part) detached from that struggle, and that it *limits* the field of the class struggle (by subjecting it to the demands of the 'whole' of society). In turn it is at most *limited* (shackled and perverted) by that struggle.[5] Thus, if these limits are overcome, it will be all the more 'free' to fulfil its universal (democratic) functions . . . But all this

---

[3] F. Hincker, in *La Nouvelle Critique*, April 1976, p. 8 (my emphasis: E.B.).
[4] *Ibid.*, p. 9.
[5] There is an opportunist variant: the idea of the 'stranglehold of private interests' on the State, of the 'misuse' of public power for personal profit. Thus the slogan: let us fight to restore to the State as quickly as possible its natural liberty and universality!

is simply based on the following fake argument: seeing that society cannot do without the State on the basis of the existing relations of production, it can never do without it, even when these relations disappear! Bourgeois ideology starts from the presupposition that the State, its State, is eternal, and – not surprisingly – that is also its conclusion.

Remember Marx's words in the *Communist Manifesto*: 'Just as, to the bourgeois, the disappearance of class property is the disappearance of production itself, so the disappearance of class culture is to him identical with the disappearance of all culture.' In the same way the disappearance of the State is to him identical with the disappearance of society itself!

In other words, it is impossible really to separate the recognition of the class struggle from the recognition of the class nature of the State *as such* – from which follows the necessity of the dictatorship of the proletariat. As soon as you admit that the State, with respect to such-and-such of its functions, may stand outside of the field of class determination, as soon as you admit that it might constitute a simple 'public service' and represent the interests of the whole of society *before* representing those of the ruling class, *otherwise than* as the historical interests of the ruling class, then you are inevitably led to admit that the exploiters and the exploited 'also' have certain historical interests in common (those of the 'nation', for example), that their struggle does not determine the whole field of social relations, that it is restricted to a certain sphere of social life or that it may disappear under the weight of certain higher demands. And to crown it all, this limitation (therefore in fact abandonment) of the class point of view is invoked precisely with respect to the *present-day development of the State*, which represents historically the expression, reinforcement and *concentration of the power of the ruling class*, in step with the development of imperialism and the aggravation of its contradictions.

I have just been speaking about the class interests of the bourgeoisie as a whole. In fact, the bourgeoisie as a class has only one fundamental interest in common. Except for *this* interest, everything divides it. The interest in question is the maintenance and extension of the exploitation of wage labour. It should therefore be easy to see what Marx and Engels intended by their argument about State power: State power can belong only to a single class just because its roots lie precisely in the antagonism between the classes, in the irreconcilable character of this antagonism. Or better: in the reproduction of the whole of the conditions of this antagonism. There is no 'third way' between the extension of this exploitation, for which the bourgeoisie is fighting, because its very existence depends on it, and the struggle for its abolition, led by the proletariat. *There is no possibility of reconciling these two corresponding historical tendencies.* Marx and Lenin were always trying to demonstrate this point: the basis of the petty-bourgeois ideology of the State – and this is true even when it penetrates socialism and the organizations of the working class – is the idea that the State represents at its own special level a site of conciliation in the class struggle between the exploiters and exploited. And the no. 1 key point of the proletarian conception of the State, an idea which is absolutely unacceptable to bourgeois and especially petty-bourgeois ideology is the idea that the State results from the irreconcilable, antagonistic character of the class struggle, and is a tool of the ruling class in this struggle. The historical existence of the State is immediately linked to that of the class struggle, even when, indeed especially when it tries to fulfil 'general social functions', whether economic or cultural: for these general functions are necessarily subordinated to the interest of the ruling class and become means of its domination. The more important and diverse these functions become, the more this characteristic of the State as a tool of class rule comes to the fore.

Has the proletariat disappeared?
Let us put the point in another way: the only 'limits' on the class struggle are set by the class struggle itself, by the material means which it provides to the exploited masses to organize and mobilize their forces. One thing ought indeed to be clear: to the extent that class struggle is ever attenuated, it is not because antagonistic class interests have been reconciled or because the conflict between them has been transcended. On the contrary, it is because a certain relation of forces has been imposed in struggle by the proletariat. To take only one example, which has sometimes provoked debates inside the labour movement and has necessitated the vigilance or intervention of the Communists: the fact that representatives of the working people are *elected* to public bodies (Parliament, municipal councils) is an index of their strength and a help to them

in their struggle, one means among others of taking this struggle further forward; but it certainly does not entail that the workers thereby hold *the least scrap of State power*, as if State power could be divided up into a number of different local or individual powers, shared out between the classes in proportion to their political strength, and thus cease to be *absolutely* in the hands of the ruling class. It is the experience of struggle itself, provided that this experience is consistently developed, which inevitably leads to the recognition of State power as the instrument of the ruling class, to what Marx called its class dictatorship.[6]

If State power really is the dictatorship of a single class, in the sense which I have just indicated, it must be either the dictatorship of the bourgeoisie or that of the proletariat, which constitute tendentially the two classes of modern society, the two classes produced and reproduced by the development of capitalism. The class State, the dictatorship of the bourgeoisie and the dictatorship of the proletariat are three concepts representing the moments of a single antagonistic process. This is illustrated once again by the discussion now taking place, for, as we have seen, the rejection of the dictatorship of the proletariat leads immediately, by the logic of the ideological reasoning which it sets in motion, to avoiding, watering down and finally revising the idea of the dictatorship of the bourgeoisie, and therefore of the State as a class instrument. Thus you can begin to see why the concept of the dictatorship of the proletariat is inseparable from the Marxist theory of the State and of the class struggle: let it go, and the rest crumbles!

The proletarian revolution is the reversal of the existing relation of social forces, the establishment in the course of the struggle of a new relation of forces, the opposite of that which previously existed. To imagine that this reversal could take any other form than the dictatorship of the proletariat is to imply that there exists in history, over against the bourgeoisie, an antagonistic force *other than* the proletariat, *a 'third force' independent of the proletariat, capable of uniting the working people against capital.* This always more improbable miracle, this 'third force' is the saviour which petty-bourgeois ideology has long been awaiting in order to escape from the class antagonism within which it feels itself to be squeezed; this force it 'discovers' successively in the peasantry, the

[6] Communists have spent enough time fighting against the myth of 'counter-powers' in order not to fall into the same trap themselves.

intellectuals, the technicians or technocrats, the 'new working class', or even (the ultra-left or semi-anarchist variant) the 'sub-proletariat', etc. All this implies, against the whole historical experience of the labour movement, that, aside from bourgeois ideology and proletarian ideology, 'another' ideology might emerge within society 'transcending' the conflict between them. Finally, it suggests the idea that capitalist exploitation might disappear otherwise than by the tendential disappearance of wage labour and thus of every class division in society. But whoever believes that, as Lenin pointed out, will have to stop calling himself a Marxist!

I know what objection will be made here: that by presenting the antagonism between bourgeoisie and proletariat as *absolute*, unavoidable and inevitable (as long as capitalism itself exists and develops), I deny the reality of history by presenting this antagonism as *immutable*. But do the 'facts' not show that the present-day bourgeoisie is quite different from its predecessors, that the present-day working class is quite different in structure and social status from the working class which Marx wrote about (or the one which we think he wrote about)? Am I, out of love for the concept itself, refusing to accept the consequences of these 'facts'? The problem about this objection, which actually means that it immediately destroys its own value, is that it is based on a complete misunderstanding of Marxist theory, and of its dialectical character. Marx's theory is not founded on the definition of some kind of 'pure' proletariat (standing against a 'pure' bourgeoisie): there is no 'pure' proletariat, there is no 'pure' revolution and there is no 'pure' communism. This theory does not depend on a picture of social classes with the fixed characteristics of a given epoch (the nineteenth century, or the beginning of the twentieth century, etc.). And for the excellent reason that the object of Marxist theory is not to paint such a picture, as a sociologist might do, but *to analyse the antagonism itself*, to discover the tendential laws of its evolution, of its historical transformation, and thus to explain the necessity of these transformations in the structure of social classes, ceaselessly imposed by the development of capital. Remember Marx, in the *Communist Manifesto*: unlike all previous modes of production, he says, capitalism is itself 'revolutionary'; it is constantly overturning social relations, including those which it has itself created.

It should now be possible to see why it is wrong to confuse the *absolute* character of the antagonism between classes (which is the root of the whole question) with the idea of the *immutability* of social classes, an idea which can then be triumphantly 'disproved by the facts': this confusion actually amounts to a denial of the antagonism between the classes, to its progressive attenuation, and consequently to the conjuring away of the need for a revolutionary break with capitalism. Just as, in other circumstances, the transformation of the knowledge produced by the natural sciences allowed idealist philosophy to proclaim that 'matter has disappeared', we are here faced with a situation in which it is being ever more openly explained that classes are disappearing: no more 'bourgeoisie', in the strict sense, no more 'proletariat', in the strict sense. Power lies, so we are told, not with the bourgeoisie as a class, but in the hands of a few families, or rather of twenty-five or thirty individuals, the Company Presidents of the great groups of monopolies; that is, it lies nowhere, or rather in a simple, abstract politico-economic *system* which owes the persistence of its influence over men, over the people, only to the backwardness of their political consciousness! The antithesis to the capitalist system is no longer the proletariat, but everyone, or almost everyone: for almost everyone, in one sense or another, is part of the working people! The proletariat is now interpreted simply as *one category of working people* among others.[7]

The facts (since they have been mentioned) are quite different. They show that, with the development of capitalism, and especially of present-day imperialism, the antagonism is actually getting deeper and progressively extending itself to all regions of the world, leaving an ever narrower margin of manoeuvre to the social classes left over from the past in their attempts to provide themselves with an independent economic and political position. The centralization of the State power of the bourgeoisie and its dependence in relation to the proletariat on the process of accumulation of capital are increasing. The transformation of more and more working people into proletarians, even if it sometimes runs up against historical obstacles which slow it down, is inexorably running its course.

Of course, the history of capitalism does demonstrate a ceaseless

---

[7] It is easy to appreciate the serious and solid nature of a theory which, having *removed* all those attributes of the working class which make it a potential ruling class, *continues* to talk about it as a ruling class.

evolution of the real relation in which the different fractions of the bourgeoisie stand to the State power of their class. There is an evolution with respect to the recruitment of the personnel which, through the State apparatus, guarantees this power in practice. There is – which is far more important – an evolution with respect to the manner in which the policies practised by the State favour the interests of this or that fraction of the bourgeoisie. But this absolutely does not mean that State power ceases to be the State power of the whole bourgeoisie, as a class, becoming in some sense the private property of a particular fraction of the bourgeoisie. This would in fact be a contradiction in terms and would inevitably lead in practice to the collapse of State power (which may happen in a revolutionary situation, provided that the proletariat and its allies know how to exploit it). State power is necessarily 'monopolized' by those who historically hold it, but it can only be monopolized by a social class.

In fact, in each epoch of the history of capitalism, there is always a profound political inequality between the fractions of the ruling class, even when this is expressed in compromises and unstable working arrangements. There is always a fraction which must, in order to maintain the State power of the ruling class, play in practice a role, a 'vanguard role', turning the State apparatus to its own profit, a fraction whose hegemony is the condition of the domination of the ruling class as a whole. The reason – and this brings us to the essential point – is that *State power has no historical autonomy*: it does not constitute its own source. It results in the last analysis from class rule in the field of material production, from the appropriation of the means of production and of exploitation. That is why, *in the imperialist epoch, monopoly capital is dominant in the State*, and transforms the instruments of the State's 'economic policy' in order to reinforce this dominant position. But it remains dominant just because, by force and material constraint, *it asserts itself as the representative of the class interests of the whole bourgeoisie*.

A very important consequence with respect to the proletarian revolution and the dictatorship of the proletariat is that the bourgeoisie as a class is not a homogeneous whole; it is crisscrossed – today more than ever – by a multitude of contradictory interests, certain of them very deep-rooted, which set the big monopoly bourgeoisie against the middle capitalist bourgeoisie and the productive or intellectual petty-bourgeoisie of proprietors or salaried employees. It is just the fact that the bourgeoisie holds State power which enables it to overcome these contradictions, obliging the middle and petty-bourgeoisie to accept the hegemony of great finance and industrial capital. As long as the bourgeoisie as a class holds State power, it is very difficult or even impossible to produce lasting divisions within the bourgeoisie, definitively to isolate the big bourgeoisie and to weld together the petty-bourgeoisie and proletariat into a revolutionary unity. In any case, it is obviously not sufficient for this purpose to *change the government*, without touching the structure of the State: historical experience shows that every government, whether it likes it or not, is always subject to the relation of class forces; it does not stand above the State apparatus of which it is a part, but in a subordinate relation to that apparatus. 'The apparatus of State power', as Lenin sometimes put it, is not *external* to the unity of struggle of the ruling class, and this is all the more true the more centralized and authoritarian its character. Though apparently, in everyone's clear view, standing at the 'summit' of the State hierarchy, a government depends for its power on this apparatus; it is powerless against it, its 'authority' is empty. The fact that the government is taken over by representatives of the working people may constitute an important moment in the political struggle, but it does not mean that the proletariat together with the rest of the exploited people *holds power*. Those Frenchmen who have lived through the Popular Front government of 1936 and the Liberation will in this connexion recall not only the victories of these periods but also what we must accept (in order to draw the objective lessons) as a fact: that they were, for the time being, defeated, for they were unable to move forward from a popular government acting in favour of the working people, and in support of its demands, to the revolutionary seizure of State power. And if we look for a moment at the history of other countries, the examples of Chile with its Popular Unity alliance and Portugal with its Armed Forces Movement are more recent reminders, among others, of the *existence of this critical threshold*, below which all the victories won by the masses in struggle, however many and however heroic these victories may be, can always be reversed, and worse. But this is also the lesson of the Russian Revolution.

We can now return to the question of the proletariat. If the class structure of the bourgeoisie is historically transformed as capital is accumulated and concentrated and extends its field of domination to the whole of society, the proletariat does not stand outside of this process, unchanged. It is all the time becoming, tendentially, the social class whose original core was created by the development of manufacture and the first industrial revolutions. In fact the *historical tendency to the dictatorship of the proletariat could never have become a reality without this historical transformation of the proletariat.* Marx realized this at the moment when the practical experience of the revolutions of 1848–50 produced at one and the same time both the problem of proletarian power and the scientific theory capable of providing the concept with which to formulate this problem: 'We tell the workers: if you want to change conditions and make yourselves capable of government, you will have to undergo fifteen, twenty or fifty years of civil war' (Marx, to the Central Committee of the Communist League, September 1850).[8] As soon as you pose the problem of the dictatorship of the proletariat, you have to provide a *historical* (and dialectical) definition of the proletariat.

To define classes, and in particular the proletariat, in a historical manner is not to come up with a sociological definition, a structure within which individuals are classified – even one in which 'economic', 'political' and 'ideological' criteria are added together – and then to *apply* this definition to successive 'historical data'. It is something quite different: it is to study the *process of their tendential constitution* as classes, and its relation to the historical struggle for State power. 'Every class struggle is a political struggle', wrote Marx in the *Communist Manifesto* – which does not mean that it is expressed only in the language of politics, but that the formation of the antagonistic classes is the effect of the struggle itself, in which the question of who holds power is from the beginning already posed as the main stake. You cannot study the 'polarization' of society into two antagonistic classes separately from the historical struggle for State power.

The proletariat is not a homogeneous, unchanging group which bears its name and its fate clearly inscribed once and for all, for all

---

[8] Marx, *The Revolutions of 1848 (Political Writings*, vol. I, Penguin ed., p. 341).

to see. It is the historical result of the permanent process by which it is constituted, which is the other side of the process of accumulation of capital. An uneven, contradictory process, but one which is in the last resort irreversible.

Is there any need to remind ourselves of the material foundations of this historical process, in its continuity? It is the development of wage labour in the sphere of production, at the cost of individual and family production. It is the concentration of the workers in the great enterprises under the impact of the concentration of capital: and therefore the subordination of labour power to the 'machine system' in which the relations of exploitation, now irreversible for each individual, take on material form. It is therefore *the formation of the 'collective labourer' of great capitalist industry*, whose productivity is ceaselessly growing to the rhythm of the technological revolutions, while these become themselves so many means of pumping out his labour power; thus the expanded accumulation of capital is guaranteed. It is also the tendential extension of the industrial forms of the exploitation of labour power to other sectors of social labour, whether 'productive' – in order directly to increase surplus value (agriculture, transport) – or 'unproductive' – in order to reduce to a minimum the inevitable 'invisible costs' of capitalist production (trade, banking, public and private administration, but also education, health care, etc.). And therefore, at the social level, it is the reduction of the individual consumption of the workers to the simple reproduction of labour power, in given historical and national conditions – not excluding the form of 'mass consumption', i.e., of *forced consumption*, in which the needs of the reproduction of capital determine not only the quantity but the 'quality' of the means of consumption necessary to the reproduction of labour power. Finally, it is the constitution of the *industrial reserve army*, developed and maintained by the relative overpopulation provided to capital by periodic unemployment, the ruin of the small producers and colonialism and neo-colonialism.

These elements do not all work together evenly, although they are linked within a single mechanism, historical effects of a single production relation. Do they seem to have become weaker, less important in the imperialist epoch in which we are living? Are we not rather experiencing an enormous leap forward in the continuing process of the constitution of the proletariat, a process each of whose new high points is marked by a 'crisis' and 'restructuring' of capital? And in particular, in a country like France, whose position in the group of imperialist powers, with its colonial preserves, allowed it for a long time to *retard* and *limit* this process, and therefore to maintain a petty-bourgeoisie which, though large and economically 'inefficient' is politically indispensable to capital, are we not faced with a breakdown in the traditional system of balances and with a brutal acceleration of the transfer of these groups into the proletariat?

Nevertheless, this process does not automatically lead to the constitution of the proletariat as an independent *class*, or rather it only leads to such a thing through the interplay of contradictions intrinsic to its tendential law. That is just why it is not possible to present the proletariat simply as the 'core' of the constellation of working people, as something unaffected by these contradictions. The exploitation of wage labour rests on the competition between working people, without which there would be no wage-earning class; this explains the essential role played by the industrial reserve army in the capitalist mode of production. This competition takes new forms in every epoch, which depend on the class struggle fought by the capitalist class (concentration, industrial revolutions, skilled workers thrown on the shelf), but also on that of the workers themselves (as soon as they combine against capital in order to defend their conditions of work and life). *Imperialism aggravates this competition.* In the sphere of production itself, the new technological revolutions and the 'scientific' organization of labour made possible by monopolistic concentration completely transform the system of qualifications, and finally deepen the division between manual and intellectual labour. At the same time employees and technicians are pulled back into the ranks of the proletariat, while we also see the formation of new 'labour aristocracies'. These divisions are complicated and exacerbated by the manner in which capital now exploits a world market in labour power, whether by exporting whole industries to 'under-developed countries' or by importing whole industrial armies of 'immigrant' workers, isolated and super-exploited. To talk about the proletariat is also to take into account *the divisions* induced by capitalism among the working people, especially within the working class.

But it is also to take into consideration the struggle of this people against such divisions, an economic and a political struggle: a struggle which, as an economic struggle, is *already* as such a decisive political phenomenon on the scale of the entire history of capitalism, because its primary objective and principal result is to transcend these internal divisions, to unite the exploited masses against capital, in short precisely to create a class antagonistic to the bourgeoisie. The existence of *organizations* of the working class, trade unions and political organizations, and their transition from the corporate to the class point of view, from sects to mass organizations, from reformism to revolutionary positions – these are not things which come to pass after the proletariat has already been formed: on the contrary, they are themselves moments in its constitution as a class, with direct influence on the conditions of exploitation and the reduction of the population to the ranks of the proletariat. The bourgeoisie has to take account of these factors, and find new means of struggle, more efficient than those used against *individuals*, even against a large number or indeed a 'majority' of individuals.

So you see: to define the proletariat in accordance with its complete historical concept leads straight to a double conclusion which is of direct importance to us.

First: the development of the State power of the bourgeoisie, the reinforcement of its material means of intervention and the increased use of such intervention is in no way the consequence of simple technical and economic requirements, nor of the inevitable evolution of political power in general, but a direct function of the historical constitution of the proletariat as a class. *The State of the imperialist epoch* is not only the product of the class antagonism built into the capitalist production relation right from the beginning: it is *the State of the epoch of revolutions and counter-revolutions*; it is expressly organized as the State of pre-emptive counter-revolution.

Second: the process of constitution of the proletariat as a class is, for the fundamental reason indicated above, an *unfinished* process, counteracted by the very capitalism which sets it in motion. This process precisely cannot be brought to a conclusion *without the proletarian revolution*: the proletariat can only finally complete its constitution *as a class* in so far as it succeeds in constituting itself *as the ruling class*, through the dictatorship of the proletariat. But this suggests that the dictatorship of the proletariat must itself be a contradictory situation, in a new sense: a situation in which the proletariat can finally succeed in overcoming its divisions and form itself into a class, yet in which at the same time it begins to cease to be a class to the extent that it ceases to suffer exploitation. Thus we can understand why, as we are now seeing, the arguments about the dictatorship of the proletariat immediately involve *arguments about the proletariat itself*, and why the abandonment of the concept of the dictatorship of the proletariat immediately causes the concept of the proletariat itself to 'disappear'. The circle is closed: the working people, if they do not constitute a proletariat, cannot hold State power as a class; they simply need the State to provide for their needs . . . It is a nice dream, but it is unfortunately only a dream.

4

The Destruction of the State Apparatus

'We are for [. . .] utilising revolutionary forms of the State in a revolutionary way.'

Lenin, Letters from Afar, XXIII, 325.

'The dictatorship of the proletariat means a persistent struggle – bloody and bloodless, violent and peaceful, military and economic, educational and administrative – against the forces and traditions of the old society. The force of habit in millions and tens of millions is a most formidable force.'
Lenin, *'Left-Wing' Communism – an Infantile Disorder, XXXI, 44.*

The State rests on a relation of forces between classes, which it develops and reproduces. It could not otherwise continue to exist. But it is not purely and simply *the same thing as* this relation of forces. It needs a 'special organ', created and perfected for the purpose. This is the second argument of Marx and Lenin: there can be no State power *without a State apparatus.* The State power held by a class takes material form in the development and action of the State apparatus.

The opportunist deviation
We can explain right away, in a few words, the manner in which the opportunist deviation on the question of the State manifests itself within the labour movement and Marxism itself. We have seen that, seduced by the constant pressure of bourgeois legal ideology, it ends by taking over the terms of this ideology. Lenin constantly repeated and demonstrated that the essential point about opportunism was its position on the question of the State

apparatus. That is, its position on the question of *the revolutionary destruction of the existing State apparatus*, and not on the simple, abstract question of the exercise of power, nor on that of the use of the *term* 'dictatorship of the proletariat' – Social-Democratic opportunism, from Kautsky and Plekhanov to Léon Blum, always formally referred to the 'dictatorship of the proletariat', while at the same time emptying it of its practical content, the destruction of the State apparatus. Lenin wrote:

'A gulf separates Marx and Kautsky over their attitudes towards the proletarian party's task of training the working class for revolution.'

Kautsky had written a pamphlet dealing with the socialist revolution, on which Lenin comments:

'Throughout the pamphlet the author speaks of the winning of State power – and no more; that is, he has chosen a formula which makes a concession to the opportunists, in as much as it *admits* the possibility of seizing power *without* destroying the State machine. The very thing which Marx in 1872 declared to be 'obsolete' in the programme of the *Communist Manifesto, is revived* by Kautsky in 1902.'[1]

And Lenin continues:

'Kautsky abandons Marxism for the opportunist camp, for this destruction of the State machine, which is utterly unacceptable to the opportunists, completely disappears from his argument, and he leaves a loophole for them in that "conquest" may be interpreted as the simple acquisition of a majority.' (XXV, 484, 489–50.)

Let us leave aside the purely historical aspect of this criticism, even though it does not lack interest, for opportunism has always, right up to the present day, ignored the rectification of the *Communist Manifesto*, and explained that the concept of the 'dictatorship of the proletariat' in Marx's writings in fact means 'nothing else' than the 'victory of democracy' referred to in very general terms in the *Manifesto*. More important is the theoretical aspect. What Lenin shows is that opportunism is not characterized by a refusal to talk about the conquest of State power, or about the need for the workers to take political power. On the contrary,

---

[1] This historical *rectification* of the *Communist Manifesto* – if you ignore it, the Marxist theory of the State and of the dictatorship of the proletariat remains unintelligible – I have tried to explain in ch. 2 of my *Cinq études du matérialisme historique*, published in the 'Théorie' series, Maspero, Paris, 1974.

opportunism is characterized precisely by the fact that it admits and proclaims that this is necessary, but *without* talking about the class nature of the State apparatus, therefore *without* talking about the absolute necessity for the proletariat to destroy the bourgeois State apparatus, and then to destroy *every* State apparatus, on the grounds that to argue for such a thing would be to take up an 'anarchist' (or 'ultra-left') position. In other words, opportunism consists precisely in the fact that it imagines that the bourgeoisie and the proletariat can exercize power by means of a similar kind of State apparatus, a State apparatus *of the same historical type*, perhaps at the cost of certain rearrangements, certain transformations in its institutions and their mode of operation, but *without any historical break*, without a revolutionary transition from one type of State to another. Against opportunism, Marxist theory does not do *more* than point this out; it does not make prophecies, it does not predict what form this historical break will take in each concrete situation, or how its forms will be *modified* with the development of the contradiction between imperialism and the dictatorship of the proletariat. But it will not settle for *less*: it insists on the need for this break. This is the precise content of the argument which I just mentioned: that there exists a material threshold below which, even if the government is taken over by representatives of the workers, State power in fact remains in the hands of the bourgeoisie, which will either make use of a 'socialist' government for its own ends or overthrow it and crush the mass movement.

Opportunism therefore consists in the belief and the argument that the State apparatus is an instrument which can be bent according to the will, the intentions and the decisions of a given class. It consists in the argument that the government is the master of the State apparatus. And of the actions which follow from this belief.

But this is complete idealist gibberish. A social class does not 'decide' anything at all; it is not an individual, even a million-headed individual. Which means that the State power of a class is not the product of a decision or of a subjective will: it is the organization, the objective practical activity of the State apparatus, a set of *social relations* independent of the will of the men who play a material role in the structure of the State apparatus. And since this is exactly the point made by the Marxist theory of the State, opportunism is obliged to ignore this aspect of Marxist theory, which is precisely the most important aspect.

But the consequences of all this are not simply theoretical. Opportunism *acts* on the basis of its idealist conception of the 'conquest of power'. The Communists must think hard about those historical experiences in the course of which the revolutionary vanguard did not succeed in casting off the illusion that it is possible to make use of the bourgeois State apparatus, or did not succeed in finding the means to construct a new apparatus. For the price of this illusion or this inability has to be paid by the masses, and they pay dearly and for a long time.

But that is not all. For, as I said just a moment ago, the problem of the power of the working people, of the real exercise of power by the working people, is not settled once and for all with the first 'seizure' of power. And since this problem re-appears throughout the whole period of the dictatorship of the proletariat, opportunism also re-appears in the course of this period, re-born in new forms. It should therefore not be difficult to work out the consequences of the inability of a revolution to install *a different* State apparatus from the bourgeois State apparatus – an apparatus tending not to perpetuate and to reinforce itself, but progressively to wither away in accordance with its own nature – or of the inability simply to conceive of the need for such a thing, though it is explained in black and white in Marxist theory. It can only lead to the distortion, the retreat and the degeneration of the dictatorship of the proletariat. It leads in fact to the transformation of the dictatorship of the proletariat into its opposite, into what I shall call the dictatorship of a bourgeois State apparatus *over* the proletariat, in spite of the objections which this term might arouse among those who insist on denying the existence of the problem.

I shall add just one brief remark on this point. You can ask the question: aside from the general cause – the tendential division of the working class, a division which is exploited and aggravated by imperialism, and the unevenness of the historical process of the constitution of the proletariat – does not the tendency to opportunism in the organizations of struggle of the working class also have an *internal* cause, related to the conditions of the class struggle under capitalism and to the form conferred by this struggle on the revolutionary party? Lenin develops precisely this hypothesis when he tries to analyze the reasons for the fact that

'German *revolutionary* Social-Democracy [. . .] *came closest* to being the party the revolutionary proletariat needs in order to achieve victory' (XXXI, 34). It came closest, but it was not in fact that party: this finally had to be admitted. The point is that any political party of the working class is inevitably caught up within a contradiction which it may succeed in mastering, if it recognizes the contradiction, but from which it can never spontaneously escape. On the one hand, it represents a form (the only form) of access of the proletariat to political independence. It represents the form in which the proletariat can itself direct its own class struggle, with the support of its own social base, and on the basis of its own ideological class positions, breaking free from the hold of the dominant bourgeois ideology, instead of simply being the 'workhorse' of this or that variety of bourgeois politics. In this way, 'the emancipation of the working class will be the task of the workers alone' (Marx). But at the same time, because the class struggle of the proletariat is not fought out independently of existing social relations – and in order to enable it to take on its full political dimensions, in the whole field of social activity – the Party of the working class cannot remain outside of the bourgeois State 'machine': in particular of the *political* ideological State apparatus (the basis of the parliamentary system, the 'party system'). Now, once it is inside that machine, it can function either like a cog, or like the grain of sand which causes it to seize up. At the level of the history of capitalism and of imperialism, at the level of the historical process of the constitution of the proletariat as a class, the party of the working class *is not*, at least tendentially, a simple element of the ideological State apparatus of bourgeois politics. But we must admit that there exists an opposite tendency, a permanent risk to which the party is subjected, and from which it cannot escape without a constantly repeated internal struggle – the tendency for it to become the prisoner of the State apparatus against which it is fighting.

On this basis, it is possible to understand why the decisive aspect of the opportunist deviation is related precisely to this point, which involves *both* the historical objective of its struggle *and* the everyday practice of this struggle. This point is of vital importance for the question of the revolutionary party. It is precisely the point at which the two roads – that of Communist politics and that of Social-Democratic politics – diverge.

The organization of class rule

What then is the State apparatus? Essentially it is that material organization, the product of a particular 'division of labour', without which no State power can exist: at one and the same time both the organization of the ruling class and the organization of the whole of society under the domination of a single class. Before making a more detailed analysis, we must first understand this double organizational function, which lies at the root of the historical efficacy of the State apparatus, but also of most of the resulting illusions concerning the nature of the State.

To say that the State apparatus is the organization of the ruling class is to imply that, without this State apparatus – the armed forces, the civil service, the legal apparatus imposing respect for the law, and all the ideological State apparatuses – the ruling class (today the bourgeoisie) could never succeed in unifying its class interests, in conciliating or overcoming its internal contradictions and in pursuing a unified policy with regard to the other classes in society. Of course, this process of unification, which takes the form of the *centralization* of State power in the system of political institutions, is not the result of a contract to which the different fractions of the ruling class freely agree, or of a peaceful discussion between them. Or rather, such discussions do take place – for example, when representatives of different parties work out a Constitution together – but these contractual discussions only ratify an already established material relation of forces.

But we must also pay attention to the second aspect: the organization of the whole of society within the State apparatus, in accordance with the needs of the reproduction of exploitation. If the State apparatus was only a closed-circuit organization of the ruling class, it would in fact produce considerable obstacles to the maintenance of the power of this ruling class, for it would immediately result in the isolation of the ruling class in the face of the mass of society. The point we made a moment ago concerning the *law* is the key to an understanding of how things work in this connexion, because the law is already, thanks to the operation of the legal apparatus (legal code, law courts, lawyers, jurisprudence . . .), an essential aspect of the State apparatus in capitalist society. This point could be illustrated in detail with reference to the history of the State. In feudal society, the State apparatus comprises *both* forms of organization proper to the ruling class (like feudal lineage relations and bondage), which constitute it as a relatively self-enclosed 'cast', *and* much more general forms of organization, which correct or compensate for this isolation by organizing the whole of the non-ruling classes, down to the humblest of wretches, *in association with* the ruling class, in a single order binding upon everyone. This is the religious order, which assigns to the Church a determinant role in the functioning of the feudal State apparatus.

What, in this connexion, characterizes the State apparatus of the bourgeois epoch? What explains the fact that, in Marx's words, it represents a continuous 'perfectioning' of the State apparatus inherited from the old ruling classes? It is precisely – apart from the enormous extension of the State apparatus, the increase in the number of its organs and the growth of its capacity for intervening in social life, together with the increase in the number of its specialized employees – the fact that it carries out much better and more completely than previous forms the function of fusion or integration of the two functions which I mentioned: the organization of the ruling class and the organization of the whole of society. The bourgeoisie, as a result of course of its direct, internal role in the production and circulation of commodities, has absolutely no need to organize itself as a closed social 'caste'. On the contrary, it needs to organize itself as a class open to individual mobility, a class which individuals may enter and leave in the course of historical development. It is true that there are indeed forms of organization specific to the bourgeoisie, 'corporative' forms, for example the employers' organizations (like the CNPF in France or the CBI in Britain), professional associations and bourgeois political parties. But this last type of organization functions more as a means of subjecting entire masses of the petty-bourgeoisie and working people to the political and ideological hegemony of the bourgeoisie than as a means of combining the fractions of the bourgeoisie in a co-operative relation. And the bourgeois political parties themselves only constitute one aspect of the operation of the bourgeois political apparatus, with its parliamentary and municipal institutions, etc.

It is important to realize that it is this double, simultaneous function of the State apparatus, brought to perfection by capitalism, which allows us to understand why the class struggle takes place not only *between* the State apparatus on the one hand and the exploited classes on the other, but also, in part, *within* the State apparatus itself. The State apparatus is held fast in the class struggle of which it is a product.

These schematic remarks allow us above all to grasp a very important fact, which Lenin constantly emphasized: the fact that each great historical epoch, based on a determinate material mode of production, comprises tendentially *one type of State*, i.e. one *general* determinate form of State. A ruling class cannot make use of any type of State apparatus; it is obliged to organize itself in historically imperative forms, which relate to the new forms of class struggle in which it is held fast. The feudal-ecclesiastical type of organization is completely ineffective as a means of organizing the class rule of the bourgeoisie. The same general point is true of course with respect to the dictatorship of the proletariat. If the class struggle fought out by the proletariat is of a quite different kind from that of the bourgeoisie, it follows that, even if it does need *some kind* of State apparatus, it cannot purely and simply make use – as if they were instruments which could be manipulated at will – of the standing army, the law courts and their judges, the secret and special police forces, the parliamentary system, the administrative bureaucracy, immune from practically any form of control by the people, or the school system, which segregates the children and is cut off from the sphere of production, etc. To picture this in simple terms, let us say that, if State power is an instrument in the service of the class interest of the bourgeoisie, the State apparatus in which it takes material form is not itself a simple instrument: it is a 'machine' in which the ruling class is held fast, to which it is in a certain sense subjected, at least with regard to its general historical forms. And this 'machine' determines the possibilities of political action open to the ruling class, just as the need for profit, for accumulation, and the compelling force of capitalist competition determine its possibilities of economic action. There is no question of escaping from either constraint: the 'will' of the capitalists, like that of the people, plays no role here.

In order to illustrate this point, let us take a small but significant example of present-day interest. A political question has recently arisen, in West Germany and in France, concerning the rights and duties of *civil servants*. The West German government and administration, in the tradition of the Prussian Empire and of

Nazism, are identifying service to the State with service to the
government in power and to its policies, and are sacking anyone
opposed to these policies on the grounds that they are 'extremists'
and 'enemies of the Constitution'. In France, in spite of the
desires of men like Poniatowski to imitate this enticing example,
the continuity of democratic struggles is still guaranteeing the
distinction between 'service to the State' and service to this or that
government, whose task is to carry out the policy of the dominant
big bourgeoisie. This makes a big difference, which must not be
underestimated, because it provides individuals living on one side
of the Rhine with rights and guarantees of which those living on
the other side are deprived. But this only means that these individuals, in their capacity as private citizens, are allowed to think
what they like about the class policy which they have to carry out –
and not that they are allowed to oppose it; for, in France as in
West Germany, they would in that case find themselves out of a
job, not because of a *Berufsverbot*, but on the grounds of 'professional misconduct', and the result is the same. But that is not
all: for what can 'service to the State' mean, historically, when it is
distinguished from service to this or that particular government?
A non-political form of service, above or beyond class politics?
Not at all: it means *service to any government whose policy is compatible with the maintenance of the existing order*, that of bourgeois
property relations and of bourgeois law. By keeping itself relatively independent of changes of government, the body of civil
servants of the bourgeois State, whatever the ideas which any of
its members might have in his head, guarantees precisely the
primacy of the State apparatus over the government itself. Thus
the bourgeoisie's hold as a class over State power, instead of being
exposed to the hazards of an election, or of a motion of non-
confidence, or to the whims or errors of appreciation of a President
of the Republic, can lean for support on the firm foundation of the
'sense of duty' and of the 'professional ethics' of thousands of civil
servants (and of course also, more prosaically, on their total
financial dependence on the State).

But let us take another example which relates to this point. In
replying to the provocative remarks of a Minister of Public Order,
who had accused high civil servants sympathetic to the Socialist
Party of having used 'for partisan purposes' information which
they had acquired in the exercise of their function, i.e. of pub-

lishing official secrets, a leader of that party retaliated with the accusation that the examination results of the students of the National Administration School had been manipulated in accordance with their political opinions. The resulting argument is extremely revealing: for behind this 'left-wing' criticism you find precisely the same ideology of the civil service as a body independent of class politics and class antagonisms. You find it in this special modified form: since non-political civil servants do not exist in reality, it is only right that the different political tendencies should be fairly represented in the administration, corresponding to their national importance! But since this ideology is precisely the one professed by top civil servants, precisely the one fed into them at the National Administration School, the accusation – whether true or false – turned out to be a blunder: it was met by a general outcry of indignation, even among the Socialist students themselves! The next part of the story is even more interesting: *L'Humanité* (May 31st, 1976) decided to explain what was really at stake in this debate; it concluded that 'one thing is certain: the social origin of the students does not reflect the class composition of the nation. The number (practically zero) of students of working class origin is ironic proof of the extent to which the vast majority of the producers of wealth is excluded from the management of the affairs of State.' Two days later, a Socialist Professor of Law put forward the same line of argument in *Le Monde* (June 2nd, 1976):

'The creators of the National Administration School (ENA) claimed that they wanted to make it an instrument for democratizing recruitment into the top levels of the civil service. This policy is a total failure. The ENA is recruiting its students from a very narrow fringe of French society, from the economically and culturally most privileged groups; and since these students will later be entrusted with the reality of economic and political power both inside and outside of the State sphere, the School appears to be one of the instruments for the preservation of the power of what we must call the ruling class. This is not a matter of opinion, but an observable fact. [. . .] This makes it easier to understand who the top civil servants educated at the ENA really are, and to guess what use they will make of their power. [. . .] This system has provided the State with civil servants of high quality, [. . .] but such a narrowly based recruitment policy necessarily leads to a profound gulf between the top levels of the administration and the great mass of citizens.'

I have quoted these texts at length because they illustrate the point so well: you see the development first of the utopian idea of an administration which would be independent of the government thanks to the counterweight exerted by the presence of civil servants holding a different opinion, and then of *the utopian idea of an administration standing at the service of the people thanks to the democratization of its recruitment policy*, reformed so as to reflect the 'class composition of the nation'. And in consequence you are, if I may say so, forced to admit the absence of a revolutionary position on the question of the civil service and of the State apparatus: for any sons of workers or former workers who became civil servants *would thereby cease, by definition, to be workers*. The 'class origin' which they carried with them would change absolutely nothing with regard to the basic characteristic of the State apparatus: the 'division of labour' between the civil service, the administration of public affairs, the government of men, and material production; *the separation between the State apparatus and productive labour*. When someone argues that, since the 19th century, the number of civil servants has increased, so that these civil servants have ceased to constitute a 'privileged' stratum – supposing that most of them ever did – and today make up a mass of employees more or less badly paid by the State, and concludes that it is now possible that the State apparatus might therefore *as such* swing over one day to the side of the revolution, he quite simply 'forgets' that this increase in numbers represents *an enormous extension of the 'division of labour' in the State*. This division of labour is a material social relation, made up of institutions, of practices and of ideological 'habits' (as Lenin put it): it must be 'broken' by a long, difficult and persistent class struggle if a political and social revolution *of the working people* is ever to become a reality. The problem of the proletarian revolution does not lie in the *recruitment* of the members of the government and top civil servants from among the working people or from former workers; it is rather, tendentially, the problem of how the working people can 'govern' and 'administer' themselves.

Lenin drew the necessary conclusion when he asked: what type of State does the proletarian revolution need in order to seize and to hold power? Not the *bourgeois type of State*, of which the parliamentary republic represents the highest, most developed historical form, whatever the extent of the 'reforms' which might be envisaged *within* this type of State. But *a new type of state* 'of the Commune type, the Soviet type, or perhaps of some third type' (XXVIII, 237, 246, 255–57, 321, etc.). Lenin constantly stressed (in particular in connexion with the famous question – whose role in Stalin's writings I have already mentioned – of the Soviet Constitution, and of the exclusion of the bourgeoisie from the right to vote) that the *particular institutions* developed by the Soviet Revolution do not themselves constitute a 'model' State. They are only an effect of the general tendency of proletarian revolutions to produce this new type of State. Their importance – the importance of the Soviets – is that they *proved* the reality of this tendency. All subsequent revolutions, even if they were defeated by a more powerful enemy, even if they were only 'dress rehearsals', have provided in their own way illustrations of this tendency: from the Italian 'factory councils' and the Chilean 'workers' cordons' to the Chinese 'People's Communes'.

What has to be 'destroyed'

The dictatorship of the proletariat means the destruction of the bourgeois State apparatus, and the construction of a State apparatus of a new type; but not *all* the aspects of the bourgeois State apparatus can be destroyed in the same way, by the same methods, and at the same rhythm.

We know that Lenin (following Marx) particularly insisted on the fact that the core of the State apparatus lies in the State *repressive apparatus*, and that in consequence the absolute priority for every socialist revolution is precisely to attack this repressive apparatus, using the objective possibilities offered in this connexion by every really revolutionary situation, in which the masses of working people are involved in the struggle for the conquest of power, against the background of a grave crisis of capitalism.

Why did Lenin pay so much attention to the repressive State apparatus, therefore to its immediate destruction, which he considered both the condition and a first consequence of the revolution? For two reasons, which are really one and the same.

First, because – in moments of open and acute class struggle – it is the repressive apparatus in which the relation of forces favouring the bourgeoisie, on which its (absolute) State and class power rests, takes material form and is guaranteed. And the same is true *every time* when, even on a limited scale – strikes, demonstrations, for example – the class struggle becomes open and acute. The law must have power in order that the ruling class, standing above the law, may retain its power.

Secondly, because the repressive apparatus is tendentially the same in all the particular forms of the bourgeois State, in all the particular political régimes whose form it takes, whether we are talking about 'democratic' republican régimes, or 'authoritarian' régimes – dictatorial, monarchical or, in the present day, fascist. Of course, it is not an 'invariant' aspect of the State apparatus, standing outside of the development of history: but it is, *in any given epoch*, an aspect whose development and reproduction is not dependent on the different kinds of political régime. It is the armies of democratic republics which take part in fascist *coups d'etat*. And the principles of organization of the French and the German police do not differ from those applied in Franco's Spain: it is not the police itself which determines whether or not these principles can be put into operation in the same way, nor does it determine the extent of its own freedom of action.

To say that the repressive apparatus is the core of the bourgeois State apparatus is not to imply that enormous differences do not exist between 'democratic' régimes and openly 'dictatorial' régimes, in the sense which bourgeois 'political science' itself gives to these terms, with regard to the forms of political and ideological domination, to the relative 'weight' of the role played by open repression on the one hand and ideological hegemony on the other, or finally to the possibilities open to the proletariat in its class struggle to develop this struggle 'freely' as a political struggle. But as far as the forms of organization of the repressive State apparatuses are concerned, the 'last resort' of the ruling class, the differences are insignificant.[2]

As Lenin says: 'It is quite easy (as history proves) to revert from a parliamentary bourgeois republic to a monarchy, for all the

___

[2] What does it mean to talk about the 'last resort' of the ruling class? It means, first, that this is the means to which the ruling class resorts in the moment of its greatest danger, when the State of the bourgeoisie finds itself faced with a mortal revolutionary danger, and second, that it can only resort to this means at the last moment, when its use has been *prepared for* by suitable tactics of class struggle. I want to quote in this connexion from Dominique Lecourt's commentary on a

machinery of oppression – the army, the police, and the bureaucracy – is left intact. The Commune and the Soviets *smash* that
machinery and do away with it.' (XXIV, 69.) History also shows,
under our very eyes, from Greece to Chile, via Spain and Portugal,
that to move back from a totalitarian and fascist régime to the
'normal' bourgeois parliamentary republic *is extremely difficult*.
This is because, *in the epoch of imperialism*, there is an enormous
development of the class struggle and of the threat posed to the
power of the bourgeoisie, while the contradictions in the struggle
for the political and economic division of the world become ever
more acute, the result being that the process of militarization and
more generally the development of the repressive aspect of the
State apparatus receive a new impetus. Thus, as Lenin pointed
out with far-sighted insistence: 'The more highly developed
democracy is, the more imminent are pogroms or civil war in
connexion with any profound political divergence which is dangerous to the bourgeoisie.' (XXVIII, 245.) The reason does not
lie in the 'strength' or 'weakness' of the democratic conditions of a
country: for democratic traditions are always strong among the
common people, and especially within the proletariat, and always
weak within the ruling class. The reason lies precisely in that aspect
of bourgeois democracy which makes it a reality (a reality with a
price): in the fact that bourgeois democracy allows the 'free'
development of the political class struggle, the 'open' formation of
political organizations of the proletariat which *may*, provided that
they maintain their ideological independence, carry out propaganda and mass action for the abolition of capitalist exploitation.
This is the immense advantage of the democratic republic from
the proletarian point of view, this is the reason why the fight to
establish or to defend it is always an aim of the proletariat – and *not*,
as opportunism believes, the supposed fact that under this system
the State apparatus takes on a form such that it can be made use of,
as it stands, by the proletarian revolution. It is simply – though
this is of great importance, and may even be historically decisive –
that the struggle for political democracy, when it becomes a class

---

remarkable film, entitled *The Spiral*, dealing with the Chilean Popular Unity
movement: 'The Chilean bourgeoisie [. . .] succeeded in creating the mass base
which it quite lacked in 1970 [. . .] Though for a short time isolated, [it] worked out
and applied its "mass line" in order to undermine the positions conquered by its
enemies . . .' (*Le Monde*, 13.5.1976).

struggle against the reactionary bourgeoisie, allows the proletariat to organize itself, to educate itself, and enrol the masses of the people in the struggle for a more advanced objective.

The argument that the repressive apparatus is the core of the State apparatus implies neither that the State can be reduced to this single aspect, nor that the repressive apparatus can function alone. And it certainly does not mean that *all* the aspects of the State apparatus can be 'destroyed' in the same way, as implied by the vulgar and mechanical image of a series of hammer blows, an image which the bourgeoisie turns against Marxism by using it as a bogy to frighten the people. The historical destruction of the State apparatus is indeed an uncompromising struggle, which can finally leave no stone of the bourgeois State apparatus standing, for the existence of this apparatus is incompatible with the real liberation of the working people. But the destruction of a whole State apparatus, and its replacement by new political forms of organization of the material and cultural life of society, cannot be *carried out immediately,* it can only be *immediately begun.* It cannot be carried out by decree or by a single violent attack, but only by making use of all the political contradictions of capitalist society, and turning them to the service of the dictatorship of the proletariat.

Lenin already pointed out in 1916, in opposition to the mechanistic conceptions of a section of 'left-wing' Social-Democracy:

'Capitalism in general, and imperialism in particular, turn democracy into an illusion – though at the same time capitalism engenders democratic aspirations in the masses, creates democratic institutions, aggravates the antagonism between imperialism's denial of democracy and the mass striving for democracy. Capitalism and imperialism can be overthrown only by economic revolutions. They cannot be overthrown by democratic transformations, even the most "ideal". But a proletariat not schooled in the struggle for democracy is incapable of performing an economic revolution. Capitalism cannot be vanquished without *taking over the banks,* without repealing *private ownership* of the means of production. These revolutionary measures, however, cannot be implemented without organizing the entire people for democratic administration of the means of production captured from the bourgeoisie, without enlisting the entire mass of the working people, the proletarians, semi-proletarians and small peasants, for the democratic organization of their ranks, their forces, their participation in State affairs. [. . .] The awakening and growth of socialist revolt against imperialism are *indissolubly* linked with the growth of democratic resistance and unrest. Socialism leads to the withering away of *every* State, consequently also of every democracy, but socialism can be implemented only *through* the dictatorship of the proletariat, which combines violence against the bourgeoisie, i.e., the minority of the population, with *full* development of democracy, i.e., the genuinely equal and genuinely universal participation of the *entire* mass of the population in all *State* affairs and in all the complex problems of abolishing capitalism.

It is in these "contradictions" that Kievsky, having forgotten the Marxist teaching on democracy, got himself confused. [. . .] The Marxist solution of the problem of democracy is for the proletariat to *utilize* all democratic institutions and aspirations in its class struggle against the bourgeoisie in order to prepare for its overthrow and assure its own victory. Such utilization is no easy task. [. . .] Marxism teaches us that to "fight opportunism" by renouncing utilization of the democratic institutions created and distorted by the bourgeoisie of the *given*, capitalist, society is to *completely surrender* to opportunism!' (XXIII, 24–26.)

If you need confirmation of this point, this time written on the eve of the seizure of power itself, re-read the *State and Revolution*, that supposedly 'utopian' and 'anarchist' text:

'The way out of parliamentarism is not, of course, the abolition of representative institutions and the elective principle, but the conversion of the representative institutions from talking shops into "working" bodies.' (XXV, 428.)

And referring back to the example of the Paris Commune, he adds:

'The Commune substitutes for the venal and rotten parliamentarism of bourgeois society institutions in which freedom of opinion and of discussion does not degenerate into deception, for the parliamentarians themselves have to work, have to execute their own laws, have themselves to test the results achieved in reality, and to account directly to their constituents. Representative institutions remain, but there is *no* parliamentarism here as a special system, as the division of labour between the legislative and the executive, as a privileged position for the deputies. We cannot imagine democracy, even proletarian democracy, without representative institutions, but we can and *must* imagine democracy without parliamentarism, if criticism of bourgeois society is not mere words for us . . .' (XXV, 429.)

In the same way, with regard to the bureaucracy:

'Abolishing the bureaucracy at once, everywhere and completely, is out of the question. It is a utopia. But to *smash* the old bureaucratic machine at once and to begin immediately to construct a new one that will make possible the gradual abolition of all bureaucracy – this is *not* a utopia, it is [. . .] the direct and immediate task of the revolutionary proletariat.' (XXV, 430.)

Many ironic and cheap remarks have been made, from apparently very different sides, on Lenin's argument to the effect that the aim of the dictatorship of the proletariat is a situation in which even cooks would take part in running the State. There is something which smells bad in this irony, not only because it shamelessly exploits, to the benefit of counter-revolution, the millions of victims sacrificed by the Soviet proletariat and people in the course of their revolution, but also because it displays an obvious contempt for cooks. And since I have just quoted the passage from *The State and Revolution* on the destruction of bureaucratism, I will quote another passage, written a few months later (and which, at root, is still just as relevant):

'We are not utopians. We know that an unskilled labourer or a cook cannot immediately get on with the job of State administration. [. . .] However [. . .] we demand an immediate break with the prejudiced view that only the rich, or officials chosen from rich families, are capable of *administering* the State, of performing the ordinary, everyday work of administration. We demand that *training* in the work of State administration be conducted by class-conscious workers and soldiers and that this training be begun at once, i.e., that a *beginning* be made at once in training all the working people, all the poor, for this work. [. . .] The chief thing now is to abandon the prejudiced bourgeois-intellectualist view that only special officials, who by their very social positions are entirely dependent upon capital, can administer the State.' (XXVI, 113–14.)

Lenin returns to this question again in 1920, when he attempts to explain what it is, in the development of the Russian Revolution, that has a universal relevance, taking account of the differences in the political history of the different countries of Europe. What is particularly interesting here is the fact that Lenin, precisely because he *never* retreated an inch on the question of the need for the destruction of the bourgeois State apparatus, entirely rejects the idea that this process of destruction could take any other form than that of a lengthy class struggle, a class struggle which is already in its preparatory stages *before* the revolution, and which becomes fully acute *afterwards*, under the dictatorship of the proletariat of which it is the condition of existence. The 'ultra-left' idea of the immediate abolition of bourgeois institutions and of the appearance out of the blue of new, 'purely' proletarian institutions is not only a myth, useless in practice; it also leads to a mechanical inversion of the parliamentary cretinism governing opportunism: it is no exaggeration to talk in this connexion about an 'anti-parliamentary' cretinism, for which particular *forms* of organization (Soviets, 'workers' councils', workers' control, etc.) becomes panaceas, whose 'introduction' and immediate 'application' is supposed to allow a direct transition from capitalism to socialism, finally abolishing the need for the political class struggle. It is this complex struggle, whose detours are imposed by the radical nature of its own tendential development, which now takes first place in Lenin's analyses. Thus a remarkable dialectic is introduced between the discovery of the immense political *tasks* confronting the dictatorship of the proletariat, following the Russian Revolution, and the analysis of the *conditions* of the seizure of power in the European 'bourgeois democracies'.

It is worth quoting these texts at length, for they clearly contradict the dogmatic and simplistic image of Leninism too often evoked.

'The experience of many, if not all, revolutions [. . .] shows the great usefulness, during a revolution, of a *combination* of mass action outside a reactionary parliament with an opposition sympathetic to (or, better still, directly supporting) the revolution within it. [. . .] The "Lefts" in general, argue in this respect like doctrinaires of the revolution, who have never taken part in the real revolution, have never given thought to the history of revolutions, or have naively mistaken subjective "rejection" of a reactionary institution for its actual destruction by the combined operation of a number of objective factors. The surest way of discrediting and damaging a new political (and not only political) idea is to reduce it to absurdity on the plea of defending it.' (XXXI, 62.)

And it is *at this point* that Lenin introduces the argument according to which 'it was easy for Russia, in the specific and historically unique situation of 1917, to *start* the socialist revolution, but it will be more difficult for Russia than for the European countries to *continue* the revolution and to bring it to its consummation.' Not in the framework of an abstract comparison between 'backward', 'uncivilized' Russia and 'advanced' 'developed' Europe, which might today be triumphantly developed in order to discover proof of the congenitally barbarian and primitive character of Russian socialism (peasant socialism!), from which our democratic and civilized culture will, thank God, preserve us (as long as we can just get started . . .). But in order to demonstrate the concrete historical link between the tasks of the Russian proletariat, attempting to find the material form of its power and constructing an effective 'proletarian democracy', and those of the European proletariat, attempting to take State power in the framework of a 'bourgeois democracy'. *Both* faced the problem of the existence of this bourgeois State apparatus, which can never disappear as a consequence of the simple *will* to 'repudiate' it, to destroy it, but only through patient revolutionary activity.

'If it wants to overcome the bourgeoisie, the proletariat must train its *own* proletarian "class politicians", of a kind in no way inferior to bourgeois politicians.

The writer of the letter [Lenin is referring to a letter from "Comrade Gallacher, who writes in the name of the Scottish Workers' Council in Glasgow"] fully realizes that only workers' Soviets, not parliament, can be the instrument enabling the proletariat to achieve its aims; those who have failed to understand this are, of course, out-and-out reactionaries. [. . .] But the writer of the letter does not even ask – it does not occur to him to ask – whether it is possible to bring about the Soviets' victory over parliament without getting pro-Soviet politicians *into* parliament, without disintegrating parliamentarianism from *within*, without working within parliament for the success of the Soviets in their forthcoming task of dispersing parliament.' (XXXI, 80.)

It is therefore necessary to be able to adopt in turn and to combine *several* forms of action, several tactics for educating the masses in the struggle, precisely because the State apparatus (and especially the ideological State apparatuses, including the political apparatus) is not a simple 'organization of the ruling class', but *also* an organization of class domination within which the exploited, oppressed classes are objectively caught, but *within* which the 'development of their class consciousness' and their struggle for socialism must in the first instance take place. Their task is historically to 'destroy' something which is however not purely external to themselves: it is the structure of the world in which they live. But it must be destroyed, to make place for a new one.

Lenin is addressing the revolutionaries of other European countries at the moment when the new Communist Parties are being set up. But he is *also* addressing the Russian Communists, he is also talking about the tasks of the dictatorship of the proletariat, tasks which have turned out to be more difficult than anyone could have imagined. Between these two struggles there is no Great Wall of China, to use one of his favourite expressions. The struggle to take power includes a struggle against parliamentarism, involving the attempt to introduce a 'Soviet form of politics' into the heart of the parliamentary system, thus bringing its contradictions to a head (a form of politics which is not restricted to the parliamentary benches: it is even more important for Communists to 'go into the public houses [. . .] and speak to the people', and to work in the factories and in working class districts!), but this struggle is not such a simple one: for parliamentarism may *re-appear* in the Soviets themselves. Lenin continues:

'You think, my dear boycottists and anti-parliamentarians that you are "terribly revolutionary", but in reality *you are frightened* by the comparatively minor difficulties of the struggle against bourgeois influences within the working class movement, whereas your victory – i.e., the overthrow of the bourgeoisie and the conquest of political power by the proletariat – will create *these very same* difficulties on a still larger, and infinitely larger scale. [. . .]

Under Soviet rule your proletarian party and ours will be invaded by a still larger number of bourgeois intellectuals. They will worm their way into the Soviets, the courts, and the administration, since communism cannot be built otherwise than with the aid of the human material created by capitalism, and the bourgeois intellectuals cannot be expelled and destroyed, but must be won over, remoulded, assimilated and re-educated, just as we must – in a protracted struggle waged on the basis of the dictatorship of the proletariat – re-educate the proletarians themselves, who do not abandon their petty-bourgeois prejudices at one stroke, by a miracle, at the behest of the Virgin Mary, at the behest of a slogan, resolution or decree, but only in the course of a long and difficult mass struggle against mass petty-bourgeois influences. Under Soviet rule, these same problems, which the anti-parliamentarians now so proudly, so haughtily, so lightly and so childishly brush aside with a wave of the hand – *these selfsame* problems are arising anew *within* the Soviets, within the Soviet administration, among the Soviet "pleaders". [. . .] Among Soviet engineers, Soviet school-teachers and the privileged, i.e., the most highly skilled and best situated, *workers* at Soviet factories, we observe a constant revival of absolutely *all* the negative traits peculiar to bourgeois parliamentarianism, and we are conquering this evil – gradually – only by tireless, prolonged and persistent struggle based on proletarian organization and discipline.' (XXXI, 114–15.)

There are several striking aspects in these remarkable formulations of Lenin, dating from 1920. They are of an essentially *descriptive* character: Lenin is discovering, for the first time, the concrete forms of a question which is decisive for the revolution, of which up to that time he had only developed an abstract notion; he had first of all to describe these forms, to grope his way towards an understanding of the tendency which they represent. With hindsight, we can say that the fact that these formulations have only a descriptive character – beyond which Lenin did not have the time, the material possibility of advancing – that this fact had a very grave result; it allowed Stalin, by relying on *the letter* of certain formulae, and deliberately ignoring the others, to introduce what are prudishly called 'administrative methods' of resolving the political problems of the dictatorship of the proletariat: *purging* the Party and the State administration as a method of ideological struggle, then combining police terror with privileges of office in order to guarantee the 'loyalty' of the intellectuals of every kind to the Soviet government. And of course, as Lenin foresaw, these methods did not resolve the historical problem at issue, they only made it worse, up to the day when, in pursuance of Stalin's policy, the reference to the dictatorship of the proletariat – i.e., the recognition of the objective *reality* of the problem – had in its turn to be abandoned in a new attempt to exorcize and camouflage this contradiction.

Lenin's formulations are descriptive, but at the same time they are extremely illuminating, in so far as they show clearly that the problem of the resurgence of parliamentarism and of bureaucratism within the Soviet institutions themselves, in other words the problem of the *resistance of the bourgeois State apparatus* to its revolutionary destruction, is not a problem of *individuals*. It is useless to raise a hue and cry about the bourgeois intellectuals, to send them to concentration camps, to replace them by workers immunized against contamination by the old society . . . The contradiction arises *from within* the 'system'. The problem does not concern individuals, but *the masses*, the practices in which the masses are held, which they must learn to understand and to master in order to be able to transform them. Consequently – but this is perhaps precisely the concept which Lenin lacked in order to crystallize his analysis – it concerns the *social relations* in which the masses are held, from the intellectuals and civil servants to the workers themselves, social relations which *oppose them* to one another and yet at the same time *associate them* by the ideological force of 'habit'. It is today clear that the different aspects of the *division of manual and intellectual labour*, constantly reproduced and deepened in every class society, and inherited by socialism together with the 'human raw material' about which Lenin speaks, is in fact the material basis of this system of social relations which provides the bourgeois State apparatus with its astonishing capacity for resistance. And it is therefore clear that the struggle ('violent and peaceful, military and economic, educational and administrative', as Lenin said) against the forms of this division of labour, *within production and outside of production*, is the key to the revolutionary transformation which will finally liberate the working people from centuries of oppression.

But Lenin's thoughts on this question involve another consequence, one which brings us back to the present-day situation. In abandoning the reference to the dictatorship of the proletariat, you necessarily evade, whether you want to or not, the problems posed by the real exercise of political power by the workers, or at least you give the impression that these problems will resolve themselves, 'at the behest of the Virgin Mary', that all you need is a good 'democratization' of the State apparatus: of the army, of the civil service, of the legal system, of the education system, etc. Thus you create a mechanical gap between the revolutionary struggles of today and the problems of tomorrow: and consequently you obscure for the workers the question of the conditions and of the stakes of their future struggle. You encourage thousands, tens of thousands of Communist militants to believe that the obstacles which they come up against every day, in practice, in the fight to unite the working class, to unite all manual and intellectual workers in the struggle against the big bourgeoisie, are only problems of individual consciousness, and therefore to be solved by *propaganda*. The idea thus grows that if each Communist would only re-double his efforts to convince everyone around him of the superiority of socialism over capitalism, and of the unshakeable devotion of the Communists to the ideal of the happiness of humanity, then the masses would finally swing over to the good side and, by an application of their will, would sweep away the obstacles to the enjoyment by everyone of the benefits of civilization. Unfortunately, however, things never follow this ideal order, nor can the masses ever be won for the struggle against capitalism by a simple process of argument, on the basis of promises or of a beautiful dream of the future, but only on the basis of their experience of the antagonism between their own vital interests on the one hand and the existing economic and political relations on the other. But at the same time it is precisely in this struggle that they progressively discover, as the size of the tasks confronting them grows, the practical means to carry them out. After the seizure of State power, these tasks become even more difficult and decisive, but they are not of a completely different kind. By maintaining, in spite of all opposition, that a revolutionary party cannot content itself with recognizing the existence of the class struggle, but must 'extend this recognition to the recognition of the dictatorship of the proletariat', Marx and Lenin provided each Communist with the means of evaluating the importance of his everyday work of organizing the mass struggle: for this work is not only *the technical means* of ensuring the seizure of power by the workers' party; it is also a first step in and a first experience of a new type of political practice, unprecedented in history, quite different from the operation of the bourgeois State apparatus, without which this apparatus could never be 'destroyed'. The dictatorship of the proletariat does not provide Communists with a ready-made answer, with a clearly marked road; it only provides them with the possibility of posing an unavoidable problem. But well-posed problems will always be more valuable than dozens of imaginary answers.

The main aspect of the dictatorship of the proletariat

In spite of the brevity of these remarks, they do draw our attention to what will turn out to be the main aspect of the dictatorship of the proletariat as a new type of State, incompatible with the maintenance of the old State apparatus. This main aspect – as Lenin indicates in the clearest possible fashion, and as the experience of all revolutions has confirmed – does not consist in the establishment of a certain type of *institutions*, in the legal sense of the term, which might be considered to possess a universal validity, and above all which might *live on unchanged*, and continue to fulfil their revolutionary role throughout the whole period of transition to the classless society. Such institutions are necessary to the dictatorship of the proletariat, since this is still a State, and they provide it with a determinate 'political form', which depends on the historical conditions under which it is established and on the stages of its development. Such-and-such a type of institution (the Soviets, for example, once they have taken a general form and been officially recognized as organs of the new revolutionary State) can only partly reflect, and sometimes in a contradictory manner, the requirements of the dictatorship of the proletariat during a given phase of the revolution, and in given historical conditions. But the necessary political foundation and the principal aspect of all these forms is what we can call *mass proletarian democracy*. Now this kind of democracy cannot be decreed, it cannot be 'guaranteed', in short, it does not depend mainly on institutions, however much freedom may characterize them; but it can be won, at the cost of a hard struggle, if the masses intervene in person on the political scene.

Since this point is really the heart of the Marxist theory of the dictatorship of the proletariat (with respect to its repressive aspect, too, its struggle against counter-revolution: the 'people in arms'), I shall look at it more closely.

First of all I want to remind those comrades who have 'forgotten' it, with the self-interested encouragement of the whole bourgeoisie, that *no real socialist revolution has ever been a 'minority' revolution*, a forcible takeover by the minority. Every socialist revolution in history, beginning with the Russian Revolution and continuing with the Chinese, Cuban and Vietnamese revolutions, which are epoch-making events in the history of the dictatorship of the proletariat, has necessarily been a majority revolution, a revolution made *by the movement of the masses* and by *mass organi-*

zations, armed and unarmed, which generally arose in the course of the revolution itself and changed with it. If this had not been so, no socialist revolution would have been able nor would it ever be able to overcome the material force of the bourgeois State apparatus, its repressive and its ideological power (the ideological influence which it exercizes on the masses themselves). And it was precisely when, in the course of the Soviet Revolution, the mass movement began to weaken and fade out, above all under the pressure of an unprecedentedly violent attack by a coalition of all the internal and external forces of imperialism, and also as a consequence of the errors of the Russian Communists themselves, when it was diverted from its revolutionary objectives, when the mass organizations were emptied of their content and in their turn became bureaucratic instruments for the control of the masses, that counter-revolutionary tendencies were able to develop at the level of the State.

The experience of the Russian Revolution did however enable Lenin to show concretely that proletarian democracy, revolutionary mass democracy, is infinitely more real, infinitely more democratic than any kind of bourgeois democracy.

It is one of the most widespread follies and calumnies of the enemies of Leninism, already spread by the 'right-wing' and 'left-wing' theoreticians of the Social-Democratic movement of his own time, that Lenin always 'underestimated democracy', the value and the usefulness of democratic institutions. This foolishness, which is in fact a complete falsification, was even recently repeated, I am sorry to say, by our comrade Jean Elleinstein, who tried to use it as one explanation of the 'Stalin phenomenon', i.e. of the destruction of proletarian democracy in the Soviet Union. And the same folly is unfortunately not unconnected with the constantly re-appearing idea that *it is impossible to talk about the dictatorship of the majority of the people*, that the notion of dictatorship is synonymous with the dictatorship of a minority. We must be careful in our use of words. To say that the dictatorship of the proletariat is impossible is to imply, like it or not, that the State power of the majority is impossible, that 'the lowest mass, the real majority' (XXIII, 120) cannot itself exercize State power. It is to imply that the power of the masses will always be *limited*, and therefore that the proletarian revolution is impossible.

The question of the majority and the minority cannot be a

formal question for a Marxist and a Communist. Which means that it cannot be answered independently of the question; *who* constitutes the majority of the population? What classes constitute the majority and how are they to be unified in a single mass movement? Every bourgeois democracy *already* relies on the fact that any of its governments represents a majority, is elected by a majority, necessarily including millions of working people. But that does not of course in any way mean that the majority classes in society, the classes making up the working people, and in particular the proletariat, in any sense hold or exercize State power: on the contrary, it means that they remain in subjection to the State. Because between the masses on the one hand and parliament or the government on the other there is all the distance and the opacity of the State apparatus and the ideological State apparatuses.

When Lenin says that proletarian democracy is *infinitely* more real than any bourgeois democracy, however progressive or advantageous the latter may be, compared with the open, brutal forms of bourgeois class dictatorship (for example, in our own day, fascism) he means that the difference between them is not simply one of degree, the difference between a narrow and limited democracy and a broad or extended democracy, but a difference of nature: the difference separating on the one hand the legal democratic forms realizing the power of a minority class, and thus *excluding* the possibility that the popular masses themselves have any hold, however precarious, on State power, and on the other hand a democracy which realizes the power of the majority class, and therefore *demands* the permanent intervention, the leading role of the masses of the people in the State.

In this connexion, the lessons of the Russian Revolution, as reflected in Lenin's analyses, constantly draw our attention to *two great practical questions*, always open and always being re-opened, never finally settled, on which the development of revolutionary mass democracy depends.

1. The first question, and it is a well-known question, concerns *the alliance of the proletariat and the petty-bourgeoisie* of intellectuals, producers (small peasants and artisans) and employees. This alliance can only be created by a struggle, a battle to overcome the contradictions opposing the proletariat to the petty-bourgeoisie, a

battle to detach the petty-bourgeoisie, in the course of the class
struggle itself, from the hegemony exercized on it by the capitalist
and imperialist bourgeoisie, in order to develop the hegemony of
the proletariat and of its revolutionary vanguard over the petty-
bourgeoisie. We must never forget that Lenin was, in the Marxist
tradition of his time, the only theoretician – I repeat: the only one,
because on this point his position is distinguished both from
Kautsky's right-wing opportunism and from ultra-leftism, and
even from the position of genuine revolutionaries like Rosa
Luxemburg – *he was the only theoretician who never held a
'ouvrierist' ('workerist') conception of the dictatorship of the proletariat*, which is in the last analysis an economistic and mechanistic conception of the State power of the working class. There can
be no dictatorship of the proletariat if the working class does not
carry with it, in the seizure and the maintenance of power, not
only the poor peasantry, and the petty-bourgeois strata which are
already being absorbed into the proletariat, but the masses of the
petty-bourgeoisie, even though their historical interests are contradictory. There can be no dictatorship of the proletariat if the
working class does not succeed in welding solid political, economic
and ideological links with these masses.

In other words, there can be no dictatorship of the proletariat if
the proletarian revolution is not at the same time *a people's revolution*. On this point too, even before October, Lenin was repeating
the true lesson learned from Marx and from the Paris Commune:
'Particular attention should be paid to Marx's extremely profound
remark that the destruction of the bureaucratic military State
machine is "the precondition for every real *people's* revolution".
This idea of a "people's" revolution seems strange coming from
Marx', continues Lenin; and he shows that this is because of the
mechanical way in which most Marxists envisage the notion of the
dictatorship of the proletariat and of proletarian revolution, for
they are simply waiting for that mythical moment when the proletariat, conceived of as a naturally homogeneous and revolutionary class, will itself constitute the great majority of society and find
itself faced by no more than a handful of capitalists superfluous to
production (XXV, 421). Elsewhere he points out: 'From the point
of view of science and practical politics, one of the chief symptoms
of *every* real revolution is the unusually rapid, sudden, and abrupt
increase in the number of "ordinary citizens" who begin to

participate actively, independently and effectively in political life and in the *organization of the State.*' (XXIV, 61.)

The dictatorship of the proletariat cannot mean the isolation of the proletariat: this idea is a contradiction in terms and in the facts – the dictatorship of the proletariat cannot overcome the counter-revolution, it cannot succeed in *disorganizing the mass base of the bourgeois State* unless it extends the real hegemony of the proletariat to the masses of the people, unless it constructs a revolutionary alliance of the proletariat, peasantry and petty-bourgeoisie. The fact that this alliance is constantly threatened, that its break-up constitutes a mortal danger to the revolution, is a fact which explains, as we know, many tragic aspects of the present history of socialism. But whoever has really read Lenin, and followed the trials and errors, the upsets of real history, whose tendency is manifested even in the contradictions of which it is made up, will understand what is going on. He will in any case understand much better than those Communists who, in order to resolve the problem of class alliances, a problem which, ever since 1917, especially in France, has proved a stumbling block to so many revolutionary struggles, think that the proletariat should be drowned in an undifferentiated mass of 'working people' having 'an interest in socialism'. The concept of the dictatorship of the proletariat certainly does not exclude the question of alliances and of the allies of the proletariat in the revolutionary process; on the contrary, *it urgently poses this question.* And it shows that it is a *political* question, in the strong sense of the term, a question of mass politics, which goes far beyond the simple framework of constitutional decisions and guarantees.

Unity between the proletariat and its allies cannot emerge spontaneously from the economic interests which they have in common, and from an appeal to those interests. 'Propaganda and agitation alone are not enough. [. . .] The masses must have their own political experience.' (XXXI, 93.) This question is central for Communist Parties today. If the emergence of the contradictions between the revolutionary struggle in the capitalist countries and the defence of the interests of the Soviet State apparatus is the negative cause of the tendency now appearing in France to 'abandon' without further ceremony the concept of the dictatorship of the proletariat, it should not lead us to ignore another, just as obvious cause: the search for a positive solution to the problem of class alliances, of the union of the people against imperialist capital.

It is because it was not possible, in spite of the efforts of the Popular Front and of the Resistance, to find an answer to this question in the period when the dictatorship of the proletariat (as it was then generally conceived) figured as a sacred principle, that the conclusion is drawn: the way forward is to abandon it. But this solution is illusory; and it can only result in self-deception if it leads the Communists to believe that the union of the people *already exists*, potentially, in the economic and sociological evolution of capitalism, and that it only needs to be brought out into the open, to be revealed by a patient effort of explanation or propaganda. The economic foundations of a revolutionary class alliance do exist in all the imperialist countries, including the most 'developed'. But as long as capitalism continues to develop (and imperialist, monopolist capitalism is developing *more quickly* than ever before), the foundations of the hegemony of big capital also continue to exist. The contradictory process leading to the isolation of big capital, to the class unity of the proletariat and its alliance with the whole of the working people, and even with certain fractions of the bourgeoisie, is not pre-determined, nor is it the simple political translation of a process of economic evolution. It is the stake of a practical struggle between the revolutionary and counter-revolutionary forces in which the revolutionary forces – proletariat, peasantry and those manual or intellectual workers who are in course of being absorbed into the proletariat – *must* exploit the contradictions of the class enemy. Lenin wrote in 1920:

'To carry on a war for the overthrow of the international bourgeoisie, a war which is a hundred times more difficult, protracted and complex than the most stubborn of ordinary wars between States, and to renounce in advance any change of tack, or any utilization of a conflict of interests (even if temporary) among one's enemies, or any conciliation or compromise with possible allies (even if they are temporary, unstable, vacillating or conditional allies) – is that not ridiculous in the extreme? Is it not like making a difficult ascent of an unexplored and hitherto inaccessible mountain and refusing in advance ever to move in zig-zags, ever to retrace one's steps, or ever to abandon a course once selected, and to try others? [. . . .] The more powerful enemy can be vanquished only by exerting the utmost effort, and by the most

thorough, careful, attentive, skilful and *obligatory* use of any, even
the smallest, rift between the enemies, any conflict of interests
among the bourgeoisie of the various countries and among the
various groups or types of bourgeoisie within the various countries, and also by taking advantage of any, even the smallest, opportunity of winning a mass ally, even though this ally is temporary,
vacillating, unstable, unreliable and conditional. Those who do
not understand this reveal a failure to understand even the smallest
grain of Marxism, of modern scientific socialism *in general.* Those
who have not proved *in practice*, over a fairly considerable period
of time and in fairly varied political situations, their ability to
apply this truth in practice have not yet learned to help the
revolutionary class in its struggle to emancipate all toiling
humanity from the exploiters. And this applies equally to the
period *before* and *after* the proletariat has won political power.'
(XXXI, 70–71.)

I would put it like this: it is by carrying out this policy in the
period which precedes and prepares for the seizure of power that
the proletariat can learn to resolve the problem in the best possible
way in the period which *follows it.* But it is by understanding why
this is necessary *even* and especially after the seizure of power that
we can also understand why it is necessary *beforehand*, if the idea of
the 'seizure of power' does not simply imply for us a moment of
adventure for which the future does not exist. That is why the
concept of the dictatorship of the proletariat, in the historical
conditions existing in each country, is not a concept *in spite of*
which the vital question of class alliances can be posed: it is in fact
the concept *with the aid of which* this question can be posed in real
terms, so that the objective foundations of this alliance and the
nature of the obstacles which it comes up against can be analyzed
in a critical way.

2. But, within this notion of mass democracy, there lies a second
question, a different question which however determines the
answer to the first: it is *the question of the mass organizations of the*
proletariat. What made possible the seizure of power in the
Russian Revolution, what enabled the Bolshevik *Party* to give
tactical leadership to the seizure of power, was the existence of an
unprecedented mass movement of workers, peasants and soldiers,
and the fact that this movement found in the Russian revolutionary

tradition the forms of organization which it needed: the 'Soviets'. This therefore is the double, dialectical aspect of the Soviets; *both*, in contradictory fashion, the embryo of a new State, of a new type of State apparatus, *and* the direct organization of the masses, distinct from *every* State, transforming political activity, on the scale of the most general questions (first of all that of war and peace) from the affair of specialists or representatives quite distant from the masses into an affair of the masses themselves. That is why the October Revolution was able to set about destroying the bourgeois State apparatus, both 'from above' and 'from below'. And that is why the Soviets are historically revolutionary, coming after the Paris Commune, and before other forms most of which are still to be invented.

As we know, this question was constantly posed throughout the Russian Revolution, as it is posed in every revolution. The nature of the problems changes, the 'front' of struggle moves, the organizations which have played this revolutionary role become incapable of carrying it through, partly because they tend, like the Soviets themselves, to be reduced to the role of simple State, administrative institutions. Now in practice you can see that something is at stake here, something whose importance, as experience shows, can never be overestimated by Communists: quite simply the 'leading role' of the Communist Party in the dictatorship of the proletariat. What can be done to ensure that this role of political leadership does not lead to the identification of Party and State, but to the constantly expanding control of the operation of the State by the masses themselves?

What characterizes Lenin's position in this period, against both 'right-wing' and 'left-wing' deviations, is on the one hand that he never fell into the illusion of believing that the dictatorship of the proletariat would be able, except after a very long time, to do without a centralized State apparatus, in which the functions of organizing the economy would have to be in large part carried out by specialists, thus perpetuating the division of manual and intellectual labour.

But at the same time, on the basis of the experience of the masses themselves, on the basis of an analysis of the obstacles which this experience ran up against, Lenin was constantly searching for the means of *abolishing the State's monopoly* – even that of the State of a new type – in the administration, management and political control of public affairs, in order to transfer these tasks in part to organizations of the masses of the people, which of course must not be confused with the Communist Party, which are distinct from the Party and much wider.

The first aspect of Lenin's answer is often interpreted as an illustration of his relentless political 'realism': not the slightest concession must be made with regard to the need for the concentration of proletarian State power; and here the reference is not simply to the 'military' necessities of a civil war, for the latter are only one of the forms of an acute class struggle characterizing every revolution.

The second aspect of his answer is often interpreted as an illustration of his 'utopianism' or even of his 'anarchism', whether in order to try to play down its importance, or on the contrary to isolate it in order to exploit it for certain specific purposes. But what must not be lost from view is that Lenin's realism lies in the unity of the two aspects: it is a dialectical, i.e. critical and revolutionary realism only because it constantly relates the two sides of this contradiction, in spite of the gigantic practical difficulties involved.

And here you find a key with which to unravel the enigmas of the history of the Soviet revolution. I shall give just a single example: Lenin's changes of position on the question of the *trade unions*, which have been abundantly commented upon. In the space of a year, from the end of 1919 to the beginning of 1921, Lenin moved from the slogan 'Governmentalization of the Trade Unions', i.e. the transformation of the Trade Unions into organs for managing the economy (and in particular for organizing the distribution of labour power and for guaranteeing discipline in production), organs integrated into the State apparatus, to the slogan of the independence of the Trade Unions from the State, for the Trade Unions, under socialism, must always represent the interests of the workers in the face of the State, even against the proletarian State itself. It is of course true – and I shall return to this point – that this change of views can be explained by the relative failure of a particular policy, by the self-criticism which this made necessary, and by the transition to the 'New Economic Policy', in which a certain 'return to capitalism' also implied that the Trade Unions would return to the role of fighting for the workers' demands. But if you look closer, these sudden changes are themselves not simple 'accidents' of socialism, and beneath Lenin's position you can discern a constant tendency, all the more persistent for the fact that it comes up against so many obstacles. To transform the Trade Unions into an element of the State apparatus and even of the civil service is to attempt to make use of their irreplaceable function in the direct organization of the masses – a function developed in the course of decades of struggle under capitalism – both in order to transmit and explain State policy to the masses, and genuinely to involve them in the exercise of power, in order little by little to create in their midst the 'leaders' of an historically new type of politics and economics. One single phrase sums up this outlook: 'the Trade Unions are schools of communism' (and are indeed, in part, the type of school which communism needs). A little later, Lenin explained, in opposition to Trotsky's militaristic attitude – but also, it should be noted, in a struggle against the anarcho-syndicalist deviation of the so-called 'Workers' Opposition' – that 'we, for our part, must use these workers' organizations to protect the workers from their State, and to get them to protect our State', and that we must 'be able to use measures of the State power to protect the material and the spiritual interests of the massively organized proletariat *from* that very same State power' (XXXII, 25). It is now a question of wielding against the 'bureaucratic deformation' the only weapon which can attack it at its root: the initiative, culture and organization of the masses, the real control over politics which they must establish in order for these politics to be *their own*. This was also Lenin's objective in his last efforts to reorganize the 'Workers' and Peasants' Inspection', made up of direct representatives of the working people, and to transform it into an organ for the permanent control of the administrative apparatus. And above all, this was Lenin's objective in his attempts to counteract the tendency for the Party to transform itself into a new body of State and ideological functionaries. For the 'bureaucratic deformation' is not a simple accident, not a simple inheritance from ancient times, which disappears in advanced capitalism (on the contrary – we have before our eyes proof of the enormous development of bureaucracy to which this leads!): it is, in different degrees and in different, evolving forms, inherent in every State, in the 'division of labour' which it involves. In fact, the contradiction is located *within* the proletarian State itself.

One last word on the question of democracy. Having understood the sense in which revolutionary mass democracy thus constitutes the main aspect of the dictatorship of the proletariat, the condition of its existence, or rather of its development, we can finally take a look at two apparent contradictions.

First of all, the fact that the objective of 'destroying the State apparatus' seems to be a purely negative aim, while in reality it implies an historically unprecedented effort of innovation and of organization, for its source lies, for the first time, in the broad masses themselves.

Secondly, the fact that the dictatorship of the proletariat, in so far as it bears on the State apparatus, cannot be defined simply in terms of the replacement of one State apparatus by another, but must be defined in a complex manner *both* as the constitution of a *new* State apparatus, *and* as immediately setting in motion the long process of the disappearance or extinction of *every* State apparatus. This second aspect, as we shall see, *determines* the meaning of the first.

Let us put the same point in another way. As long as it is presented only in abstract fashion, this idea of the 'destruction of the State apparatus' remains difficult, and open to any number of arbitrary interpretations (and of outbursts of sham indignation). It is precisely this idea which leads certain people to claim that the concept of the 'dictatorship of the proletariat' is 'contradictory', even dangerously mystifying, that it plays on two images at the same time, pushing forward the bad side under cover of the good: Statism behind the mask of democracy. But this is to ignore *the real contradictions* of which the dictatorship of the proletariat is the product, and which the concept of the dictatorship of the proletariat allows us to analyze. In order to make such an analysis, however, we must provide the concept with a concrete definition, that is, we must avoid splitting up the two aspects. These two questions – that of the 'destruction' of the bourgeois State apparatus, and that of the 'extinction' or 'withering away' of every State – are recognized in the Marxist tradition. But as long as they remain artificially separated, they remain equally scholastic and insoluble. And Marx's definition, taken over by Lenin, according to which the State of the dictatorship of the proletariat, the State which allows the proletariat to 'constitute itself as the ruling class', is at the same time already a 'non-State', becomes a mystery or –

what is even worse – appears to be a trick. A State (a State apparatus) which is not from the very first moment in course of 'withering
away', i.e., of handing over political leadership – by various means
which can only be learned from experience – to the masses themselves, has no chance of ever being a *new* kind of State apparatus:
it can only result in the resurgence or the extension of the old one.
In this sense, the notion of the *proletarian State* itself designates,
not an absurdity, but a contradictory reality, as contradictory as
the situation of the proletariat in its role as the 'ruling class' of
socialist society. The proletariat has to turn against the bourgeoisie a weapon forged by the bourgeoisie itself, a double-edged
weapon. The experience of the socialist revolutions shows that
this is possible. It also shows that it is terribly difficult, always
more difficult than anyone believes, and that you can never rule
out mistakes, or deviations, or reverses. It is a real contradiction,
which develops in history and in practice, which grows deeper
until it is finally solved; a contradiction which it is impossible,
except in utopian ideology, to resolve except by developing it to its
final point.

The existence of every State apparatus is linked to the continued existence of classes, i.e. of class struggle, of antagonistic
social relations. It is held fast within this antagonism. Every State
apparatus is (always) bourgeois, even when the workers succeed in
using it against the capitalists. Communism means the end of the
State, and not the 'State of the whole people', an expression which
is nonsense for a Marxist. Between the proletariat and the bourgeoisie there is both a relation of symmetry (both need the State),
and a relation of dissymmetry (the proletariat aims at the destruction of every State, it practises class struggle with a view to the
abolition of classes). What defines the dictatorship of the proletariat is the historical *tendency* of the State which it establishes:
the tendency to its own disappearance, and not towards its
reinforcement.

Lenin explains that the dictatorship of the proletariat must push
democracy 'to its limits' – which means: it must push it forward to
the point where there is no longer any State, not even a democratic
State. Lenin never claims that proletarian democracy is a 'pure'
democracy, an absolute democracy; he never falls into the least
legal, liberal *illusion* in this connexion: he always insists, following
Marx and Engels, that every democracy, including proletarian

democracy, is a form of the State, deriving from the fact that class relations still exist, and that in consequence *this democracy is not freedom*. Freedom can only be equated with the disappearance of every State, in other words, only with communism, which has its own social foundations. But communism is already present, as an active tendency, within socialism: socialism cannot really be constructed except from the standpoint of communism. The proletarian revolution already entails, right from the beginning, the *development of communist social forms*, in particular in the shape of the political intervention and organization of the masses themselves, without which it would never have been possible to make the transition from the bourgeois State to proletarian democracy. In other words, proletarian democracy is not the realization of full liberty for the working people, but it is the struggle for liberation, it is the process and concrete experience of liberation as materialized in this very struggle.

From this point of view it is possible to explain why the dictatorship of the proletariat is feared or rejected. The reason does not lie in a principled attachment to democracy, in a determination to preserve democracy while bringing about socialism by democratic means. On the contrary, it lies in *the fear of democracy*, the fear of *the mass forms* of democracy which overshoot and explode the extraordinarily narrow limits within which every bourgeois State confines democracy. Or perhaps in despair that history will ever make it possible for these forms to develop.

Let us not forget that what defines opportunism is not too great an attachment to democracy but, behind the abuse of the *term* democracy (understood in accordance with the legal conception of democracy), its revulsion in the face of the extension of democracy represented by the dictatorship of the proletariat, even when this dictatorship has to defend itself in the face of imperialist counter-revolution by mass revolutionary violence. In the last analysis, opportunism means the defence of bourgeois democracy, *which is a form of Statism*, and conceives the intervention and organization of the State as a means of overcoming social antagonisms.

At least, that is undeniably the way in which Lenin presented the question. So let no-one say, after that, that he ever 'underestimated' the value of democracy!

5
Socialism and Communism

Thus we arrive at the third aspect of the dictatorship of the proletariat: what I called in the beginning Lenin's *third argument*. We shall examine it in its own right: the above discussion already shows how important it is. It is ultimately only on the basis of this third argument that we can understand the two preceding arguments. It shows why they are necessary, and it allows us to understand the historical role of the dictatorship of the proletariat. Even set out in schematic form, as it must be here, given the space available to us, it has a more concrete and a more dialectical form than these first two arguments.

I presented this thesis in a very allusive manner: I said that *the dictatorship of the proletariat is the period of transition from capitalism to communism*. It follows that the dictatorship of the proletariat is not the period of 'transition to socialism', and even less is it a particular political 'road' taken by this transition to socialism: *it is socialism itself, an historical period of uninterrupted revolution and of the deepening of the class struggle, the period of transition to communism*. Thus, the dictatorship of the proletariat cannot be correctly defined except by referring it *right from the beginning* to the theoretical and practical standpoint of communism; it cannot be defined by reference to the standpoint of socialism, considered as an independent objective.

We have to show of course that we are not dealing here with a simple question of words, a question of definitions. What is of primary importance is not the use of such and such a word (even if the terms involved do have a connotation which, in the light of experience, is not at all accidental): it is their historical content which is crucial. It is not a question of *calling by the name* 'dictatorship of the proletariat' what others call socialism, for the pleasure of upsetting some people, but of demonstrating, at least in principle, why the problems of socialism cannot be posed in a revolutionary manner except in terms of the dictatorship of the proletariat, and of making use of this knowledge as a touchstone and as an instrument for the analysis of the real history of socialism.

It is not irrelevant in this respect to pose the question, first of all, of why Lenin came to place such principled importance in this argument, not in an 'academic' manner – to use a phrase which is supposed to frighten us – but as a guide to practical action: recognition of this argument might become a question of life or death. This problem deserves a whole work of research to itself; it would tell us a lot about the historical conditions of Leninism. I shall mention only two facts, two episodes of the revolutionary process, which may serve as reference points, since they are decisive.

The first is that in 1917 Lenin posed the problem of the Russian Revolution in these terms, to the great surprise of the Bolsheviks themselves. And this he did because he recognized that the revolution in course really was, in spite of a number of exceptional characteristics and of paradoxical conditions, a proletarian and *therefore* a communist revolution. It was not a 'purely' proletarian revolution: as I have already pointed out, according to Lenin there are no 'pure' revolutions in history. But it was a revolution whose main aspect was proletarian, and whose leading force was the proletariat, for its enemy was the imperialist system, the 'imperialist chain' in which Russia was a link. In the world of imperialism, there was no longer any place for another kind of revolution. Only the proletariat could therefore lead it, by itself taking power, in spite of the difficulties of this enterprise (Lenin was to say later: 'Under the influence of a number of unique historical conditions, backward Russia was the first to show the world [. . .] that the significance of the proletariat is infinitely greater than its proportion in the total population' C.W., XXXI, 90). That is why, in *State and Revolution* (a 'simply circumstantial' work!), Lenin directly poses the problems of the proletarian revolution, whose historical epoch has now opened: it is the problems of *communism* which must urgently be brought to light and taken in hand.

Let us look at this first fact a little more closely. It will allow us to understand that there is nothing speculative about this question.

The biographies of Lenin and the histories of the Russian Revolution have recounted a hundred times the anecdotal side of the events of April 1917, when Lenin returned to Russia, having crossed Germany in his famous 'sealed carriage' and arrived at the Finland Station in Petrograd, where delegations of the Bolshevik Party and of the Provisional Government were awaiting him. The speech which he made was to amaze his comrades, those who had experienced on the spot the fall of the Tsar, the establishment of the Soviets and of the Provisional Republican Government, and the new conditions of political work. He was however to repeat it again and again in the course of the following days, before meetings of the leaders and members of the Party. He was to publish his theses, the famous *April Theses*, in *Pravda*: but the editorial board, though it was made up of his best comrades in arms, added an introductory paragraph to the effect that Lenin was only expressing his *personal* opinion. During these discussions, Lenin was interrupted, and treated as a madman and as an anarchist: the very man who was later to be presented as the founder, the teacher, the only master theoretician of the Party, was in this period completely alone, isolated in his own Party, apparently in complete disagreement with his own previous line. It was to take him a month, in the heat of events, while the masses of peasants, workers and soldiers entered into acute struggle with the 'revolutionary' government of the bourgeoisie (of which the Socialists were members), in order to win the Party over to his analyses and his slogans and therefore in order to make possible, as far as its 'subjective conditions' are concerned, the October Revolution.

What were these theses for which Lenin was arguing, whose unlikely and unexpected character I have just drawn attention to? Would Lenin himself, a few months beforehand, have been able to formulate them exactly in this way? They resulted from a particular analysis, according to which the revolution which had just begun in Russia, as a consequence of the imperialist war, was – in spite of all its special characteristics – the beginning of a world proletarian revolution. It thus became necessary to envisage the objective of the seizure of State power, which would open the period of the dictatorship of the proletariat. This was the reason for the new slogan: 'All power to the Soviets'; for the Soviets represented, in the face of the bourgeois State, the embryo of a proletarian State. And it was also the reason for proposing, at the organizational level, that the Party should cease to be and to be called a *Socialist*, 'Social-Democratic' Party, in order to call itself and to become in reality a *Communist* Party, the first detachment of a new 'Communist' International. There is much more in these revolutionary theses which, for the first time since Marx, once again linked the question of the dictatorship of the proletariat to the concrete perspective of communism, than the simple intention to 'draw a line' in words between the Communists and the opportunist Socialist Parties whose imperialist war had illustrated their historical 'bankruptcy'. We are talking about theses concerning matters of principle, but which are nevertheless indispensable to and immediately applicable to practical problems.

In order to understand this point, we must glance briefly backwards. Why, up to 1917, did Lenin talk *so little* about the 'dictatorship of the proletariat'? Why did he even construct, in order to grasp the political tasks of the revolution of 1905, a concept which can in many respects be described as 'hybrid' and quite monstrous: namely the concept of the 'revolutionary democratic dictatorship of the proletariat and peasantry', a concept borrowed in part from the example of the French Revolution, which *is not* exactly the 'dictatorship of the proletariat' (even if it anticipates certain aspects of this latter concept), and which still formed the basis in 1917 of the thought of most of the Bolshevik leaders? Contrary to what one might think (and to what, after the event, 'Leninist' orthodoxy has suggested), the reason was not that Social-Democracy in this epoch, in general, ignored or refused the term 'dictatorship of the proletariat'. On the contrary, it was in fact defending this term in its own way against Bernstein's revisionism. The reason was precisely that Lenin, during the whole pre-revolutionary period, *shared certain theoretical premises with Social-Democracy*, while at the same time drawing *in practice* diametrically opposed conclusions and coming into conflict with its principal Russian theoreticians. In other words, Lenin originally shared the conception of the dictatorship of the proletariat as a form of transition to socialism, just as he originally shared the idea that a 'backward' country like Russia was not 'ready' for socialist revolution, that it would have to pass through a more or less lengthy phase of 'bourgeois' revolution. To put it differently again, he had not yet been able to free himself explicitly and radically from the mechanistic and evolutionist conception according to which, for each particular country, it is the 'level of maturity' of the economic and social development of capitalism and this alone which can create the conditions for socialism in that country, which can render capitalist property in the means of production 'superfluous' and harmful, and which thus makes political and social revolution 'inevitable', a revolution which would transform the producers into the collective owners of their means of production. The conclusion was of course that the dictatorship of the proletariat had nothing to do with the particular historical 'situation' of Russia.

But two things then happened: on the one hand, this economistic and evolutionist conception of socialism proved itself incapable either of analyzing imperialism or of genuinely opposing it; and on the other hand, the objective conditions of revolution, under the impact of imperialism itself, were suddenly present in a country where, 'in theory', such a revolution should never have been possible . . . From that moment on, Lenin had to revise his position: not to renounce the materialist idea according to which the objective conditions of a revolution and of a new society are engendered *by capitalism* itself; but to give up the idea – the dominant idea of Social-Democracy – that one must wait for the conditions of socialism to 'mature'. It had to be understood that capitalism does not create the conditions of a new society by a kind of pre-established harmony, in such a way that the capitalists can be removed simply by a vote or by a *coup d'état*, the new society then appearing in the full light of day, having already been *prepared* within capitalism itself. It had to be understood that if 'socialism is knocking at the door of every present-day capitalist State', this is only because the *contradictions of capitalism* have become insuperable; it is these contradictory elements which socialism has to correct, to develop, to complete and to assemble. From this moment on, it became possible to understand that the proletarian revolution, though it is linked to the *general development* of capitalism in the world, which has reached its imperialist stage, is not mechanically linked, in this or that of its phases, to the 'advanced' capitalist countries, to the leaders in the 'development' of capitalism. For these advanced countries are not necessarily, in a given conjuncture, those whose contradictions are most acute.

By re-introducing and rectifying the concept of the dictatorship of the proletariat, by relating this concept directly to the perspective of *communism* (and therefore to the insuperable contradictions of capitalism, which will not finally disappear until classes themselves disappear) – rather than relating it only to the perspective of socialism, conceived as the result of the spontaneous development of the most advanced forms of capitalism – Lenin was able to explain and to grasp the concrete and unique character of the historical conditions in which the proletarian revolution began.

That is also why, once the real history of this problem in Marxist theory is understood, it is impossible not to be astonished by the argument now being put forward to the effect that the 'dictatorship of the proletariat' is an idea adapted by nature to the 'backward' conditions of the Russian Revolution (with its 'minority' proletariat, forced to make use of abnormal means of struggle because it did not represent a majority of the population, etc.): nothing is more contrary to the facts than this idea that the concept of the dictatorship of the proletariat is only a provisional response to, and a reflexion of, an historical situation which today no longer exists. The truth is that Lenin, *arguing against* the whole Marxist orthodoxy of his time, was able to rescue the concept of the 'dictatorship of the proletariat' from the sphere of reformist socialism, and *to discover* the conditions of its unexpected 'application' to the conditions of the Russian Revolution: thus at the same time he was able to submit it to a provisional theoretical rectification, whose full importance still has to be appreciated today, by making it into the concentrated expression of the *communist point of view* – and not simply of the socialist point of view – on the development of class struggle in history. I shall return to this point in a moment.

But I must right away, and just as briefly, say something about the second fact which I mentioned. For a Marxist, who wants to reason dialectically, this fact is even more important than the preceding one: it provides its confirmation. When Lenin in 1922 drew up the provisional balance-sheet of five years of uninterrupted revolution, he had to take into account its victories (in the face of armed counter-revolution), but also its defeats, including those which seemed to be the result of a mechanical application of Marxist theory. The simple fact that the Soviet power had triumphed over the whole coalition of its internal and external enemies, that it had maintained itself in spite of its isolation, of the devastating effects of the war and of the famine, was an immense historical victory: not the victory of a system of government technically and militarily more efficient than others, but the victory of a class, the proof that the epoch of proletarian revolutions had finally been opened. However, the period of 'war communism' also produced dramatic consequences which very nearly led to the destruction of the Soviet power: the 'disappearance of the proletariat' (because hundreds of thousands of proletarians had been killed at the front in the Civil War, and also because an important part of the proletariat had been forced to take over military and administrative tasks, tasks of controlling the management of enterprises, etc., and had *left* the sphere of production); the collapsing alliance between the proletariat and peasantry, in particular as a consequence of the policy of requisitioning the harvest and of the methods of constraint which had to be employed in order to carry this policy through; finally the 'reappearance of bureaucracy within the Soviet régime', the full dangers of which can be understood if it is related to the two preceding phenomena; thus the picture emerges of an isolated and decomposed revolutionary proletariat, impossibly trapped between, 'up above', the old State apparatus which was still in place, and 'down below', the hostility of the peasant masses, of the petty-bourgeoisie of producers. That is why Lenin then undertook and enrolled the Communists in a thorough self-criticism. At least, he desperately tried to do so. It is true that the situation can be explained by objective causes, which no-one had the power to eliminate: but objective causes only produce particular effects through the mediation of practice, by aggravating contradictions internal to that practice. Lenin showed how great was the error that he had committed in believing that it was possible to *move directly* from the existing capitalist system to communism, underestimating the inevitable 'delays', therefore ignoring the stages of transition, and confusing communism with different, more or less viable forms of State capitalism. 'We have to admit', said Lenin, 'that there has been a radical modification in our whole outlook on socialism.' (*On Co-operation*, 1923, C.W., XXXIII, 474.)[1]

[1] On all these points, and on others which I only treat allusively in this work, one must refer to Robert Linhart's analyses in his book *Lénine, Les Paysans, Taylor* (Le Seuil, Paris, 1976). Linhart is perfectly right to point out that 'Lenin continually contradicted himself' – unlike his contemporaries among Marxist theoreticians and most of his followers. The idea that 'Lenin never contradicted himself' is the *leitmotiv* of Stalin's *Problems of Leninism*. Linhart's book is a valuable guide, helping

We must look closely at the *precise point* on which Lenin made his self-criticism, and therefore in what direction this self-criticism led him, and leads us. Lenin's self-criticism was not at all – contrary to what certain Bolsheviks believed – directed against what we called the need to define the socialist revolution in terms of communism: for it is this need which in the last analysis accounts for the fact that the world socialist revolution began in that country where, at a precise moment, the most acute contradictions were concentrated.[2] In spite of all the pressures continuously exercized on him in this connexion, Lenin never accepted, and with good reason, the idea that he should return to the mechanistic schema according to which socialism arrives when its 'conditions have matured'; that the socialist revolution 'should have', if everything had gone 'properly', taken place *elsewhere, in another way* . . . than there where it became a reality, where it confronted the hard test of reality! That is why Lenin's self-criticism, which deals precisely with the need to give up all illusions, to recognize against all forms of voluntarism the nature of the obstacles thrown up on the road to communism, is not a kind of renunciation or of subjective repentance, but a great step forward in objectivity, as a result of which there emerged in this epoch a force capable, in spite of all its defects and all its errors, of transforming the world: the International Communist Movement.

This becomes even clearer if you follow the development of Lenin's self-criticism, and if you study it in terms of the direction in which it moves. Originally, Lenin conceived of the New Economic Policy, involving commodity trade with the peasantry, 'concessions' to foreign capitalists and the development of co-operatives, as a 'step backwards' imposed by the temporarily

---

us to escape from the alternative: *either* the good old dogmatism *or* the superficial relativism into which Elleinstein leads us. Any careful reader will realize how ridiculous are definitions like 'Leninism = the spatio-temporal conditions of the Russian Revolution'; such arguments demonstrate an ignorance of the object of study (we get only a few remarks about the backwardness of the Russian peasantry, drunk on vodka and duped by the priests, plus a few statistics) equalled only by the pomposity of their tautological appeals to History.

[2] Among the most important of which was the contradiction between the young Russian imperialist bourgeoisie and the Russian proletariat, which – in spite of its relative numerical weakness – had been able to create a stronger bond with revolutionary Marxist theory than any other European proletariat: both of these classes had developed out of the old, rapidly decomposing semi-feudal régime and against the background of the 'national crisis, affecting both exploited and exploiters'.

ruinous condition of the Russian economy, which could not be overcome by purely administrative measures. But later, more and more, Lenin modified and rectified this view: he showed that the NEP in fact represented a step forward and, with all its special 'Russian' characteristics, a necessary step towards communism. For the causes of the errors and the illusions of the Bolsheviks were more profound and more general than these special conditions taken separately; the dramatic circumstances of the Civil War only served as a revelation in this respect. It had to be recognized that capitalist relations of production had actually not disappeared, but that a 'communist' – in fact, statist – legal form had been imposed upon them, and that the whole task of transforming them remained. More exactly, these relations had only been reproduced, in a new form imposed by the State, by means of constraint and of ideology. That is what had to be recognized and analyzed, and that is why, taking full account of the contradictions of the dictatorship of the proletariat as the form of transition from capitalism to communism, and full account of the delays and the stages which this transition involved, it was *more than ever* necessary to set out from the standpoint of communism, and step by step to apply this standpoint in practice. Lenin's theses in *State and Revolution* were thus confirmed: they were rectified in practical experience.

At each step of this experience, Lenin thus defended and developed Marxist theory, at the cost of a difficult and unfinished internal struggle, in the Party and at the level of theory itself. Against the current. Against the manner in which the socialism of the Second International had deviated in its principles towards economism and statism. Against a tendency which was already, within the Bolshevik Party itself, making itself felt – the 'posthumous revenge of the Second International', to use the expression proposed by Althusser. Against evolutionism, for the revolutionary dialectic.

Whoever makes a first-hand study of the conditions in which the concept of the dictatorship of the proletariat was first produced, then developed and rectified, of the enemies which it had to face at each of these stages within the Labour Movement itself, of the terms in which it had to be presented, given these conditions and given these opponents – he will certainly come to the conclusion that the concept of the dictatorship of the proletariat has always been *ahead of its time*, just as revolutions themselves, in which the

mass movement suddenly raises its head where it is not expected,
are themselves ahead of their time. Sometimes this concept,
apparently under its own power, would surpass everyone's hopes;
sometimes it would disappoint the expectations of those who were
precisely counting on it, and had spent their lives patiently working
it out, putting it together. It is ahead of its time, just as the real
dialectic of history is ahead of its time, as opposed to the mechanical schemas of social evolution, even when these are formulated in
a Marxist language. In this connexion, Gramsci would be right
(*cf.* 'the revolution against *Capital*!') . . . if it were not for the fact
that the whole of *Capital* only becomes intelligible in connexion
with the dictatorship of the proletariat, whose necessity it demonstrates. Nothing is more revealing, in this respect, than a comparison between the situation in which Lenin found himself fifty
years ago and that in which we find ourselves today. Then, *in the
name of* the 'dictatorship of the proletariat', the most orthodox
Marxists proclaimed the impossibility of a socialist revolution in
Russia, demanding of the workers, peasants and intellectuals that
they should wait until imperialism, following the horrors of the
war, had provided a few decades of capitalist industrial development. Today, there are Communists who believe that we have
waited long enough, that capitalist industrial development has
advanced so far that we *no longer need* the dictatorship of the
proletariat, that we have reached a point *beyond* that at which it
plays a necessary role. Two apparently opposite conclusions. But
their theoretical foundations are exactly identical. I leave it to the
reader to draw the conclusion: if it is *not true* that the dictatorship
of the proletariat was, historically, a concept invented specially to
describe the difficult transition to socialism in a 'backward'
capitalist country, what value can there be in the thesis supported
by this pseudo-historical argument, according to which we no
longer need the dictatorship of the proletariat today in order to
deal with the particular problems and dangers thrown up by *our
own* revolutionary situation?

The historical tendency to the dictatorship of the proletariat

We have just made an apparent detour *via* the history of the conditions in which the Leninist concept of the dictatorship of the

proletariat was constituted. We can now return to the question of
what this thesis implies, as far as the relations of socialism and
communism are concerned.

What the concrete analyses carried out by Lenin show, with all
their rectifications, is in fact the following: that the dictatorship of
the proletariat is not a 'slogan' summing up this or that particular
tactic, even though it does determine the choice of correct slogans.
It is not even a particular strategic line, whose meaning would be
relative to certain transitory historical conditions, even though it
does determine strategy and allow us to understand why a given
strategy must be transformed.[3] It is neither a tactic nor a strategy
to be *applied* after having first been invented; the dictatorship of
the proletariat is above all a *reality*, just as objective as the class
struggle itself, of which it is a consequence. It is a reality which
Lenin tried to study scientifically, to the extent that it revealed
itself in practice, in order to be able to find his bearings in the
struggle.

But what kind of reality? Not a reality like a table or a chair,
which you can simply 'touch' and 'see'. It cannot be an unmoving,
unchanging reality, any more than the class struggle itself can be.
It is *the reality of an historical tendency*, a reality subject to ceaseless
transformations, which cannot be reduced to this or that form of
government, this or that system of institutions, even of revolutionary institutions, established once and for all.[4] A tendency does
not cease to exist because it meets with obstacles, because its
direction has to be corrected under the impact of the existing
historical conditions. On the contrary, this is precisely the manner
in which it exists and develops.

In order to understand this point, and to act accordingly, we
must relate the dictatorship of the proletariat to the whole of its
conditions, on the scale of the history of human societies: it is a
tendency *which begins to develop within capitalism itself*, in struggle

[3] It is *in this sense* that I referred, during the Pre-Congress debate for the 22nd
Congress, to 'a line of reasoning' tending to 'assign new historical objectives' to the
action of the Communists. Georges Marchais's reply – 'Our goal has not changed:
it is still socialism' – leads me to make my point in a more precise manner, and brings
us directly to the basic question: what is socialism, from the Marxist point of view?
[4] This is Stalin's point of view, as expressed in his definition of the 'system of the
dictatorship of the proletariat': for Stalin, the dictatorship of the proletariat is
simply a hierarchical structure of institutions, dominated by the Party, and linking
the masses to the Party by means of a certain number of 'transmission belts'.

against capitalism. Just as, formally, capitalism is originally an historical tendency which begins to develop within feudal society, in struggle against it, in different, first of all fragmentary and hesitant forms. This tendency therefore precedes by far the first victorious revolutions, and this is what allowed Marx and then Lenin to argue that *communism is not an ideal*, not a simple, abstract historical stage *of the future*, which might be predicted or prophesied, but a real tendency present in the existing contradictions of capitalist society, even though in fragmentary and still hesitant forms, which are nevertheless growing progressively stronger.

In what sense is communism thus a real tendency, already present in capitalist society itself? The answer, schematically, is the following: in two senses, which are not originally directly related.

– On the one hand, in the form of *the tendency to the socialization of production* and of the productive forces. It is capitalist accumulation itself which constantly develops this tendency, in the form of the concentration of capital and of the State;

– On the other hand, in the form of the *class struggles of the proletariat*, in which first the independence, and then later the ideological and political hegemony of the proletariat are manifested. These struggles allow the proletariat to organize itself as a revolutionary class, to place solidarity on a higher level than competition and division. These struggles do not – and for a good reason! – find an ally in the State, but they do result from the very conditions of life and of work and begin to make possible the collective mastery of these conditions.

Throughout the whole development of capitalism, these two tendencies constantly exercize an influence on one another, but they remain quite distinct. They do not merge with one another; on the contrary, they stand in mutual opposition. In order for them to begin to merge, you need a real proletarian revolution, the seizure of State power by the proletariat.

History has shown that the conditions for such a revolution are only produced by capitalism when it has arrived at the stage of imperialism, and unevenly from country to country, though the movement is globally irreversible (which does not mean that it is irreversible in any particular case). Only then, in determinate social conditions, which must differ from case to case, first in one and then in many countries, can the historical epoch of the dictatorship of the proletariat begin. And Leninist theory reflects this fact by showing that the epoch of imperialism is also the epoch of socialist revolutions, i.e. by explaining the characteristics of the epoch, in the last analysis, in terms of the *simultaneous, contradictory development of imperialism and of the dictatorship of the proletariat*. A contradiction which operates at the world level, but which is necessarily reflected, in an extreme variety of forms, within *each* social formation, before and after the socialist revolution.

In the course of the historical period of the dictatorship of the proletariat, the two opposed forms in which, for a long time, communism has been tendentially present in the development of capitalism itself, themselves begin to merge. It is possible to say, as Marx already pointed out, that they are present *right from the beginning* of the history of capitalism: which does not mean that the conditions for their effective combination could be satisfied except after a very long period, in spite of the attempts which took place in this connexion (like the Paris Commune). But it is just because Marxist theory was present from the beginning that it was able to prepare so far in advance the theoretical foundations of the revolution. With the revolution a new period opens, when these originally opposed forms begin to link up and to transform each other, *under the domination of the second form*, which represents the directly proletarian element. The socialization of production tendentially ceases to take the capitalist form, but only at the end of a long struggle, to the extent that the direct administration of society by the workers becomes a reality, together with the forms of communist labour. This fusion of the two forms can therefore not take place immediately, without contradiction. The history of the dictatorship of the proletariat is the history of the development and of the resolution of this contradiction.

But if this is true, it follows that we must now rectify an idea which is profoundly rooted in the whole of the International Communist Movement, an idea which, as we saw in the beginning, weighs heavily on the analysis of the problems raised by the present discussion. It is the idea of a simply 'external' contradiction between socialism and imperialism, the idea that socialism (or the 'socialist camp') and imperialism constitute *two worlds*, not simply foreign and opposed one to the other, but without any common point or line of communication between them, other than 'external relations' of a diplomatic character, which may be, depending on the case, either hostile or peaceful. It is true that the imperialist bourgeoisie of the 'Cold War' always presented things in this way (together with, in counterpart, the opposite thesis: that these two worlds are at root the same, two variants of 'industrial society'), but that is no good reason for us to take over such a non-dialectical and non-materialist idea. Socialism and imperialism are neither 'two worlds' impervious one to the other, nor one single world. This notion of the 'two worlds' places Communists in an impossible position: the socialist world represents 'the future', the imperialist world represents 'the past'; between this past and this future there can by definition be no interdependence, no inter-action, simply the tenuous thread of a moment of transition, all the more difficult to grasp because it is still to come, and yet has already taken place. In order to find a way out of this maze, you would need nothing less than a good idealist philosophy of the indefinite repetition of history, of the 'eternal circle' . . .

It is not astonishing that, in such a perspective, the *new revolutions* which must occur *outside of* the 'socialist camp', and further aggravate the crisis of imperialism and its historical decomposition, become strictly speaking impossible to imagine!

But it is also not astonishing that, from the same point of view, *the recent history* of the socialist countries appears to be inexplicable – at the very moment when we are forced to try to explain it: we can explain neither the social contradictions which come to the surface in this or that country, nor those which characterize the relations between different socialist countries. How can we possibly explain them if socialism is that 'other world' in which the historical tendencies of capitalism and of imperialism represent no more than an inert and almost forgotten past, whose return can be prevented by a good army stationed on the national borders? And how, on the other hand, can we escape the idea that capitalism will indeed be (purely and simply) *restored* when, the contradictions having become more acute, socialism, in its 'pure' and ideal form, which we used to imagine already existed beyond the frontiers of the imperialist world, can no longer stand the test of the facts? Finally, how can we any longer justify the idea that, although the labour and Communist movement of the socialist countries has influenced and still does influence that of the capitalist countries, the opposite is not true, and that the Communists of all countries can only watch as passive spectators the development of the history of socialism, in spite of the fact that they have daily experience of its direct repercussions on their own class struggle?

Things begin to look a little less irrational – I repeat: they *begin* to do so – once we rectify this mechanical notion, once we understand that the contradiction between socialism and imperialism is not an 'external' contradiction, but an *internal* contradiction, and once we try to draw the consequences of this fact. It is an internal contradiction, first of all because it is *one of the forms* in which, in the present epoch, the antagonistic contradiction between capital and wage labour, or bourgeoisie and proletariat, is developing. The second reason is that, as always, neither of the two terms of the contradiction can remain 'pure', independent of the other: in the development of the contradiction, each exercizes an influence on the other and transforms it, giving birth to new situations and social structures. No-one will deny that the very existence of socialism in an increasing number of countries has had a profound influence on the history of imperialism, even providing it with certain means of developing the tendency to State Monopoly Capitalism. It is time to recognize that the development of imperialism – which did not come to a halt in 1917 – has continued to have political and economic effects on the history of the socialist countries, playing on the *internal bases* provided for it in this connexion by the existence of contradictory *social relations* within the socialist countries themselves.

If we do not want the recognition of this fact – which implies the urgent need of a concrete analysis – to lead, as certain people fear, to reactionary conclusions, to the idea that there exists a relation of *symmetry* between socialism and imperialism, to the idea that the two terms of the contradiction are equivalent, an idea which imperialism makes use of in order to undermine the revolutionary movement, we must precisely relate the whole of the problem to the framework of the general tendency out of which this contradiction arises. We must, as Lenin saw, define imperialism as the stage of capitalism *in which* the history of communism itself begins, in the dangerous and contradictory form of the dictatorship of the proletariat.

What is socialism?

What I have just outlined in a very general manner can be explained in another way, by starting out from the simple but very topical question: what is 'socialism'?

It is nowadays common to define socialism in terms of a combination of the 'collective property of the means of production' and the 'political power of the working people'. But this definition is insufficient. Or worse: it is false, because, by ignoring the question of the class struggle, of the place of socialism in the history of the class struggle and of the forms taken by the class struggle after the socialist revolution, it leaves room for enormous ambiguities. It does not allow us to distinguish clearly between proletarian socialism and bourgeois or petty-bourgeois 'socialism', which really does exist in the ideological and political field. The mistake becomes even more serious when socialism is *defined* in terms of planning, economic rationality, social justice, the 'logic of needs', etc.

Let us first therefore say a word about what socialism cannot be, from the Marxist standpoint: *socialism cannot be a classless society*. And, since it is not a society without classes, it cannot be a society without exploitation, a society from which every form of exploitation has disappeared. Socialism can only be a society in which every form of exploitation is *on the way to* disappearing, to the extent that its material foundations are disappearing.

Lenin explained this very clearly, in 1919, in a remarkable text, entitled *Economics and Politics in the Era of the Dictatorship of the Proletariat* (XXX, 107ff.), whose formulations can be usefully compared with those of the article '*Left-Wing*' *Communism – an Infantile Disorder* (1920) and with those, among others, of his Report on the NEP presented to the Eleventh Congress of the RCP (B) in 1922 (XXXIII, 259ff.). Lenin writes:

'Theoretically, there can be no doubt that between capitalism and communism there lies a definite transition period which must combine the features and properties of both these forms of social economy. This transition period has to be a period of struggle between dying capitalism and nascent communism – or, in other words, between capitalism which has been defeated but not destroyed and communism which has been born but is still very feeble.'

Let us pause here for a moment, in order to look more closely at these remarkable formulations: this inevitable transition period, which takes a whole historical epoch (even if, in 1919, Lenin and the Bolsheviks underestimated its length), *is socialism itself*. This means that socialism is not an independent economic and social formation, and *even less* is it an independent historical *mode of production*. There is no socialist mode of production in the sense that there is a capitalist mode of production or a communist mode of production, contrary to what mechanistic Marxists like Kautsky or Plekhanov believed (they were always trying to work out the degree of its 'maturity'), and contrary to what a certain number of Communists believe today. To imagine that there can be an independent socialist mode of production, distinct both from the capitalist mode of production and from communism is either to imagine, in a utopian manner, that it is possible to move immediately from capitalism to the classless society, or to imagine that *classes can exist without class struggle*, that class relations can exist without being antagonistic. And the common root of these utopian ideas is generally the confusion between *relations of production*, in the Marxist sense of the term, which are relations of men to one another and of men to the material means of production in productive labour, with simple legal property relations, or again with relations of income *distribution*, of the distribution of the social product between individuals and classes, as regulated by the law.

Let us make this point more precisely, for questions of terminology can play a decisive role here. *The* basic production relation of the capitalist mode of production is the 'immediate relation of the labourer to the means of production': it is the relation of exploitation, which rests on wage labour, the buying and selling of labour power, which is then 'consumed' in the production process. It is the social relation (concerning classes, not individuals; and the function of the legal forms which it takes is precisely to subject individuals to the basic relation itself) which transforms the means of production into just so many means of 'pumping' labour power and causing it to produce a certain amount of surplus labour. As Marx showed, this production relation is the *last possible* relation of exploitation in history: once having arrived there, you can neither return to former modes of exploitation – in which the labourer enjoys a certain form of possession of his means of production and a certain individual control over their use – nor go forward to a 'new' mode of exploitation. For capitalism is characterized precisely by the absolute separation of the labourer from the means of production, with which he only comes into contact through their owner, who controls them. Capitalism may last a very long time, it may undergo a long series of transformations with respect to the (legal) form of the (individual or collective) property of the means of production. And it may undergo a long series of transformations based on a number of technological revolutions, and of revolutions in the organization of the labour process, with all the necessary consequences on the system of qualifications, and therefore on the education of working people and on their relation to the labour market, etc. But all these transformations are always historical developments of the *basic* production relation: capitalist wage labour. Socialism is not a new mode of exploitation (whatever some may think). Nor is it a mode of production without exploitation and without classes: it can only be grasped as a period of transition.

Is this an unprecedented idea within Marxism? By no means. On the contrary, it is part of Marxism. It is the key to the theoretical work of Marx, from the *Communist Manifesto* to *Capital*, in which its scientific foundations are laid down. Finally, it is made explicit in the text of the *Critique of the Gotha Programme*, where Marx works out its first consequences, precisely in order to criticize the opportunist deviation of Social-Democracy: he shows that 'socialism' is only the first phase of communist society, therefore a period of transition to communism. Certain of Marx's formulations are very interesting in this connexion. For example, he explains that socialism is a communist society which has not yet 'developed on its own foundations', i.e., to borrow the rigorous terminology of *Capital*, on its own mode of production. He adds to this argument the fact that, under socialism, it is still 'bourgeois law' – we could just as well simply say *law*, because all law, from the beginning of capitalism onwards, is bourgeois – which inevitably regulates the relation of the workers to the means and to the product of their labour. Equally interesting is the fact that he lists the transformation of the social division of labour (and in particular of the division of manual and intellectual labour) as one of the conditions of the progressive transition from socialism to communism in the strict sense, i.e. to the higher phase of communist society, within which, once the transition has been accomplished, and to the extent that it is accomplished, it will find 'its own foundations'.

In order to understand our present situation, it is particularly important to recall the historical fate of these formulations of Marx. On the one hand they were immediately *criticized* by the German Social-Democratic Party and by its 'Marxist' leaders, *at the same time* and for the same reasons that these leaders criticized the 'rectification' of the *Communist Manifesto*, whose importance with respect to the question of the State apparatus I mentioned earlier. All this was very logical. Then, having been taken up again and commented on at length by Lenin,[5] they became canonical formulae, constantly quoted but in fact used in a non-dialectical way, within the framework of the 'theory of stages'. I cited, at the beginning of this book (in chapter 1) a typical example of this theory in Stalin's work. There is no doubt, if you look first for theoretical reasons contained in the letter of the texts themselves, that this problem is related to the fact that Marx's formulations are still – and for a good reason, given that Marx was no prophet, contrary to a popular legend – of a very general and abstract nature. That is why they leave room for ambiguity. They leave room for a non-dialectical conception of the relation between socialism and communism, in which this relation can appear to be a matter of a simple, mechanical succession. It is true that in order to get this idea you have to read the texts very superficially, i.e. to concentrate above all on the 'general idea of transition', while more or less ignoring the *content* which Marx gives to each of these stages, and therefore the *motor* of the transition linking them. In this way a fetishism concerning the formal *number* of these stages is produced, and you are back in a utopian ideology.

Of course, any present-day 'Marxist' is prepared to admit that after the 'end' of socialism there will be something else – communism – and that consequently socialism, in the long term, in the very long term, is not an end in itself, etc. The fact that Marx, in order to characterize the difference between socialism and communism, borrowed two old revolutionary slogans of utopian socialism which put the accent precisely on distribution and not on

[5] The reader should refer, in this connexion, to the full text of Lenin's commentary, in *The State and Revolution*, ch. V.

production ('To each according to his work'/'To each according to his needs'), this fact has paradoxically contributed to relegating the questions of communism to a kind of golden age, or to an indeterminate 'end of history'. It has been used to define so-called 'general laws' of the socialist mode of production and of the communist mode of production, and to construct on this basis a whole imaginary political economy of these modes of production. In this non-dialectical, mechanistic and evolutionist interpretation of Marx, 'socialism' and 'communism' become successive *stages*, the second of which only begins when the first is complete. And it is in this perspective that the dictatorship of the proletariat is re-defined as a 'path of transition to socialism', thus becoming little by little unintelligible. It is in the logic of such an evolutionist approach, which is incapable of thinking in terms of tendencies and of contradiction, to multiply the 'intermediate stages' in order to evade the resulting theoretical difficulties: to the transition period between capitalism and communism is added another, between imperialism and the transition to socialism, and another within the stage of socialism itself, etc. But why precisely *these* 'stages'? Why not more, or less? And how are they to be distinguished from one another, if they all represent forms of the 'classless society'? The circle is closed.

Let us therefore return to Lenin's formulations:

'The necessity for a whole historical era distinguished by these transitional features should be obvious not only to Marxists, but to any educated person who is in any degree acquainted with the theory of development . . .'

What are these 'transitional features'? Lenin has just said: they concern the struggle between capitalism and communism. He then adds:

'Yet all the talk on the subject of the transition to socialism which we hear from present-day petty-bourgeois democrats [. . .] is marked by complete disregard of this obvious truth. Petty-bourgeois democrats are distinguished by an aversion to class struggle, by their dreams of avoiding it [. . .]. Such democrats, therefore, either avoid recognizing any necessity for a whole historical period of transition from capitalism to communism or regard it as their duty to concoct schemes for reconciling the two contending forces instead of leading the struggle of one of these forces.' (XXX, 108.)

Since we want to abolish the class struggle, they argue, let us not *encourage it*! Let us make up some plans. Up to now, history has always moved forward by its 'bad side', by struggle, or by violence: now it can move forward by its 'good side' . . .

By defining the phase of transition as a phase of struggle, of contradiction between the surviving elements of the capitalist mode of production and the nascent elements of communist relations of production, Lenin, though he does not indicate what concrete forms this struggle must take, does make it quite clear (except to fools) that it must continuously change its form in the course of its development. He does not content himself with 'making up some plans'. He does not try to forecast how long it will last, or how easy or difficult it will be. But he does provide the key which allows a Marxist to escape from a paradox as crazy as the attempt to square the circle: the paradox of the existence of classes and of class relations without class struggle!

On precisely this point Lenin continues:

'Classes still *remain* and *will remain* in the era of the dictatorship of the proletariat. The dictatorship will become unnecessary when classes disappear. Without the dictatorship of the proletariat they will not disappear.

Classes have remained, but in the era of the dictatorship of the proletariat *every* class has undergone a change, and the relations between the classes have also changed. The class struggle does not disappear under the dictatorship of the proletariat; it merely assumes different forms.' (XXX, 115.)

I note in passing that in reality this 'simply' indicates the enormous theoretical task which Marxists face, a task which is however vital for all Communists: the analysis of the *new forms of the existence of classes* and of the class struggle under socialism, bearing in mind of course that these new forms always have their roots in *capitalist* relations of production and of exploitation. We cannot say that much progress has been made on this task since Lenin's time. There is no doubt that this 'delay' is not unconnected, once again, with Stalin's position, which vacillated in the 1930s between two equally false theses: one arguing for the continuous sharpening of class struggle under socialism, the other claiming that the class struggle had come to an end in the USSR.

If you re-read the analyses sketched out by Lenin in the course of the years of the revolution, you will soon come to the conclusion that this problem is precisely the one which he was trying to pose in a correct form in order to understand the nature of the obstacles met with in the course of the struggle, and in order to rectify the line of the Party. Lenin was slowly discovering the enormous complexity of this problem, which did not derive from the particular conditions existing in Russia (especially, from its economic and cultural 'backwardness'), but in the first place from the nature of the socialist revolution itself, of which no-one had any previous experience. He returns to this question when talking about the NEP:

'When I spoke about communist competition, what I had in mind were not communist sympathies but the development of economic forms and social systems. This is not competition but, if not the last, then nearly the last, desperate, furious, life-and-death struggle between capitalism and communism.

... It is one more form of the struggle between two irreconcilably hostile classes. It is another form of the struggle between the bourgeoisie and the proletariat.' (XXXIII, 287–89.)

But in this struggle 'we are not being subjected to armed attack', yet 'nevertheless, the fight against capitalist society has become a hundred times more fierce and perilous, because we are not always able to tell enemies from friends' (*ibid.*). *New forms* of classes and of class struggle, in which it is no longer possible simply to attack the 'political power' of the capitalists ('We have quite enough political power'!), nor their 'economic power' ('The economic power in the hands of the proletarian State of Russia is quite adequate to ensure a transition to communism'!); it is *capitalist relations* themselves, as materialized in commodity production, in the State apparatus, which have to be attacked. New forms of the class struggle, in which, as a provincial Communist wrote: 'It is not enough to defeat the bourgeoisie, to overpower them; they must be compelled to work for us.' (Cited by Lenin; XXXIII, 290.) Thus the mass line of the dictatorship of the proletariat, unity and struggle inseparably linked, becomes even more necessary, because it is essential 'to build communism with the hands of non-Communists'. Lenin points out: 'The idea of building communist society exclusively with the hands of the Communists is childish, absolutely childish. We Communists are but a drop in the ocean' (*ibid.*).

And what happens when the Communists do not succeed in

hammering out and then in applying this mass line? Then *they are not directing* [and cannot direct], *they are being directed* [and will continue to be directed].' Lenin is not so complacent as to ignore this fact; he even admits that there is some truth in the analysis made by some émigré bourgeois politicians intelligent enough to grasp the real tendency making up *one of the sides* of the contradiction, and who thus conclude: 'The Bolsheviks can say what they like; [. . .] they will arrive at the ordinary bourgeois State, and we must support them. History proceeds in devious ways.' Such is the 'plain class truth uttered by the class enemy'!

Thus Lenin's words of 1920 take on their full meaning: 'Dictatorship is a big, harsh and bloody word, one which expresses a relentless life-and-death struggle between two classes, two worlds, two historical epochs.' And what is socialism, if not precisely *two* worlds within the *same* world, two epochs within one single historical epoch? Lenin adds: 'Such words must not be uttered frivolously.' (XXX, 355.)

This expression has two senses: on the one hand it implies that you do not say such things on the spur of the moment; and on the other hand that you cannot, from one moment to the next, get rid of the reality which they express.

The real 'problems of Leninism'

When you re-read Lenin's texts today, or perhaps in fact really read them for the first time, you not only render to Leninism its revolutionary due, and rediscover its critical power, so long buried under the weight of dogmatism. You also begin to understand his real political position. There is no *complete* theory of socialism and of the dictatorship of the proletariat, there is no dogmatic system in Lenin. Nor do his writings consist of a set of simple empirical *responses* to the demands of a very particular historical situation. It is *just because* Lenin never leaves the sphere of the concrete analysis of the revolutionary process that he is able progressively to grasp the general meaning of the problems which it runs up against. Lenin's theory of the dictatorship of the proletariat is not a system of dogmatic or empiricist responses (dogmatism and empiricism go together); it is a system of *questions* posed in the face of a contradictory reality, in response to the contradictions of this reality, an attempt to escape from utopianism and adventurism in all their forms. In this respect, it is now easy to see why what I called Lenin's 'third argument', in which the standpoint of communism comes to the fore, is absolutely indispensable: only this standpoint can guarantee the coherence and the development of revolutionary Marxism. Far from 'closing the circle' of a theory which falsely imagines itself to be complete, it is an element of progress, which opens new perspectives. It is a thesis *whose function* is precisely to open such perspectives, to develop and to rectify the analysis of the dictatorship of the proletariat – an analysis which, though it has begun, is only in its first stages. It is therefore also possible to understand, at least in part, why the *suppression of this third argument lies at the heart of the Stalinian deviation* which had such profound effects on the whole of the International Communist Movement. That is why, in the present conjuncture, in today's world, a world combining new forms of imperialism with the first forms of socialism, a correct understanding and a creative application of the Marxist theory of the State and of the dictatorship of the proletariat depend – this must be openly recognized and openly stated – on the recognition and the development of Lenin's third argument: that socialism only makes sense from the standpoint of communism, as a phase in its concrete realization.

Thus, to stand on the basis of the principles of Leninism is indeed, as we have been told so many times and for so many years, to *develop* Leninism. But this phrase has no real content unless it implies that we seriously take up the questions posed by Lenin, discuss the way in which they are formulated and, taking account of the conditions under which they arose and of the need of practical direction to which they corresponded, try to discover what problems they imply. To develop Leninism is not simply to make use of some vague 'method' or to justify the substitution of one concept for another by invoking 'concrete reality', which is supposed to throw up all the new concepts which we need, leaving us only the task of turning to marvel at their appearance.

I should like, at my own risk and peril, to mention two of the problems which arise out of the above arguments.

1. The first problem derives from the fact that socialism is always based on *commodity* production and circulation in course of transformation towards *non-commodity* production. If you pose the problem – and I have just tried to show that you must do so – in

148

terms of the *mode of production*, it seems to follow that the existence of commodity relations under socialism produces a permanent *tendency* to the re-constitution of relations of exploitation, and of the development of the still existing forms of exploitation. This is above all a consequence of the fact that labour power itself remains a commodity, that labour remains wage labour (subjected to 'bourgeois law'). The means of production cannot cease to be commodities, even if they are produced and distributed by the State, as long as wage labour remains. But now the question arises: is socialist planning itself a *non-commodity* form of the organization of production? Under what historical conditions might it become such a form? Given the historical experience of the Five-Year Plans and the 'economic reforms' in the socialist countries, there is now good reason to believe that planning, together with the collective property of the means of production, is first of all, and throughout a long historical period, in fact a new (modified) form of *commodity* production and circulation, and not its absolute opposite.

Lenin did not 'jump ahead of his time'; he by no means resolved this question. But he did make it possible for us to pose it. For obvious reasons, linked with the situation of the Soviet Union of the 1920s, Lenin usually brings up this question in connexion with the problem of peasant *petty-commodity production*. His general, continually repeated arguments about the persistence of classes under socialism are usually directly referred to the problem of the persistence of petty peasant production, the massive and concrete form of commodity production with which the Russian revolution had to come to terms. We also know that it is this reference which allowed Stalin to argue, following collectivization, that class antagonisms had 'disappeared', and to link the 'survival of commodity categories' to simple legal differences between the sectors of production (co-operative property, State Property).

But on several occasions (*cf.* in particular the article *'Left-Wing' Communism – an Infantile Disorder*, part of which I have already quoted; XXXI, 114–115) Lenin overcame the limits of this point of view. And he did so by posing a remarkable question, precisely concerning classes: it is not *only* from petty commodity production that capitalist relations tend to re-emerge, but also from another 'habit', that which is engendered by the existence of bourgeois ideological relations within the State apparatus and within the productive apparatus. We are talking about 'intellectuals, political representatives, school-teachers, engineers, skilled workers, etc.', therefore about the petty-bourgeois *and* proletarian masses caught up in these relations of which they are – to use Lenin's phrase, which is sure to give our humanist friends the shivers – the 'human raw material'. Or rather, we are talking about these very relations, which are directly bound up with political and economic relations, and which are reproduced by the whole system of qualification and education: you cannot abolish them by decree.

Lenin's remarks suggest that the question of commodity production, and in particular the question of the commodity form of human labour power, must be *coupled* with that of the forms of the division of labour, and of the antagonistic relations implied by this division in the form in which they are inherited by socialism from capitalism. Now collective property and planning, in themselves, do nothing to modify this division of labour: on the contrary, they continually come up against the persistent contradictions between different 'social categories' which are its result.

That is why it produces nothing but confusion to picture socialism in terms of the simple 'rationalization' of the organization of social labour, the parasitic capitalist class having been eliminated (even if this process is supposed to be accompanied, at the social level, by a fair distribution of the products of labour, and at the political level by greater liberty and increased 'participation' for the masses). Such a picture leaves out the essential point: that socialism, as an historical process, can only develop on the basis of a profound, progressive transformation of the division of labour, on the basis of a conscious political struggle against the division of manual and intellectual labour, against 'narrow' specialization, for what Marx called 'all-round competence'. Socialism cannot consist in the permanent *association*, in the service of their common interest, of the various social strata and categories of 'working people' existing in capitalist society: it cannot perpetuate, or even 'guarantee' the distinctions in function and status which divide them, as if there always had to be engineers on the one hand and unskilled workers on the other, professors, lawyers and labourers ... It can only be the continuous process of the *transformation* of these divisions, which will finally suppress the foundations of all *competition*, in the capitalist sense of the term, between working people, therefore the very foundations of wage labour and consequently the bases of *commodity* production, whether planned or not. In an earlier chapter I talked about the constitution of the proletariat as a class in terms of a process which can only 'end' with the constitution of the proletariat as the ruling class. It seems to me that it is therefore now time to propose the following argument: socialism is a process in the course of which the condition of the proletariat *becomes generalized* at the same time as it is transformed and tends *to disappear*. This is, in both senses of the term, *the end point of the formation of the proletariat.*

2. But this first question leads us on to a second, more precise question, that of the relation between *socialism and State capitalism.*

What is remarkable here is that, although Lenin right from the first considered State capitalism, the product of the insurmountable contradictions of imperialism, to be the 'threshold of socialism', he needed to go through the whole experience of revolution in order to discover the practical consequences of this direct relation. In the economic field, socialism first takes the form of State capitalism, itself in course of development. You will remember the famous formula from *The Impending Catastrophe and How to Combat It*:

'Socialism is merely the next step forward from State-capitalist monopoly. Or, in other words, socialism is merely State-capitalist monopoly *which is made to serve the interests of the whole people* and has to that extent *ceased* to be capitalist monopoly.' (XXV, 362.)

As becomes clear not only from the context of this quote, but also from the whole of Lenin's later thoughts on the matter,[6] to say that capitalist monopoly *has ceased* to be capitalist monopoly is to imply that it has ceased to be a class monopoly of the bourgeoisie; but that does not mean – on the contrary – that it immediately loses the whole of its capitalist character. Or, if you like, it means that it will only have lost the whole of its capitalist character at the moment when it will be genuinely possible to talk about the appropriation of the means of production by the whole people, because the whole people will be made up of productive workers, and because the antagonistic forms of the division of labour, inherited from capitalism, will have disappeared – in other words,

[6] *Cf.* the pamphlet on *The Tax in Kind* (1921), which cites, summarizes and rectifies the arguments of 1917 and 1918 (XXXII, 329ff.).

because, to the extent that the whole of society will have been absorbed into the proletariat, the proletariat as such will have finally disappeared.

Normally, when this formula is cited from Lenin's writings, only *one* aspect is generally taken up: the idea that the objective foundations of socialism lie in capitalism itself, in the form of the (capitalist) socialization of the productive forces and of production. Thus the revolutionary point of the argument is often missed: namely that there is no other possible solution to the contradictions of monopoly and State-monopoly Capitalism except the proletarian revolution and socialism. But above all the dialectical consequence of his argument, as it bears on socialism itself, is generally ignored: there is no attempt to analyze the fact that the contradictions of this process of capitalist socialization – contradictions which only represent the material form of the intensification of exploitation by capitalism – are inevitably 'inherited' by and carried over into socialism. They cannot miraculously disappear as a simple result of the seizure of power.

Of course, the forms taken by State Capitalism under socialism are necessarily profoundly contradictory and of an unprecedented kind. Lenin pointed this out in 1922:

'We philosophize about how State capitalism is to be interpreted, and look into old books. But in those old books you will not find what we are discussing; they deal with the State capitalism that exists under capitalism. Not a single word about State capitalism under communism. It did not occur even to Marx to write a word on this subject . . .'

And he added:

'State capitalism is the most unexpected and absolutely unforeseen form of capitalism [. . . .] We passed the decision that State capitalism would be permitted by the proletarian State, and we are the State. [. . . .] We must learn, we must see to it, that in a proletarian country State capitalism cannot and does not go beyond the framework and conditions delineated for it by the proletariat, beyond conditions that benefit the proletariat.' (XXXIII, 278, 310–312.)

The complexity of contradictions: State capitalism is at one and the same time both the representation, in the face of commodity production, of the general struggle between socialism and capitalism, and also something to be controlled, limited and finally suppressed and eliminated by proletarian socialism. From what point of view does State capitalism, *in opposition to* the previous forms of capitalism, 'represent' socialism, to what extent is it a revolutionary tendency? From what point of view is it on the contrary the main enemy in which all the fundamental characteristics of capitalism tend to be 'concentrated', and against which the proletariat must struggle? And how are these two aspects combined, in a given country, in a given conjuncture?

This is a typical example of the kind of question which it is *impossible* either to ask or to answer unless you start out from the theoretical standpoint *of communism*, of the struggle between capitalism and communism. Starting out from the concrete conditions existing in Russia ('Nobody could foresee that the proletariat would achieve power in one of the least developed countries, and would first try to organize large-scale production and distribution for the peasantry and then, finding that it could not cope with the task owing to the low standard of culture, would enlist the services of capitalism') Lenin came to stand, in fact, more and more consistently on this standpoint. With the benefit of hindsight, we can see why: socialism is in the first instance the collective property of the means of production; this form of property cannot be equated primarily with the appropriation of these means of production *by the State*, whatever the particular legal form which it may take. To restrict socialism to State appropriation would entail, from the point of view of the workers, that this appropriation remained formal, since it would not itself abolish the separation of the worker (of labour power) from the means of production.

But at the same time State appropriation does produce a substantial transformation of the previous situation. It does first of all suppress the separation characteristic of capitalism between the political sphere and the economic sphere, or more exactly the sphere of labour (the term 'economic' is ambiguous here; bourgeois politics and bourgeois economics have never been separate!).

On the one hand, it turns the problems of the organization of labour and of the transformation of labour relations into directly political problems.

On the other hand, it enables all the forms of the mass movement, of revolutionary mass democracy, to become means of revolutionizing labour itself and the relations of production. And at the same time it *ties the 'political' problem of the withering away*

of the State to the '*economic*' *problem of the abolition of exploitation.*
Because although these problems cannot be solved *separately*, they
can be solved through one another, together.

In this connexion, I shall re-introduce an expression which I
have had occasion to use before, and say that socialism, the historical period of the dictatorship of the proletariat, is necessarily
characterized by the unprecedented extension of a new form or
new practice of politics. And this of course also means that
socialism can only exist and can only develop *to the extent that* this
new (mass) political practice also exists and develops. It is in this
context that, in my opinion, Lenin's famous formula defining
socialism as 'electrification plus Soviet power' must be explained,
not by ignoring but precisely by *taking account* of the conjuncture
in which it was put forward. It does not mean that you have
electrification (and more generally the planned development of
the productive forces) *on the one hand*, and Soviet power *on the
other*, one alongside the other, one in the economy, the other in the
State: it implies that each is dialectically related to the other, so
that electrification and planned development take place *within the
framework* of the development of the power of the Soviets and of
the mass organizations. And in consequence State capitalism *is
subjected to* the development of communist social relations and
communist forms of organization.

A Few Words in Conclusion

These are some of the questions concerning the dictatorship of the proletariat. Not the only ones, no doubt.

Since the occasion of the 22nd Congress of the French Communist Party, our comrades – and the revolutionary working people and intellectuals who stand close to us – have had to pose the question (because they did not really get a chance to pose it *before* the Congress): when the perspective and the concept of the dictatorship of the proletariat is 'abandoned', what *changes* actually take place in Marxist theory, in the theory which provides the labour movement with a scientific basis for analyzing reality and acting on it? The discussion on this question is now open.

If the Leninist arguments are correct, and if it is not just a question of words that is at stake here – which no-one really believes any more – then the dictatorship of the proletariat is indeed a concept which constitutes an essential part of the Marxist theory of the class struggle, and cannot be separated from it without bringing this whole theory into question. The very idea that, in the history and the strategy of the Communist Parties, the dictatorship of the proletariat might be 'out of date' can have no meaning for a Marxist. For, as we have seen, the dictatorship of the proletariat is not a particular method, a particular model or a particular 'path of transition' to socialism. It is the historical tendency which leads from capitalism to communism, through the transition period of socialism, in the conditions of imperialism.

That is why it is both possible and necessary to rectify and to enrich our understanding of the dictatorship of the proletariat by studying the real history of the socialist revolutions which have taken place up to the present day. But this investigation, indispensable to the Communists of every country, can only be carried out on the basis of the principles of *analysis* discovered by Marx and Lenin. Not by 'relativizing' the concept of the dictatorship of the proletariat, by trying to restrict it to a primitive, remote and defunct period – that old epoch of imperialist wars, of violent revolutions and counter-revolutions – but by developing the internal dialectic of its contradictions, by concrete analysis. The real history of socialism, which is, as I pointed out at the beginning of this book, the unspoken question haunting this whole discussion – whether it is a question of 'socialist democracy', of 'peaceful co-existence' or of proletarian internationalism – cannot be understood except in terms of this dialectic. *Without* the concept of the dictatorship of the proletariat, what today appear to us and tomorrow will appear to us as the errors and deviations of the socialist revolutions can only be seen as a sum of accidents, of strokes of bad luck, of inexplicable set-backs or as a new kind of infantile disorder from which our own maturity will, we hope, miraculously preserve us. Their victories, which have opened the way to our own, can only be looked on as lucky chances. But *with* the concept of the dictatorship of the proletariat, we can analyze and rectify the errors of the past, and we can try to recognize and to correct in good time those of the future.

Above all, it is possible and necessary progressively to work out, in the light of experience and the critical examination of that experience, the paths of revolutionary transformation in the conditions of *our own* capitalist country. The principles of Marxist theory, on which the arguments concerning the dictatorship of the proletariat are based, will no doubt undergo some unprecedented transformations as a result. That is precisely what makes them materialist principles, and not dogmas, 'fixed ideas' or commonplace 'catchwords'.

Let us put it another way: it must today be obvious to anyone who has not closed his eyes on the world outside that we are experiencing a very grave historical crisis of Leninism, as a form of organization and as the principle of unity of the International Communist Movement, therefore as a form of the fusion of revolutionary theory and practice. This historical crisis has dramatically weakened the Labour Movement, at a moment when the imperialist system is itself entering a new period of general and acute crisis, thus opening revolutionary possibilities and demanding revolutionary solutions. But this historical crisis of Leninism also has its positive side: it means that, at the level of practice, the elements of a new form of revolutionary theory and practice are already emerging. This crisis is so acute that it can hardly be resolved by a simple 'return' to previous forms of organization, to the old methods of political and theoretical work. Everyone is aware that it is necessary to work out new forms. And the whole effort, the whole of the constant pressure of bourgeois ideology is tending precisely to exploit this crisis in order to present Leninism as a gigantic 'historical error' of the Labour Movement, in order to liquidate it (and Marxism with it): and above all to liquidate the Leninist theory of the State, therefore the dictatorship of the proletariat, by replacing it with the ideology of reformist and technocratic socialism, with a dash of its eternal by-product, anarchism, thrown in for good measure.

It seems to me that the importance of this offensive, coupled with the importance of the present tasks of the proletariat, clearly entails that the Communists have an urgent duty: to study Leninism in a critical manner, and to develop it.

I have proposed some weapons for our struggle, some themes for collective and public consideration. The question, as we have seen, is by no means of mere historical interest: it is of immediate importance. It is by no means speculative: it is a practical question, like every real question in Marxist theory. But let us not forget: this question is not one for an armchair discussion, for a fire-side chat about the reasons for our preferences and desires. It arises in the course of a confrontation in which each of our errors, each of our retreats is immediately exploited by the enemy. And this enemy, imperialism, *has already*, a long time ago, *chosen for us* the position *which suits its own ends*. Its own class dictatorship, the dictatorship of the bourgeoisie, has no interest – on the contrary – in being called by its real name and understood in terms of its real historical power. To suppress the dictatorship of the proletariat is at the same time to suppress the dictatorship of the bourgeoisie . . . in words. Nothing could serve it better, in practice.

It is never too late to draw the conclusion.

Dossier

Extracts from the Pre-Congress Debate and the Proceedings of the 22nd Congress of the French Communist Party (January–February 1976)

On the question of the dictatorship of the proletariat*

Georges Haddad

*(Secretary of the Pablo Neruda branch,
Epinay-sous-Sénart)*

Although the question of the Party Statutes does not figure on the agenda for the 22nd Congress, we [L'Humanité] think that readers may find the following contribution interesting, in so far as it deals with a problem which is relevant to the work of the Congress.

I should like to make my contribution to the debate which is now involving large sections of the Party in connexion with the preparations for the 22nd Congress, by proposing a new version of certain paragraphs of the Preamble to the Statutes of the French Communist Party.

As far as paragraph 9 is concerned, I want to suggest a new wording which, while avoiding the use of the expression 'dictatorship of the proletariat', clarifies this notion and brings it into closer touch with the present-day class struggle.

Why is it better to avoid the term 'dictatorship of the proletariat'?

– Because, although it is an old and fundamental notion, the 'dictatorship of the proletariat' corresponded to particular circumstances of the class struggle, to particular historical, social and economic conditions.

– Because the term 'dictatorship' does not have the same connotations nor even the same content now, as compared with before the appearance of the fascist régimes in Germany and Italy, and of the Spanish, Greek and Portuguese dictatorships, the last two of which have recently collapsed . . . not to speak of the dictatorships

* From the pre-Congress debate for the 22nd Congress; as published in *L'Humanité*, 7.1.1976.

in Latin America, and in particular in Chile.

– Because, after all, 'dictatorship' is the opposite of the continuously widening democracy and continuously expanding liberties for which we are fighting.

– Because the idea of the 'dictatorship of the *proletariat*' is no longer completely true today. It was absolutely true towards the end of the nineteenth century and at the beginning of the twentieth. It does still have some truth today, but it does not reflect the whole of present-day reality, since the possibilities of victory do not depend *entirely* on the struggle of the working class and of the agricultural proletariat, but *essentially* on the struggle of the working class *in alliance* with the *broad* anti-monopolist social strata, and not only with the proletarian peasantry, within a broad *grouping* of forces around the working class, the decisive force behind the *Union* of the French People.

Thus paragraph 9 could be worded in the following way:

'This new political power, whose form may vary, guarantees the widest possible democracy, in particular for all working people, at both the economic level and the political level. It will ensure both the extension of liberties and the satisfaction of economic, social and human needs. This new political power of the working people will open up the road which will lead progressively from the government of men to the administration of things, to communist society.'

And then, I would propose adding to or completing paragraph 11 with the following phrase:

'Only the working class can successfully lead the revolutionary struggle, because it is the leading force of the struggle to change society.'

Liberty and socialism*

Georges Marchais

G. Marchais – Your [*the interviewer's*] question poses a general problem to which I must reply. In the construction of socialist society a number of principles must be taken into account.

You cannot build socialism without the collective appropriation of the means of production and exchange; without the State being ruled by the working class and its allies; without democratic planning; without the participation of the citizens in the administration of public affairs at every level; without a great Communist workers' party.

From Cuba to China and the USSR, socialism already offers a great diversity of possibilities throughout the world. This diversity will increase as other countries reach socialism.

Socialist society is genuinely superior because it truly guarantees the liberation of man, puts an end to his alienation and allows him to enjoy real freedom.

The text submitted for discussion by the Party with a view to the preparation of the Congress underlines the fact that democracy must be taken to its limits.

Socialism is synonymous with liberty.

This notion is valid for every country and for every circumstance. It is quite wrong to use repression or administrative measures against the expression of ideas, and there can be no other way of looking at this question.

That is why the French Communist Party has decided to express its disagreement with certain other ways of behaving. We think that there is no justification for attacking liberties. We shall remain

* From the interview given to 'Antenne 2' (French Television). As published in *L'Humanité*, 8.1.1976.

attentive to the question of liberty and of respect for socialist democracy.

It is within this general framework that our standpoints must be interpreted. There is a difference of opinion between ourselves and the CPSU on the question of socialist democracy. [. . .]

Question: Your condemnation of the attacks on liberties in the USSR – is this a new thing?

G. Marchais – For you it is new, for me it is not. The question of liberty and of respect for socialist democracy is for us of the first importance.

We are more demanding now that the considerable successes of the Soviet Union and of the Socialist countries – and I draw your attention to the fact that 25 million Soviet citizens are participating in the administration of public affairs – have created new conditions in which socialist democracy can be pushed forward and further developed.

The CPSU has criticized the crimes, tragedies and errors of the past – which by the way demonstrates the superiority of socialism – and certain necessary corrections have been made, but these are not yet complete and more corrections have to be added. The necessary conditions exist for the Soviet Union to bear the banner of liberty ever higher and further.

G. Marchais is next asked about the pre-Congress discussion for the 22nd Congress of the French Party.

The branches are meeting, the debate is lively, *says G. Marchais, who remarks*: no party in this country prepares its congresses so democratically as we do. In our Party discussion is free; when the decision has been made, everyone applies it!

But, *he continues*, it is always difficult to reproduce before the Congress itself the same lively to-and-fro as in the discussion in the branches. . . .

. . . With 1,500 delegates present, the Congress always gives a rather solemn impression; but we must ensure that the Congress debate reflects the tremendous discussion now taking place in the Party.

Christian Guy then questions G. Marchais about 'the democratic road to socialism'.

G. Marchais – It means transition to socialism without civil war. What is the solution? STRUGGLE. We reject civil war, but there can be no transition to socialism without a bitter struggle, taking various forms, based on the Union of the French People and its central pillar, the Union of the Left, and whose means lies in the system of elections. The majority must at each step make its will known through the election system.

G. Marchais is then asked: Is this a gamble?

G. Marchais – No, it is a serious political strategy: shall we or shall we not succeed in obtaining a majority grouping of the people and thus in isolating the big bourgeoisie? Yes, of course!

The General Secretary of the French Communist Party then details the 'three necessary levers' of change:

1. – The working class, which has the greatest interest in change. The working people makes up 44% of the population. It has a great experience of struggle, a powerful Communist Party, and a great, experienced Trade Union federation.
2. – The Union of the French People, a grouping whose main pillar is the Union of the Left.
3. – The French Communist Party, the revolutionary party of the working class.

These are the three forces, the three levers of struggle. At each stage, universal suffrage will decide!

J.-M. Cavada – Well, that's clear enough!

Next, C. Guy questions G. Marchais about the discussion contributions published that morning by L'Humanité, *and in particular about the opinion expressed there according to which the term 'dictatorship of the proletariat' should be eliminated from the French Communist Party's Statutes.*

George Marchais expresses his agreement with this proposition. He says: 'The Congress will decide.' *He continues:* 'Here is my opinion . . .'

G. Marchais – . . . We are living in 1976 . . . The French Communist Party is not rooted in the past. It is not dogmatic. It knows how to adapt to present-day conditions. Now, the word 'dictatorship' no longer corresponds to our aims. It has an intolerable connotation, contrary to our aspirations and to our arguments . . .

Even the word 'proletariat' will no longer serve, because we want to unite together, with the working class, the majority of wage-earners . . . But this does not mean that we are abandoning our objective: socialism in French colours . . . For without socialism there is no way out of the crisis . . .

G. Marchais underlines the need to struggle step by step for each immediate demand, but he is emphatic in pointing out: 'We must transform society. We need a socialist society . . .'

The broadcast then links up with Rome for the next item.

'Ten questions, ten answers, to convince the listener'*

Georges Marchais

Question 2 – You have enlivened the pre-Congress debate by con-
demning the dictatorship of the proletariat. If this expression is
eliminated from the Party Statutes or replaced, will you not appear
as a revisionist of Marxist-Leninist doctrine and be called to
order?

Answer – As you know, we are preparing our Congress on the basis
of a draft document entitled 'What the Communists want for
France'.

The 'dictatorship of the proletariat' does not figure in this draft
document to designate political power in the socialist France for
which we are fighting. It does not appear there because the
'dictatorship of the proletariat' does not properly characterize the
reality of our policy and of what we are proposing to the country
today.

We are living in 1976. We are living and struggling in a France
and in a world totally different from the situation fifty or even
twenty-five years ago. We take the fullest account of this fact. To
do otherwise would be to replace the precise and living study of a
real situation by quotations or examples erected into a dogma. The
French Communist Party has been formed in a quite different
school.

We believe, as our draft document clearly points out, that the
power which will have to carry out the socialist transformation of
society will be – with the working class playing the vanguard role –
representative of the whole of the manual and intellectual workers,

* From the interview broadcast by France-Inter (French Radio): 'Ten questions,
ten answers to convince the listener', January 19th, 1976; as published in *L'Humanité*,
20.1.1976.

therefore of the great majority of the people in *France today*.

This power will bring about the most extensive democratization of the whole of the economic, social and political life of the country by drawing support from the struggle of the working class and of the masses of the people.

Finally, at each stage we shall respect and ensure respect for the decisions of the people as freely expressed by universal suffrage.

Very briefly, we are proposing to the people the democratic and revolutionary road to socialism, taking account of the conditions of our epoch and our country, and of a relation of forces which has profoundly changed in favour of the forces of progress, liberty and peace.

Now, it is evident that this road, which we are now proposing to the working people, to our people, cannot be called a 'dictatorship of the proletariat'. That is why this term does not appear in our draft document. Half a million Communists have been engaged in a democratic discussion on this question for more than two months. If their representatives at the Congress agree – and this is probable, on the evidence of the branch, section and federation meetings already held – then the problem will certainly arise of drawing up the necessary modifications to the Preamble to the Party Statutes. The Congress will have to decide what procedure to adopt.

Question 3 – Mr Marchais, were you or were you not guided in your decisions by tactical considerations and by the attitude of other political forces, for example by the progress of the Socialist Party?

Answer – The idea that the reason why we are proposing a democratic road to socialism, without the dictatorship of the proletariat, lies in pressure from other political forces, is quite simply absurd. I will tell you why. All the other political parties are now or have in the past been involved in government. What have they done?

The right-wing parties, especially under Giscard d'Estaing, are using their power in an anti-democratic, authoritarian manner, for the benefit of a privileged minority.

The Socialist Party and François Mitterand, when they entered the government without us, also served the interests of big capital. And you can see today how in certain countries, like West Germany, the Social-Democratic Parties in government are carrying out numerous and grave attacks on liberties, and undermining democracy.

In short, if we were to give way to pressure from other political forces, the consequence would be that we should change for the worse, we should enter the government to maintain capitalist rule and restrict democracy. But we are proposing exactly the opposite, as I have just explained to you.

The reason for our position is very simple: we have taken account of the changes which have occurred in national and international reality. In short, these positive changes allow us to envisage less severe roads to socialism, different roads from those followed by the peoples who have already built socialism. It is our good fortune that these possibilities exist in the French conditions. Our attitude is therefore not a tactical but a principled one. Taking account of the situation, we are pointing out the best and quickest way of arriving at socialism.

On the dictatorship of the proletariat*

Etienne Balibar

(Gabriel Péri branch, 5th Ward, Paris Federation)

Several discussion contributions published in *L'Humanité* and in *France Nouvelle* have taken up position either *for* or *against* referring to the 'dictatorship of the proletariat' in the document which the Congress must consider; and even for or against the presence of this notion in the Party Statutes. Interviewed on Antenne 2 [French Television] on January 7th, Georges Marchais declared himself in favour of rejecting the 'dictatorship of the proletariat', neither term of which any longer corresponded either to the present situation or to the objectives of the Communists. He added: 'Congress will decide.'

We therefore find ourselves faced with the following situation: the 22nd Congress may officially ratify a radical change in the principles on which, from the very first, the political action and organization of the Communist Parties has been based. Citing Marx's unambiguous arguments, Lenin wrote: 'To confine Marxism to the theory of the class struggle means curtailing Marxism, distorting it, reducing it to something acceptable to the bourgeoisie. Only he is a Marxist who *extends* the recognition of the class struggle to the recognition of the *dictatorship of the proletariat*' (*The State and Revolution*).

1. First of all, it must be pointed out that a theoretical change of this importance cannot be carried out *ad hoc*. How does it come about that the draft document of the Congress, the basis of the present discussion, did not even mention the problem? Are Communist militants incapable of facing a clearly posed question

* Discussion contribution for the 22nd Congress; as published in *L'Humanité*, 22.1.1976.

head-on, and of organizing a thorough discussion about the principles of their politics? Would it not have been correct to set out in detail, *precisely on the occasion of the Congress*, the whole line of reasoning justifying the decision to establish the action of the Communists *on new foundations*, to assign it new historical objectives, and *to drop* the dictatorship of the proletariat, so that the Communists might make their decision with full knowledge of the facts, and not simply on the basis of a feeling of repulsion inspired by the word 'dictatorship'.

In fact, and this is my second point, there is unfortunately reason to fear that we Communists – i.e. the Party – are at the moment incapable of discussing the problem at depth. For the necessary conditions do not exist.†

[. . .] French Communists are being invited to reject, at short notice, and without having made a scientific analysis of the problem, a concept which is an integral part of the Marxist tradition, and which cannot be reduced to a question of words. Can we, in that case, be sure that we have an objective understanding of what we are going to put in its place?

2. I quoted Lenin. I could have produced a thousand other quotes. Quotations prove nothing. Reduced to quotations, Marxism becomes a form of sterile dogmatism, a religion of formulae: painful experience has taught us something about the consequences. Let us remember one fact, however: that the 'dictatorship of the proletariat' is not a *theoretical invention*, conjured up by Marxist intellectuals; it is a *discovery* which had to be made, which expresses the lessons of years of activity. And this

† The following paragraph was omitted by *L'Humanité*:
Even if the Congress document had been differently conceived, conceived not as a 'manifesto' for the future, but as an analysis of the political problems confronting the present theory and tactics of the Party, these conditions could not have been created from one day to the next. It would in fact have been necessary for the Party in the preceding years to have fixed for itself the task of studying in depth the problems of the dictatorship of the proletariat, systematically confronting them with the lessons of its everyday experience. Instead of which, voluntarily or not, it has kept silent on this question, and thus allowed a gap to develop between its analyses, its projects for a programme and Marxist political theory. So that *the particular* 'dictatorship of the proletariat' which is now to be cast off like a worn-out piece of clothing is no more than a ghost, a caricature of the concept worked out by Marx and Lenin, which they had made the touchstone of the revolutionary class position and which they had tried, not without difficulty, to explain to the labour movement of their own time in the hope that the movement would adopt it.

activity teaches us, in particular, that the revolutionary class must not accept the blinkers, the mystifying alternatives on which bourgeois legal ideology rests: 'dictatorship' in itself *or* 'democracy' in itself; organization of the workers as a ruling class through the use of State coercion *or* democratic mass struggle for their emancipation. But these are precisely the alternatives within which we are now trapping ourselves.

You have to understand what is at stake here. If the labour movement in the course of the class struggle had to fix the dictatorship of the proletariat as its objective, with all the difficulties and even formidable contradictions which go with it, and could not 'simply' define this objective as happiness, liberty, democracy, etc., it is for a material reason. It is because capitalist exploitation inevitably brings with it the *class dictatorship of the bourgeoisie*, and rests on it, whatever the more or less violent and openly repressive forms taken by this dictatorship in particular historical conditions; and it is because it is impossible to destroy the historical foundations of this bourgeois dictatorship *without* immediately undertaking the destruction of the existing *State apparatus*, which can never as such function 'in the service of the working people'. To imagine that we can fight for 'real' democracy, for democracy for the masses of the people, *without* passing through the dictatorship of the proletariat is to *ignore the existence of the dictatorship of the bourgeoisie*, to ignore the role of the State apparatus as an instrument of exploitation. Does this really correspond to the experience of the working people of France in their present-day struggles?

3. We are faced with an enormously important fact, about which we have finally had to admit that it has been a big obstacle to the mass movement. This fact is that the history of the socialist countries (or of certain socialist countries) *has disfigured and discredited the 'dictatorship of the proletariat'*. It has confused it with a dictatorship *over* the proletariat, by identifying party and State; it has in practice *opposed* the dictatorship of the proletariat to mass political democracy. It has led to grave political crises and to deep-rooted splits in the International Communist Movement. But it is no good for us simply to express our regrets about this situation or to hope to avoid it by ignoring and then finally openly abandoning the problem of the dictatorship of the proletariat. On the contrary, this situation must be *analyzed*. An historical phenomenon has

historical causes. What are the historical causes which *prevented* (leaving aside all questions of individual 'personalities') the peoples of the socialist countries from fully realizing the dictatorship of the prolateriat, and which have thus tended to turn it into its opposite? What are the historical causes which prevented the effective destruction of the bourgeois State apparatus and therefore the complete solution of the gigantic social contradictions inherited from centuries of class oppression? What form do these causes take *today*, in the socialist world, and in the capitalist world, and *how* can they be counteracted? What in consequence are the *additions* (including the *rectifications*) which have to be made to the notion of the dictatorship of the proletariat in order to guide the revolutionary action of the Communists?

4. The absence of these questions is greatly distorting the present debate in the Party. Its effects can be felt in every line of the draft document, sometimes producing astonishing results. I shall give just one example. The document devotes one small paragraph to the 'international context'. The impression is given on the one hand that the world situation is evolving *uniformly* to the detriment of imperialism and to the benefit of the socialist camp, the national liberation struggles, the labour movement and the *unity* of these forces for progress; and on the other hand that France, because of its 'world importance', *has the means* to carry out its internal social transformation *while escaping* the intervention of imperialism. But the facts show this simplistic and over-optimistic view to be completely wrong. *The only* peoples who, in the course of the last decades, have succeeded in liberating themselves from imperialism and starting out on the road to socialism have been able to do so only at the cost of prolonged struggles against imperialist intervention: Cuba and Vietnam. The point is obviously not to underestimate the historic importance of these victories, for they show that revolution *can be made* by the peoples of the world and by the workers. And this *in spite of* the obstacles resulting from the *disunity* of the socialist camp and from the *fragility* of the alliance between socialism and the national independence struggles (*cf.* the Middle East!), which imperialism ceaselessly plays on.

But what are we to think of the argument invoked in order implicitly to meet this objection, the argument about France's 'world importance'? It can in fact mean only one thing: that *because France is an imperialist country*, it finds itself in a *more favourable position* to neutralize any intervention in its internal affairs by the world imperialist system (of which it is a part), or even to escape such intervention completely! But this argument is quite unacceptable, and that is why, in fact, no-one has ever formulated it openly in this way; because it is the *opposite* which is true: the nearer a country is to the heart of the imperialist system, the more vital it is for imperialism to prevent its revolutionary development, and the greater the means available to imperialism – economic, ideological, political and military – to do so. There is therefore less need for it to make immediate use of the extreme remedy of an external attack, which in the end only welds against it the national unity of the forces of the people. Once before, in 1945–47, a movement of the people was thus isolated and defeated in France. But the extent to which French society nowadays *depends* on the world imperialist system has not been reduced but considerably increased.

What are the lessons, in particular, of Chile, of Portugal and at the present time of Italy? Surely that imperialist intervention never takes exactly the same form, that it has to adapt itself to the existing conditions. In this respect it is remarkably successful, making use in one place of the military putsch, in another of economic pressure exercized through the Common Market, mediated and guided by the counter-revolutionary action of European Social-Democracy, and everywhere exploiting the specific weaknesses of the mass movement. These examples reveal a basic fact, characterizing the present-day situation: the fact of the still enormous *power* of imperialism, its *capacity for initiative and pre-emptive action*. As soon as the *masses*, in any country in the world, begin to intervene *in person* on the political scene, even if they are only fighting for limited social changes, even if they are not yet completely united politically, even if they are quite unaware of the fact that in order to bring their struggle to a successful conclusion they need to overthrow capitalism itself, nevertheless imperialism will be there to intervene and even, forestalling its enemies, will begin to plan and to organize counter-revolution.

That is why we must realize that when the need and the conditions for a real social change in this country begin to develop, we cannot rest content with a strategy based on counting up all those social groups who are *at this moment* being trodden down by big capital and who *in principle* ought to be capable of uniting against it; we cannot content ourselves with putting forward a few general slogans and universal ideological themes which are supposed *spontaneously* to conjure up such a majority. We have to *forecast* the forms which imperialist intervention will take, which are related to its very existence; we have to take into account in the analysis the contradictions in the camp of the people on which imperialism can play, and the means at its disposal – it will use *everything* that it has got – to mobilize entire masses of the people, including sections of the *exploited* masses, against change, even when their own interests suffer thereby (in the case of Portugal it succeeded in using as its shock troops those very same poor peasants which it had itself reduced to poverty and forced into emigration). To put it briefly: we do not simply need to take into account *the foundations of the popular union* for change and for the transition to socialism; we *also* have to take into account – this is the whole problem – *the potential foundations of counter-revolution*, in order to analyze them and to work out corresponding forms of struggle. Any strategy which fails to deal with *both* aspects of the problem must be utopian; it will bring not victory but defeat.

Thus – and the above is only one aspect of the problem, which I have singled out in order to remain within acceptable limits of space – we arrive back at the question of the dictatorship of the proletariat. Not at the question concerning the simple *term* 'dictatorship of the proletariat', but at that which concerns the *problems* raised by the dictatorship of the proletariat, which we must ask and answer in our own fashion, and which no-one could or can answer *for us*. The question is not that of the alternative: *either* the dictatorship of the proletariat *or* mass democratic struggle; this alternative is the one which the bourgeoisie wants to force upon us. The question is: how to develop the forms of mass struggle, broad and democratic, which can *make the dictatorship of the proletariat a reality*, uniting the workers and the whole people against the exploiters and the bourgeois State. I am for my part completely convinced that the transition to socialism, with its own original stages, is 'on the agenda' for French society, as in other capitalist countries. But I do not think that we have any chance of making this transition if we give way to the ideological pressure of the enemy, or if we underestimate the contradictions involved in the process, and deceive ourselves as to the acute nature of the class struggles which it implies and the high stakes which it involves.

Comrades – let us not lightly reject the slogan of the dictatorship of the proletariat! Let us prove ourselves, in theory as well as in practice, to be real Communists!

On the dictatorship of the proletariat (Reply to E. Balibar)*

Guy Besse
(Corrèze Federation, Guy Moquet Branch (Brive), Member of the Political Bureau)

Some remarks on Etienne Balibar's discussion contribution (*L'Humanité*, 22.1.1976).

1) To question the right of the General Secretary of the Party to take part in the pre-Congress discussion is to put in question the rights of every member of the French Communist Party; it is to ignore the duties of every Communist leader and to reduce his role to that of an arbitrator, or a simple spectator. Besides which, G. Marchais has said nothing which might suggest (as one might think, reading the opening lines of E. Balibar's contribution) that the Communist Party's 'aims' have changed: today, as it has always done, it is fighting for a socialist France.

The power of the big bourgeoisie today

2) E. Balibar writes: 'To imagine that we can fight for "real" democracy, for democracy for the masses of the people, *without* passing through the dictatorship of the proletariat is to *ignore the existence of the dictatorship of the bourgeoisie*, to ignore the role of the State apparatus as an instrument of exploitation.'

In fact it is *on the contrary* just because we are fighting against the domination of big capital, the power of the monopolies and that of the State uniting together in what we call *State Monopoly Capitalism* that we are led to define in French conditions a form of socialist power which cannot be properly expressed by the notion of the dictatorship of the proletariat.

---

* Pre-Congress discussion contribution; as published in *L'Humanité*, 23.1.1976.

If we want to unite all the forces of the working class, to group around it the whole of the working population against the money aristocracy, then we cannot satisfy ourselves with a general denunciation of the 'dictatorship of the bourgeoisie'. Unless we locate the different aspects of the economic, social and political power held by the great industrial and finance companies, unless we analyze the crisis of State Monopoly Capitalism, unless we analyze the class struggles of present-day France, then we shall be condemned to impose on contemporary reality texts of Lenin abstractly torn from their historical context.

The crisis has its source, says the draft document, in a fundamental contradiction between the 'economic, social and political structures' of our society, dominated by big capital, and on the other hand the 'vital needs of the workers and of the people', the 'requirements of economic progress and of national development'. There exists an oligarchy which, in order to hold on to power and to force the whole of the French working people to accept the consequences of the crisis, is concentrating the levers of power ever more closely into its own hands. It is attacking the liberties dearly won by our people since 1789. It wants to imprison France in a supra-national Europe, under American supervision.

In such conditions, is it not the task of a Leninist Party to help all the social strata victimized by big capital to recognize their common enemy, to form that unstoppable 'majority grouping' which alone can isolate the régime and defeat it? And which, already, is forcing it onto the defensive in this or that sector of the class battle – when for example, supported by the population, workers prevent the closure of an enterprise decided on by some big company, protected and supported by the State.

This is the revolutionary meaning of our struggle for the Union of the French People around the Common Programme of the Left. A Union whose motor is the working class, for reasons which the document explains. The needs, the aspirations which have become globally an essential characteristic of French society are today in fact witnesses (even if many French men and women are not yet conscious of the fact) to the *objective necessity* of the socialist transformation of our country. The working class therefore cannot play its full part except by assuming all the responsibilities which fall to it with respect both to the everyday economic struggle and to the unification of all the forces which will make our country into a *socialist democracy*.

If this was not the case, it would be impossible to understand why the régime wants to isolate the Communist Party, win back the Socialist Party to class collaboration, and set the different sections of the working population against one another. It would be impossible to understand why it is so worried by the successes of our action for the defence and extension of liberties. One thing which Marx and Engels taught us, and which Lenin repeated in his time, followed by French Communists like Maurice Thorez and Waldeck Rochet, is that the struggle for socialism and the struggle for democracy are inseparable.

Democratizing the State

3) According to E. Balibar, the draft document ignores the need, in order to put an end to the 'class dictatorship of the bourgeoisie', to destroy 'the existing *State apparatus*, which can never as such function "in the service of the working people"'.

Balibar reproaches the draft document for reducing the debate on the dictatorship of the proletariat to a question of 'words'; I should like to ask him to measure the terms which he employs against contemporary reality.

The evolution of the State in present-day France faces the labour movement with new problems. For example – to take only one case – State power is nowadays being used to undermine the big public service industries (e.g. the Post Office); and it is the postmen who have been fighting to preserve for the French people a public service which is truly 'public' and truly a 'service'.

But, above all, the transition from the State of the monopolies to the State of the working people as envisaged by the draft document (Part 3) cannot be made in a single step; it will not be like a sudden mutation. It will be a process of democratization, the very process which we are already preparing for today in working for the Common Programme.

The application of this Programme will deprive the monopolies of their control of the banking and finance system, and of the key sectors of the economy. It will thus constitute an 'important step forward' on the road to democratic change. And the struggles of all those groups whose interest lies in the application of the Common Programme will lay the foundation for other struggles, those which, when the majority of the French people has decided for it, will take democracy 'to the limit' and transform the country into a socialist democracy.

How can E. Balibar therefore write that we are trapping our-selves within mystifying 'alternatives'? We do not believe, as Bernstein used to believe, that the movement is everything and the goal nothing. The democratic mass struggle does not exclude but paves the way for the victory of socialism. And the new govern-ment, which will for the first time be a government of the working class and of all working people, will improve its work and defend itself not by restricting democratic activity but by providing it with every possible facility.

Defending socialism
4) E. Balibar believes that the draft document underestimates the forces and means available to the bourgeois counter-revolution; he suggests that it cannot be overcome except by the dictatorship of the proletariat.

These worries would be justified if the Document had forgotten that a socialist democracy must watch over its conquests. But the whole document in fact helps us to understand that the *defence* of socialism is one of the components of *socialist democracy*.

I shall not repeat here the arguments already developed in the present discussion by those comrades who are of the opinion that, in our country, the 'representative government of the working people' will have a broader base than that of a dictatorship of the proletariat. This government will not forbid opposition move-ments to participate in public life; it will exclude no single social group from the voting booths. It will provide for its own defence, in every domain, by means of the indispensable 'action of the working class and of the broad masses of the people'. And the conquests of socialism – on the workshop floor and in the various institutions, in life and in law – will provide the working class and its allies with greater possibilities of intervention against any attempt, whatever its form, to drag the country back into the past. One of the functions of a democratized system of universal suffrage will be to demonstrate the will of a people resolved to give way neither to pressure nor to violence.

It is therefore in *its own way*, in direct application of its princi-ples and aims, that socialist democracy will provide itself with the means to ensure that it is 'respected'. In this way the links between the working class and the other strata of working people will be reinforced. In this way more favourable conditions will be created for the mobilization of all the help which a socialist France will need in order to guarantee its progress – even against threats of subversion and armed violence.

The working people of our country understand the meaning of the word 'fascism'. But it was only in the struggle for the people's demands and liberties that, thanks to the initiatives of the Communist Party, fascism retreated in the face of the single front, in the face of the Popular Front.

If today the practical activity of the men of government proves their liberalism to be no more than a matter of words, it is because they find democracy more and more impossible to accept. The struggle to preserve the democratic heritage, to extend the sphere of liberties in accordance with the demands of our epoch – this struggle is imposing on the modern feudalists a battle which is becoming more and more difficult for them. And it is preparing the ground, today, on which millions of Frenchmen will be able to come together in defence of their socialist democracy. To act now, today, for the democratization of the system of administration, of justice, of the police, for an army of citizen-soldiers and of citizen-officers – this will enable our working class and our people to make the best possible use tomorrow of all the weapons of liberty.

And, since the defence of socialism (Balibar stresses this point) implies the need to hinder any attempt to hold up its economic development, here too the most effective defence will be the full exercise of socialist democracy. The new government will interest the whole working population in the protection and perfectioning of the means of production and exchange; in their enterprises the working people (including the employees of the banks) will be the best defenders of the socialist economy. Is it not already obvious that they know how to protect the national heritage against the big bosses and their State? Will they not find this task all the easier when State power is their own?

Fighting anti-Sovietism

5) The history of the socialist countries is open to study. It is in any case certain that, without the dictatorship of the proletariat (as Lenin understood it), the first socialist State would have been

unable either to defeat its enemies or to transform old Russia.

Never could a 'dictatorship *over* the proletariat' (an expression unfortunately taken over by E. Balibar) have found the strength to break Hitler's offensive. The Soviet Union's victory over fascism, the murderer of peoples, was the victory of a *socialist society*, of a people solidly united around its Soviet State and its Communist Party.

We condemn those practices which are – in spite of the decisions of the 20th Congress of the CPSU – still holding up the development of socialist democracy. Our attitude is based on the conviction that such practices are in conflict with the principles of a society whose goal can only be the happiness and brotherhood of men.

It is this society itself which provokes the steadfast hostility of international reaction; a society in which the working people have conquered and developed that fundamental liberty which is still to be born in 'advanced liberal society': they are no longer subjected to capitalist exploitation.

To fight against anti-Sovietism is today, as it has always been, a revolutionary task.

The evolution of the relation of forces
6) E. Balibar has a different view of the international context from that set out in the draft document. *L'Humanité* has on several occasions presented the analyses on which this document is founded, and I shall not repeat them in detail.

Peaceful co-existence, which has been imposed on imperialism, is working in the interest of the liberation of the peoples, whatever the form of their struggle (from Cuba to Vietnam).

Imperialism has not changed its aggressive nature, and the fact that it has been weakened does not lead us to conclude that the international situation is irreversible.

But I cannot imagine that Balibar has not noticed the positive evolution of the relation of forces. And how can he disregard the role and the effects of the movement of the people in this country, today and in the future?

Imperialism (and above all American imperialism) is hostile to a socialist France? But the draft document does not hide this fact, and our Party is at the head of the struggle for the right of the

French people to decide its own future. Balibar pleads for us not to ignore 'the potential foundations of counter-revolution' in our country, not to underestimate the ability of imperialism to turn to its own profit 'the contradictions in the camp of the people'; but it seems to me that the only strategy capable of foiling these manoeuvres is precisely the one defined by the draft document.

It warns against the temptation to try and take short cuts; and here again the importance attached to the system of universal suffrage will be a substantial guarantee against the impatience of anyone who thinks that he can force the pace. It envisages the most sensible means of resolving at the proper moment, and to the advantage of socialism, the contradictions thrown up by its development.

A thoroughgoing debate

In the conditions of present-day France, the notion of the dictator-ship of the proletariat is out-of-date. Only the strategy defined by the draft resolution offers the working class the possibility of bringing about the 'Union of the French People', an indispensable condition of victory. Only this strategy offers the French Communist Party the possibility of further strengthening itself and assuming all its responsibilities at the head of the struggle for a socialist France.

E. Balibar believes that the French Communists are not in a position to make a decision on these questions because they lack 'full knowledge of the facts'. But does the debate not demonstrate – a debate in which tens of thousands of our comrades are taking part, in branch meetings, section congresses and federal congresses – that the moment has come when the problems under examination are ready to be solved? And they are being solved, by the vast majority of our militants, both manual and intellectual workers, in the spirit of the draft document presented to the 22nd Congress.

'In order to take democracy forward to socialism, two problems are decisive.' (Extracts)*

Georges Marchais

1. Property and administration

Now, just because we are Communists, we do not consider that putting the Common Programme into effect would constitute an end in itself. We want to take democracy further forward, we want socialism.

The draft document defines the characteristics of socialist society as we are proposing it to the country. I should like to take a closer look at two problems which are decisive for a correct understanding of the kind of society for which we are fighting.

As our document points out, we believe that the 'great means of production and exchange should become as a whole the property of society itself'. This is one of the foundations of socialist society, and there can be no socialism if this condition is not realized. This is shown by the experience of the Social-Democratic Parties which, recoiling before the need to put an end to the stranglehold of big capital on the principal resources of the countries which they have ruled or are presently ruling, have nowhere been able to bring socialism into being. Does this mean that we want France to be what reactionary propaganda calls 'collectivist', i.e., that we want to dispossess everyone, to submit them to uniformity and constraint? Our reply is a categorical *no*.

In the first place, we obviously do not intend to interfere with personal property – with the various kinds of consumer goods and articles of personal use – or with the right to bequeath it. This applies for example to home ownership, either of a house or flat.

In the second place, the objective of socialism is the satisfaction

* From the Report presented to the 22nd Congress of the French Communist Party on February 4th, 1976; as reported in *L'Humanité*, 5.2.1976).

of the needs of the members of society. In order to meet this requirement, there will be various forms of social property: nationalized property, co-operative property, municipal, provincial and regional public property. At the same time, in a number of fields, small-scale private property (artisan-type, commercial and industrial) and family-based farming will be the best way to satisfy the people's needs; taking account of international experience, we intend to maintain these forms in a socialist France.

In the third place, it is the monopolies which are exercizing a real dictatorship over the enterprises; it is the present régime which is developing a technocratic bureaucracy trying to domineer over all aspects of national life; it is the State of big capital which is meddling with the local communities and trying to keep them under its thumb. We are today struggling against this authoritarianism, this suffocating centralism. And not in order to re-introduce it tomorrow, under socialism! On the contrary, we want the nationalized enterprises to be independent in their administration; we want planning to be carried out democratically, with the participation of the working people and consumers; we want the administration of enterprises to be itself democratic, so that those employed there – workers, white-collar employees, engineers, managers – can participate more and more actively in this task. And we also want the parishes, provinces and regions to become real centres of democratic decision-making and administration.

The same preoccupations lie behind our conception of cultural life. We stand for a culture liberated from the rule of money, a culture which will no longer be a commodity nor a luxury but the property of everyone, men and women, in our country. In a socialist France, culture will be broad and lively, open to every advance in knowledge, research and creation. Developing the great traditions of our people, it will be enriched by the diversity of talents and also by the possibilities provided for each individual freely to develop the faculties which lie in him.

In short, we do not want a mutilating uniformity but an enriching diversity. Nothing is more foreign to our conception of socialism than what is called 'barracks communism', which pours everyone and everything into the same mould. We picture the socialist system which we are proposing for our country in lively, flexible and inventive terms, as favouring a variety of solutions and appealing to the expansion of initiatives. (*Applause.*)

2. The question of the 'dictatorship of the proletariat'
This leads me to another question.

The document defines a second decisive problem of socialism, inseparable from the first: 'Only a political power representing the working people will make it possible to bring about the necessary radical transformations in economic and social life.'

The importance of this problem has provoked a discussion all the richer for the fact that the 'dictatorship of the proletariat' does not appear in the draft document. We must therefore take a closer look at this question.

The reason that the 'dictatorship of the proletariat' does not appear in the draft document in order to designate political power in the socialist France for which we are fighting is that it does not characterize the reality of our policy, the reality of what we are proposing for the country.

What do we say in the draft document? We say the following:

– The power that will lead the socialist transformation of society will be that of the working class and of the other categories of working people, manual and intellectual, of city and countryside, i.e. the great majority of the people.

– This power will be based on and will act according to the freely expressed results of the system of universal suffrage; its task will be to carry out the most extensive democratization of the economic, social and political life of the country.

– Its duty will be to respect and to ensure respect for the democratic decisions of the people.

In contrast to all this, the term 'dictatorship' automatically evokes the fascist régimes of Hitler, Mussolini, Salazar and Franco, i.e. the very negation of democracy. That is not what we want.

As far as the proletariat is concerned, today it represents the core or heart of the working class. Though its role is an essential one, it does not represent the whole of this class; still less does it represent the whole of the working people whose power will be expressed in the socialist society which we envisage.

It is therefore obvious that what we are proposing to the working people, to our people, cannot be called a 'dictatorship of the proletariat'.

On what basis do we define our position on this question? We base ourselves on the principles of scientific socialism elaborated by Marx, Engels and Lenin.

The first point is that the working class must play a leading political role in the struggle for the socialist transformation of society.

Even if the working people, the masses of the people, are already able to force the government to take urgent social measures, and even to win certain new privileges, the genuine and permanent satisfaction of their economic, social and political rights is totally impossible *without a change in the class nature of the régime*. The participation of the working people and of their representatives in the administration of the country's affairs, *their access to the control centres of society constitutes the key problem of the struggle for socialism*. Among the working people, the working class is the most numerous, militant and experienced class in the struggle for social progress and also – this has to be underlined – for the national interest. It must therefore take its full place in the socialist State and play a determining role within it.

In this connexion, the draft document states: 'Only the working class can lead the revolutionary struggle to victory. Its vital interests, its numerical power, its great concentration, its experience of the class struggle and its organization make it, today and tomorrow, the leading force in the fight for a new society.'

The second point is that the manoeuvres of the big bourgeoisie cannot be defeated without the revolutionary struggle of the masses.

In this connexion the draft document declares: 'The big exploiting bourgeoisie will never willingly give up its domination and its privileges. It will always tend to use every possible means to defend them or to win them back.' I would even add that this is particularly true of the French bourgeoisie. For, although there exists a revolutionary tradition in our country, there also exists the reactionary tradition of Versailles, which is certainly not dead, as the behaviour of the men now in power reminds us every day.

That is why the draft document shows that the working people, the masses of the people, must 'at each stage gather their forces and struggle very actively in order to foil reactionary manoeuvres . . . and to paralyze or defeat any possible attempt by reaction to resort to illegal action, subversion and violence'.

Having said that, we must in conformity with the spirit of our own doctrine take into careful account 'the real process', in other words the conditions in which we live in this epoch and in this country. These conditions allow and require us to envisage other paths to socialism in France than those followed by the peoples which have already brought about the socialist transformation of their country.

In the conditions of Russia in 1917, and then of the young Soviet Union, the dictatorship of the proletariat was necessary in order to guarantee the construction of socialism. It is true to say that without this dictatorship the working class and the peoples of the Soviet Union would have been able neither to undertake nor to persist in the unprecedented task of liberation which they carried out. That is why the Communist Parties, when they were founded, drawing the lessons of the bankruptcy of international Social-Democracy and of the victory of the October Revolution, were correct in the conditions of the epoch to adopt this slogan.

The world has changed
In the most recent period of history, the world has profoundly changed. The relation of forces has been transformed and continues to develop in the direction of independence and the liberty of the peoples, of democracy and socialism. Peaceful coexistence has been strengthened. In the course of complex and bitter struggles, marked by advances and sometimes by retreats, it is finally reaction and fascism which have had to give ground, while democracy is progressing, as shown by the events in Greece, Portugal and also in Spain. It cannot be denied that never have the peoples of the world had such great possibilities of deciding their destiny and of advancing on the road of national and social liberation. These possibilities are based on the existence and progress of the socialist countries, on the development of the struggles of the working class and the masses of the people in the capitalist countries, on the rapid advance and the rise in the level of the struggle of the national liberation movements, and on the solidarity between all these revolutionary forces. The people of our own country will find in these movements a factor of support, which does not of course mean that it is exempt from the need to take action for itself, but which does provide it with unprecedented means of independent action. Moreover, if the position of France in Western Europe and the relations linking it with its neighbours

pose problems which must not be ignored, they also offer possibilities of co-operation and common action between revolutionary and progressive forces in the struggle to open new roads – based on the concrete conditions existing in our country – to democracy and socialism. Our Party has already, for several years, been working in support of such common action. It is in this spirit that we contributed to the success of the Conference of Communist Parties of Capitalist Europe held in January 1974, and to the implementation of its decisions, and it is in the same spirit that we have just adopted, together with our Italian comrades, an important joint declaration.

Now both the Communists and all the forces of progress are of course very concerned about what happened in Chile. They are also attentively following events in Portugal. Beyond the important differences between these two sets of events, they both provide brutal confirmation of the fact that reaction will never shrink from the use of violence. No-one who is really interested in the progressive transformation of society, its transformation in the direction of the interests of the working people, can afford to forget or to neglect this fact. But events also show that reaction has not always turned and cannot always, in all conditions, turn to violence; it requires a relation of political forces which is moving in its favour.

In Chile, the Popular Unity alliance took government power in an absolutely legal and normal way. However, we must not forget that it did not in the beginning enjoy the support of a majority in the country. In the face of the machinations of internal reaction and of imperialism, nothing was more important than to change this relation of forces in its own favour, by getting down to the problem of winning and extending the majority support of the population. Our Chilean comrades did in this connexion, even if they produced some positive results, commit gravely damaging errors which did not help them to realize this aim. In Portugal the overthrow of fascism allowed the popular movement to win some important successes. But the division of democratic forces, for which Mario Soares' Socialist Party must bear an overwhelming responsibility, led to a retreat of this popular movement. The struggle to defend, and to extend in the future the democratic achievements of the Portuguese people is today being fought out in more difficult conditions.

In drawing attention to these events, we do not intend to lecture others but to draw the necessary conclusions for our own struggle.

In this connexion, what we conclude from these two sets of events is that it is necessary to be on permanent guard against two dangers:

– The danger of not carrying out, when this becomes possible, the necessary democratic transformations of the economic and political structures, with the support of the mass movement;

– The danger of putting forward adventurist slogans or of taking adventurist actions which do not correspond to real possibilities, which are inspired by the desire to 'take short cuts', and which in fact lead the revolutionary forces to isolation and defeat.

The most important conclusion is that *the decisive condition of success is the existence and self-assertion of a popular movement sufficiently broad to encompass a large majority of the people, solidly united around the need for change.*

This fundamental lesson adds weight to the conclusions which we have drawn with respect to France from the analysis of the conditions existing in our country.

What is this analysis and what are its conclusions?

French reality

As you know, the working class now makes up 44.5% of the working population of France, i.e. about 10 million persons. In addition, several million other wage-earners, above all among the employees, live and work in conditions close to those of the working class. Together with the working class in the strict sense, this makes at least three-quarters of the active population. Moreover, the crisis is not only damaging the interests of the mass of wage-earners but also those of the other strata of the working population. The convergence of the basic interests of all these social forces therefore offers unprecedented possibilities of winning over the majority of the people to the cause of changing our society, of grouping around the powerful pole constituted by the working class a movement representing the vast majority of the people. Should we make use of such a possibility? There is no doubt about it.

In this connexion we must return to the question of 'bourgeois liberties'. It is claimed that we are opposed to certain liberties on the grounds that they are bourgeois or formal in nature. This is to deform not only our position but also that of the founders of Marxism.

There is one and only one liberty to which Communists are and always will be opposed: the liberty to exploit the working people. This liberty is the only real bourgeois liberty, if you can talk about a right of oppression as a liberty.

For the rest, we openly refuse to give the credit to the bourgeoisie for the existence of liberties. It is true that the French bourgeoisie, when it took power nearly 200 years ago, did carry into daily life some of the democratic principles proclaimed by its philosophers. But very soon, a very long time ago, it stopped arguing for or putting into practice any principle which did not correspond to its own nature and to its needs as an exploiting class.

In reality there is no liberty in France which has not been paid for by the sufferings and sometimes the blood of our people. The working people, the masses of the people, have indeed had to struggle for – among other things – universal suffrage, freedom of opinion, expression, association and publication, for the right to strike, for trade union rights, and for the right to organize their own political parties. And they waged these struggles because all these liberties correspond to their own interests and aspirations. That is why they are so attached to them, and why the Communist Party will defend them to the end. The task of the Communists – and their ambition is only to improve their work in this respect – is to continue in the line of all the workers, peasants, intellectuals, simple citizens or statesmen who have for so many centuries been fighting for liberty in our country.

If certain liberties today have a formal character, it is because the bourgeoisie in power has been trying to empty them of their content. Far from coming to their aid and holding these liberties in contempt, we intend on the contrary to restore them to their full meaning, to renovate them. Socialism is not an arbitrary construction of the mind. It is born in the real movement of history, out of the real struggles of the people such as it is, with its own traditions and aspirations. We are convinced that *socialism in our country must be identified – otherwise we shall remain at the level of words – with the defence and extension of the democratic conquests which have been made possible by the great and persistent struggles of our people.* This must be so and this can be so.

As I have pointed out, the draft document rules out any illusions about the attitude of the big bourgeoisie and its willingness to respect the verdict of universal suffrage.

But at the same time it guards against the idea that it might be possible, taking a short cut, to substitute for the political will of the majority of the people the action of 'small, highly-motivated groups' or of the weapons of repression. This is an equally dangerous illusion, because it can only give internal and external reaction an excuse for violence; it can only lead the revolutionary movement to isolation and defeat.

Struggle of the masses and liberties

In the struggle for socialism, nothing, absolutely nothing can – in our own epoch and in a country like our own – replace the popular majority will, expressed democratically in struggle and *by means of universal suffrage*. Whatever the forms taken by the advance to socialism in this country (and of course we cannot predict in detail what these will be) we are convinced that at each stage there must be both a political and an arithmetical majority. This is possible.

How are we to create the best conditions for the development of this indispensable majority movement of our people, to make it broad, strong and effective? This is the real question; to pose any other is either empty talk or provocation.

To this question, the democratic road to socialism which we are proposing offers a serious answer.

In struggling today for the democratic transformations foreseen in the Common Programme, we are offering the best possible foundation for uniting the broad masses of the people, a foundation which will make it possible to replace the power of the monopolies by a new, democratic power.

Tomorrow, the application of democratic reforms will enable the positions and the means of struggle of the big bourgeoisie to be weakened, and the positions and therefore the means of struggle of the working class and of the people to be strengthened.

Beyond that moment, it is by developing economic, social and political democracy, and by still further extending individual and collective liberties, that the popular movement will be reinforced and that the socialist régime will win the support and participation which it needs. In return, the struggle of the masses will continue to produce

changes in the relation of social and political forces, to the benefit of
the working people and of all the other sections of the people.

In fact, in order to guarantee the success of socialism, the problem is not to deprive the minority making up the reactionary forces of its liberties, but to provide these liberties to the working people constituting the great majority of the nation. The reactionaries might of course organize a reactionary party. But this they already possess today, it will not be a novelty. What will indeed be a great novelty is for example the fact that the working people will have extensive rights in their places of work, or that their representatives will be allowed fair access to the television, or that the police will be democratized. Thus they will possess effective means of struggle against any economic sabotage carried out by reaction, they will be able to extend and defend their positions, ideas and actions far and wide, and they will be able to defeat their enemy politically and ideologically. The workers will be strengthened, ever more strengthened by the liberties they will enjoy.

It is by drawing support from these liberties that they will be able to develop their struggle, to force the big bourgeoisie on to the retreat and then to defeat it. And it is by drawing support from this broad-based struggle that the socialist government will be able to force the reactionaries to respect the choices freely made by the great majority of the people.

This means that, far from renouncing socialism or holding it back, we are proposing the best and quickest means of bringing it into being.

In so doing, we are absolutely faithful to the teachings of Marxism-Leninism, which has no use for a collection of dogmas, and to the creative experience of the world Communist movement and of our own Party.

We know for example that Lenin, analyzing the situation at the beginning of the century, developed the argument that, contrary to what Marx had imagined, socialism could triumph first of all in a single country. This all-important conclusion was to be the basis of the Bolshevik Party's strategy in 1917. In the same way, the world Communist movement put forward in 1960 the new idea that world war was no longer inevitable in contemporary conditions. And the fact is that thirty years have passed since the Second World War, and that peaceful coexistence is advancing, though of course it is not irreversible.

Turning now to the case of France, the idea of the Popular Front, which became a reality in 1936, cannot be found ready-made in Marx or in Lenin. It was based on the general principles of scientific socialism and on 'a concrete analysis of concrete reality'. Many other examples could be taken, all showing that our present approach finds its inspiration in the living source of the revolutionary theory and practice of our movement.

Such are the foundations of our position, the reasons leading us to propose the democratic road defined in the draft document.

That is also why the 'dictatorship of the proletariat' does not figure in the draft document.

In consequence, and as requested by all the federal congresses of the Party, we are proposing to the National Congress that this notion should be abandoned (*applause*). We are also proposing to Congress that the Central Committee to be elected there should be instructed to present to the following Party Congress a suitably modified version of the Preamble to the Statutes.

The Historic Significance of the 22nd Congress

by Louis Althusser

I want to thank the UEC Philosophy Branch for having invited me to take part in this debate.[1] I was left free to choose my subject. And I thought: there is no subject in France more important than the 22nd Congress of the French Communist Party, not only for Communists but for everyone who wants to put an end to the dictatorship of the bourgeoisie, to its exploitation, cynicism and lies.

I shall therefore present a series of remarks on this Congress.

In order to make my political position clear to everyone, let me first say that I consider the 22nd Congress to be a decisive event in the history of the Communist Party and of the French labour movement.

I should add that, in order to understand an event of such importance, we must not concentrate our attention on this or that detail of French political history, on this or that particular circumstance of the Congress, or even on the letter of the formulations adopted there.

We must rather try to grasp *the general problems* to which the 22nd Congress constitutes a response, problems which are posed not only on the national scale but also on the world scale. We must look at matters in the necessary perspective, and place the Congress in the history of imperialism, the 'period of revolutionary movements' (Lenin), which are themselves inseparable from the general forms of crisis of the international revolutionary movement.

We must place the Congress in this long and dramatic history,

[1] This paper was first presented as a speech in a debate organized by the Sorbonne Philosophy Branch of the French Union of Communist Students. [*This and the following notes are added by the translator.*]

a history full of problems and contradictions. And we must understand that the initiatives taken by the Congress do, in their own way, tend *to break with this history and to open new perspectives.*

As a first approximation let me say that it is impossible to understand the 22nd Congress without taking account of two important facts which dominate the political situation and are of crucial interest to millions of men and women in the world: *on the one hand* the aggravation of the crisis of imperialism, and *on the other hand* the aggravation of the crisis of the International Communist Movement.

For the third time in its history, following the revolutionary crisis opened up by the First World War and the great crisis of 1929, whose revolutionary premises imperialism swept away by fascism and a Second World War – each time however paying the price of a revolution (USSR) or revolutions (China, Cuba) – we can say that this same imperialism now finds itself once again in a pre-revolutionary crisis, whose forms are quite new.

Paradoxically, the revolutionary movement has never been so powerful in the world, now that the Third World movements for liberation and economic independence have been joined to the anti-capitalist struggle in the imperialist centres. But, *paradoxically,* at the same time the crisis of the International Communist Movement, both open (the Sino-Soviet split) and masked (the conflict between the Western Communist Movement and the USSR) has never been so acute.

Unless we place the 22nd Congress within the framework of this fundamental contradiction and of its effects, we run the risk of failing to understand its significance, together with the problems which it posed and its own contradictions.

But I would also say, as a second approximation, that in spite of its own crisis, imperialism – playing on the crisis of the International Communist Movement – *still has at its disposal considerable resources and forces* in order to make the international working class, the countries of the Third World, their emigrant workers and the dependent capitalist States pay the cost of the crisis and of the maintenance, re-establishment or reinforcement of its supremacy. In the present context it would be dangerous to underestimate the power of imperialism, *just as it would be dangerous to underestimate the power of the bourgeois State:* the fact that it is dominated by its monopolist fraction does not prevent it

from defending and strengthening its mass base. When the reputa-
tion of a political figure is damaged (Giscard), the bourgeoisie can
always find another one to replace him (Chirac): you must not
believe that it is always a case of 'Tweedledum and Tweedledee',
because it may be that the second man can, by a more dangerous,
semi-fascist form of demagogy, win back the mass base of the
bourgeoisie which was collapsing as a consequence of the class
struggle. We must pay great attention to these *differences in the
political forms* taken by the dictatorship of the bourgeoisie: they
can have important consequences. And in the first place they may
precisely allow the bourgeoisie to survive and to maintain itself
in power.

In the same way, but on a quite different front, *it would be
dangerous to underestimate*, in spite of the acute crisis which it is
going through, *the capacities of the International Communist
Movement*, and its chances of resolving this crisis. And this too is
an historical phenomenon of great significance.

In order to understand the initiatives taken by the 22nd
Congress, we must take all these aspects together, in their always
complex and sometimes paradoxical dialectic.

It is in this context that I shall examine, one by one, the initiatives taken by the 22nd Congress.

First initiative

The Congress itself claimed to be of historic importance, a turning
point in the history of the Communist Party. Why was it an
historic Congress? Because for the first time it dealt with the
present stage in the class struggle in terms of the *strategy for
socialism* and of the *peaceful* and *democratic* means of transition to
socialism.

The document adopted by the Congress[2] is not a concrete
analysis of the state of the relation of class forces in the world in
general and France in particular, but a political *manifesto* picturing
to the French people, and not only to the working class, 'the
society which the Communists want for France: *socialism*'.

You will notice an important difference here: for the 21st
Congress did not talk so much about socialism, but above all

[2] *Ce que veulent les communistes pour la France*; published together with other
Congress documents in *Le Socialisme pour la France*, Editions sociales, 1976.

about the Common Programme.[3] The whole document adopted
by the 22nd Congress is however *centred around socialism.* By
this reference to socialism, the Congress intended to move beyond
the tactical and electoral point of view centred on the Common
Programme alone in order to say something about the 'strategy'
which, beyond the Common Programme, must lead to socialism.

The great innovation of the 22nd Congress is that it argues that
this whole strategy will be democratic and peaceful. In every case
the Party promises to respect the verdict of universal suffrage,
and therefore the possibility of the democratic alternation of
governments. The French people will not make the transition to
socialism by force, but democratically, by the vote, in full liberty.

But at the same time the Party does not hide the fact that it will
not be a passive witness to the class struggle. It is launching a great
recruiting campaign on the basis of lofty objectives, intervening
'on all points of the compass' in the class struggle, and doing
everything to unite the masses of the people around their class
demands, in order to achieve socialism with liberty.

But since nothing is without its contradictions and problems,
we must point out here that the ambitious character of this
initiative, *which does not hesitate to sketch out a picture* of the
socialist society of the future (one leading comrade used the
phrase 'a practical utopia'), is accompanied by a very scanty
account of the existing class power of the bourgeoisie in France.
Here is where the absence of a concrete analysis of the concrete
situation makes itself felt. Because you cannot solve *politically* the
problem of the bourgeois class State by just *pointing out* that the
French economy is dominated by 25 giant trusts + 600 great
auxiliaries + 500,000 members of the great bourgeoisie, for this
State always takes the form of a 'power bloc', *associating several
class fractions* under the domination of the bourgeoisie as a class;
so this is no way to solve the fundamental problem of the *mass
base* of the domination of the bourgeoisie as a class, which, as a
class, cannot be reduced to its monopolist fraction. If the bourgeoisie, *as a class*, was reduced *politically* to its monopolist
fraction, it would not last for a quarter of an hour.

I am not making a simply 'abstract' or 'theoretical' objection

[3] For Georges Marchais' Report to the 21st French Communist Party Congress,
see *Marxism Today*, January and February 1975; for Althusser's contribution to the
pre-Congress discussion, see his *Essays in Self-Criticism*, NLB, 1976, pp. 208–15.

here; I am talking about terribly concrete realities which find their expression in the famous 'electoral barrier' and other similar stumbling-blocks, and which cannot be explained just by blaming the 'television system', etc. – on the contrary, we have to analyze with great care in each particular case the precise class limits, functions and effects involved.

Second initiative

It is to the credit of the 22nd Congress that, in the definition of its political line, it pays attention to the important changes which have taken place in the world. If this political line sketches out a new perspective it is because class relations have changed, and because the masses, in the course of their own struggles, however hard these struggles may be in a period of inflation and unemployment, *have become aware of this fact*. Georges Marchais expressed this historical experience of the masses by insisting on the fact that *if things have changed, the Party must change too*.

And the Cold War has indeed begun to fade away, though very dangerous sparking-points remain, like the Middle East and South Africa, where American imperialism intervenes either directly or through its lackeys. The economic crisis of imperialism is indeed undermining the political power of the bourgeoisie and creating new possibilities for the struggle of the working class and of the people. New social strata are indeed drawn into the ranks of the wage-earners and joining the struggle of the working class. An unprecedented relation of forces is appearing on the horizon of this struggle: for the first time in history the transition to socialism *may* take a peaceful form. For the first time in history a form of socialism is appearing different from the 'grey' variety built on force or even repression: a *mass democratic socialism*.

The 22nd Congress was able to draw the lesson of the objective demands, of the experience and claims of the people of this country. That is why it talked about 'socialism in French colours'. In its own way it echoed the long revolutionary tradition of the French people, which has always linked liberty and revolution. It went much further than the repudiation of the military occupation of Czechoslovakia. It launched a gigantic campaign for the defence of existing liberties and for their future extension. This development is irreversible.

But since nothing is without its contradictions and problems, we must point out that this same Party, which talks at such length and with such generosity about liberties for others, nevertheless remains *silent* on the question of the present forms and practices of democratic centralism, *i.e.* on the forms of liberty of Communists in their own Party. Yet there is a lot to be said about this question. I shall come back to it in a moment.

Third initiative
The 22nd Congress adopted a new position in response to the crisis of the International Communist Movement.

The paradox is that the Congress made allusive references to the problem without providing an analysis of this crucial phenomenon: silence reigns over the history which is now being made. The paradox is that the crisis of the International Communist Movement was dealt with obliquely, indirectly: *in the form of the abandonment of the dictatorship of the proletariat.*

This is one of those cases where you must not take declarations *literally.* What is at stake here is of *much greater importance* than would appear from the official explanations.

The official standpoint was that, following the Hitler, Mussolini and Franco régimes, the word 'dictatorship' has become 'intolerable'. The official standpoint was that the proletariat, the 'hard core' of the working class, is now 'too narrow' to be identified with the broad popular union which we want.

Now this last argument – the proletariat as the heart of a broad alliance – is in the tradition of Marx and Lenin. The 22nd Congress takes it up in the form of the idea of the 'leading role of the working class' at the heart of a broad union of the people. There are no serious problems on this point.

On the other hand it is difficult to take seriously the argument about 'dictatorship', since it does not say what it means: it says *something different,* and something very important. Because the official list of examples (Hitler, Mussolini, etc.) simply omits any mention of Stalin: not just of the individual called Stalin, but of the structure of the Soviet State and Party, and of the economic and political line imposed by Stalin over a period of thirty years, not only on the Soviet State and Party but on the Communist Parties of the whole world. Fascism is fascism: the workers quickly learned what they could expect from it. But they expected something quite different from Soviet socialism, in which they had placed all their hopes of liberation, from that régime of terror and mass extermination, which is still awaiting a Marxist analysis.

The exponents of the abandonment of the dictatorship of the proletariat *said*: dictatorship = Hitler, Mussolini, etc. *In reality* they *meant*: dictatorship = *Stalin, Soviet socialism*. In reality they meant: *we do not want anything to do with that kind of socialism, ever*.

There is no doubt that in the unexpected form of the abandonment of the dictatorship of the proletariat the 22nd Congress killed two birds with one stone: *while adopting a new strategy for socialism it also at the same time adopted a new position with regard to the crisis of the International Communist Movement*, thus furnishing the proof that, at least to some extent, it is possible to find a way out of this crisis. In spite of its present limits, agreed to at the Berlin Conference, this initiative may prove fruitful.

It is in this perspective that the abandonment of the dictatorship of the proletariat played its part, by allowing a *spectacular presentation* (the abandonment of a hallowed formula . . .) of the idea that a different kind of socialism is possible from that now holding sway in the USSR and Eastern Europe.

As far as the concept of the dictatorship of the proletariat is concerned, in particular its irrefutable scientific core, I am not too worried about its future prospects. They will not be settled by its political abandonment. Every materialist knows that a scientific truth which objectively reflects a real relation is hard to kill off, and has time on its side. We shall soon see the proof of it.

Fourth initiative

On this matter too the 22nd Congress was not explicit, but it is an important matter, one which has to be deciphered.

I am talking about the slogan of the *Union of the French People*, which Georges Marchais proposed to the 21st Congress and which the 22nd Congress readopted in its full force.

This slogan is not the same as that of the Union of the Left. It is wider, because it designates more than a Union of the political organizations of the Left, parties and trade unions.

How are we to understand this slogan of the Union of the

French People? Interpreted in the most favourable sense it might be taken to be or to be destined to become something quite different from a slogan designed to restore the 'electoral balance', namely to be directed, beyond the organizations of the Left, *to the masses of the people themselves*. Why address the masses of the people? In order to suggest to them, even if at first only by hints, that it will one day be necessary for them to organize as an autonomous force, in new forms, in factories, in neighbourhoods, around questions of housing, education, health care, transport, etc., in order to define and defend their demands, to support and stimulate the people's government in power or to prepare for its coming. Such mass organizations already exist in Italy and in Spain, where they play an important political role.

If the masses take up the slogan of the Union of the French People and interpret it in this *mass sense*, they will be joining up with a living tradition of popular struggles in this country and will be able to contribute to giving a new content to the political forms in which the power of the working people will be exercized in this country, under socialism.

Something may come to fruition in the Union of the French People, something which was eliminated in the practices of the Stalin type, and yet lies at the heart of the Marxist and Leninist tradition: the practice of letting the masses which make history speak for themselves, of not simply attempting to serve the people but of listening to them, learning from them and understanding their aspirations and their contradictions, and being attentive to the powers of imagination and invention of the masses.

The present broad recruiting policy of the Party can favour such mass democratic practices, and others of a daring kind (*e.g.* the opening of the Party press to workers who are not Party members: *cf. France Nouvelle*),[4] and in general everything which might serve the common debates and actions of Communists and non-Communists.

But since nothing is without its contradictions and problems, we must point out the risk involved here: the risk that this slogan will remain a matter of words alone, without giving rise to the corresponding forms of practical activity, the risk that it will serve

---

[4] Weekly journal of the French Communist Party; the nearest equivalent in the CPGB would be the fortnightly *Comment*.

to express a kind of political voluntarism designed simply to extend the influence of the Party beyond the Union of the Left. Not that an electoral gain is an insignificant matter, but it is far from exhausting the wealth of ideas contained in the slogan of the Union of the French People. There is thus a political battle to be engaged and won if the slogan of the Union of the French People is to be interpreted in its strongest sense: *its mass sense*.

Fifth initiative

The 22nd Congress has taught us several times over to be very careful with words. And here is the most surprising case.

My opinion is that we have to give paradoxical credit to the Congress on one point. In deciding to abandon the dictatorship of the proletariat, which had become a ritual formula, empty except for the Stalinian parody with which it was identified, the Congress placed *publicly on the agenda*, for the first time since the Tours Congress,[5] the theoretical and political ideas linked to the dictatorship of the proletariat. And yet the formula of abandonment did not itself appear in the Congress document.

The details of the events of the Congress do not in the last instance matter too much. We have other things to do than undertake a legal examination of the procedure followed there. Here again, facts are more important than words. The problem which concerns us is the following: willy-nilly, the 22nd Congress forced us all to think about a question which had remained obscure or been obscured for many comrades. It has already provoked and will continue to provoke thought about the concept of the dictatorship of the proletariat on the basis of the *concrete questions* which it talked about: not only the dictatorship of the proletariat but also for example the nature of socialism and the 'destruction' of the State.

There can be no telling the workers that the conditions of life described by the document are not in fact imposed on them by the dictatorship (or class rule) of the bourgeoisie, or that the dictatorship of the bourgeoisie can be reduced to its merely political forms, called 'democratic', that it does not extend to the worst

[5] The Congress of the French Socialist Party (1920) at which a majority of the delegates voted for applying to join the Communist International, thus creating the French Communist Party.

forms of economic exploitation, to the most vulgar forms of ideological influence and blackmail. The workers have everyday experience of the intervention of the bourgeois State in economic exploitation and in ideological propaganda. There can be no telling the workers that the proletariat does not exist, whether you call it 'the core of the working class' or something else. Georges Marchais, talking recently about the unskilled workers in automated industry, called them 'the proletariat of modern times'.

It is this experience of the 'dictatorship', or, if you prefer the old phrase of the *Communist Manifesto*, of the class '*domination*' of the bourgeoisie, an experience repeated daily for the working class, which contains the 'secret' of the expression 'dictatorship of the proletariat' or 'class domination' of the proletariat and its allies. The political form of this domination is mass democracy, democracy 'taken to the limit', but as a form of class domination it cannot be reduced to its political forms – it is also class domination in the economy and in ideology. This quite new kind of class domination runs counter to the bourgeois class dictatorship: it begins little by little to transfigure the bourgeois forms of exploitation and the corresponding political and ideological forms by 'destroying' or revolutionizing the bourgeois State, which is nothing but the State of the dictatorship (or domination) of the bourgeoisie.

As long as we understand this point, we shall also understand that the expression 'dictatorship of the proletariat' contains both relatively *contingent* elements and *necessary* elements. We shall understand for example that the question of the peaceful transition to socialism is a *contingent* element: if, in the class struggle, the relation of forces is very favourable to the proletariat and to the working people in general and very unfavourable to imperialism and the national bourgeoisie, *then* a peaceful transition is possible. You must not forget about imperialism in the analysis, because it can intervene without the slightest scruple, though it may on the other hand find itself relatively paralyzed. All this depends on the relation of forces, on the conjuncture: all this is contingent.

The achievement of the broadest possible class alliance around the 'hard core' of the working class, although it is an ever-present objective of the revolutionary struggle, is also a *contingent* element of the dictatorship of the proletariat. If the strength of the forces of the people and the relation of forces *allows* it to be constructed, then this alliance is quite simply indispensable, and it would be criminal not to exploit the possibility.

To say that these two conditions – relation of forces permitting the peaceful transition to socialism/broadest possible alliance around the proletariat – are 'contingent' elements of the dictatorship of the proletariat means that they *may or may not* be present. We know that they were not present in the 1917 revolution, although the situation did pose the task of a revolutionary breakthrough. The revolution thus took place in non-peaceful forms, on the basis of an alliance of workers and peasants which proved rather fragile.

As far as these two questions are concerned – peaceful transition, broadest possible alliance around the proletariat ('leading role of the working class') – the 22nd Congress did, in the paradoxical form of the abandonment of the dictatorship of the proletariat, *correct certain errors* to which some comrades might have fallen victim with regard to the seizure of power and to socialism, errors induced by the Stalin deviation. But precisely on these two questions, the 22nd Congress added nothing new: it only repeated arguments about things which Marx and Lenin themselves had claimed to be *possible* (peaceful transition) or politically *desirable* (broadest possible alliance around the working class).

On the other hand there are elements of the dictatorship of the proletariat which are not *contingent* (dependent on the circumstances) but *necessary*, if the revolution is not to get bogged down and come to grief.

The essence of the dictatorship of the proletariat today lies in the *question of socialism* and in the *question of the State*.

Now when the 22nd Congress presents socialism in the way which it does, a society governed by a *generalized democracy* and by the generalized satisfaction of *needs*, it imagines that it has resolved what is in fact an imaginary problem. The introduction of the term 'practical utopia' is no accident. The problem is quite imaginary because it does not correspond to the reality of socialism as it can be understood both in theory and in real-life experience.

Socialism is not presented as what it really is: a *contradictory transition period* between capitalism and communism, but on the contrary as a *goal* to be attained, and at the same time as the end term of a process – that is, to put it bluntly, as a *stable mode of production*, whose stability, like that of every mode of production, lies in particular *relations of production* which, according to the classic formula, resolve the contradiction between the developed productive forces (at this point there comes a hymn of praise to the 'scientific and technical revolution') and the old, out-dated relations of production.

Now this conception is foreign to the ideas of Marx and Lenin, and also, we must add, if we want to try to understand these ideas together with all the difficulties which they raise, foreign to the historical experience of the socialist countries.

For Marx and Lenin, *there is no socialist mode of production*, there are *no socialist relations of production*, no socialist law, etc. Socialism is nothing other than the dictatorship of the proletariat, i.e., a new *class domination*, in which the working class fulfils the leading role with regard to its allies in the broadest possible mass democracy. Socialism is the transition period (the only such period which Marx and Lenin talk about) between capitalism and communism, a *contradictory* period in which capitalist elements (*e.g.* wages) and communist elements (*e.g.* new mass organizations) coexist in a relation of conflict, an essentially unstable period in which the class struggle persists in modified forms, unrecognizable from the standpoint of our own class struggle, difficult to decipher, and which may – depending on the relation of forces and the 'line' which is followed – either *regress* towards capitalism or *mark time* in frozen forms or again *progress* towards communism.

Everything which the historical experience of socialism has taught us (and we should be very wrong to condemn it from on high simply on the basis of obviously 'blameworthy' 'short-comings in democracy', as they are called in order to avoid having to look further) also proves that this historical period, *far from being a society in which problems resolve themselves* (on the basis of the satisfaction of 'needs'), is on the contrary one of the most difficult periods in world history, because of the contradictions which have to be overcome at each step – as if humanity, in order finally to bring communism to birth, was obliged to pay a heavy price in struggles, intelligence and initiatives for the right to see it come to pass.

This original conception of socialism brings with it an important consequence. Contrary to modes of production, which are defined in terms of their relations of production, socialism cannot be defined in its own right, in terms of its relations of production, since there are strictly speaking no socialist relations of production, but only in terms of the contradiction between capitalism, out of which it emerged, and communism, of which it is the first phase: thus in terms of its relation to communism, which is its future and end point.

Very concretely, this reminds us of Marx's phrase: communism is not an ideal but a *real movement* taking place under our own eyes. Very concretely it means that the strategy of the labour movement has to take account of this dialectic; *it cannot be a simple strategy for the transition to socialism*, it must be a strategy for the transition to communism – otherwise the whole process may run aground.

It is only on the basis of a strategy for the transition to communism that socialism can be conceived as a transitory and contradictory phase, and that a strategy of struggle can thus be put into effect *right now* which will fall into no illusions about socialism (of the kind: 'last stop: everyone get off!') but will treat socialism as what it really is, without getting bogged down in the first 'transition' which it meets up with.

Now the 22nd Congress replied to this question, it must be said, in the form of a disappointing definition, supported by a kind of super-optimism. Far from putting the emphasis on the decisive *contradiction* characterizing this transition phase called socialism, the Congress presented socialism, which does indeed bring enormous advantages to the workers, as a *general, non-contradictory* and quasi-euphoric solution to every problem. It is clear that instead of thinking in terms of a strategy for *communism, which alone allows us to grasp the contradiction*, to size it up and take bearings, it was concerned with a pseudo-strategy for *socialism*, thus running the risk of conjuring away the contradiction, not only under socialism but in consequence also in the period of the application of the Common Programme, if the Left wins the next general election.

The same goes for the question of the State.

I am not talking about the seizure of State power, which, if the national and international relations of forces permit it, may take a peaceful form. Nor am I talking about the bourgeois State, which will remain in place during the period of application of Common Programme. I am talking about the State of the socialist revolution, supposing that a peaceful transition to this State is possible.

Now here is where the dictatorship of the proletariat makes its *necessary* effects felt, just as it does with respect to the case of socialism.

For this bourgeois State, the instrument of bourgeois class rule, must – as Marx and Lenin constantly repeated – be 'smashed'; moreover, in an even more important argument, they linked this process of 'breaking up' the old State with the later 'withering away' of the new revolutionary State, something which is indispensable if socialism is not to mark time indefinitely but is to arrive at communism. In other words, they understood the 'smashing' of the bourgeois State against the background of the withering away and end of every State.

The Congress obviously could not avoid confronting the argument concerning the 'smashing' of the bourgeois State. Here again, we must pay careful attention to words, because 'smash' is a strong word which, like 'dictatorship, can frighten people if its sense is not properly understood. Now if you want to get an idea of this sense, here is a concrete example. Lenin says: we must 'break up' the bourgeois parliamentary State apparatus. In order to 'break it up' (or 'smash' it) Lenin proposes: (1) to suppress the separation of powers between legislature and executive; (2) to suppress the division of labour on which it rests (in theory and practice), and above all (3) to suppress the bourgeois separation between the masses of the people and the parliamentary apparatus.

This is a very special use of the term 'smash', nothing to do with annihilation, but rather with recasting, restructuring and revolutionizing an existing apparatus in order to ensure the triumph of the domination of a new class, firmly linked with the masses of the people.

In fact – and I should like particular attention to be paid to these words – in order to 'smash' the bourgeois State and to replace it with the State of the working class and its allies *it is not enough simply to add the adjective 'democratic' to each State apparatus*; it is something completely different from this formal and potentially reformist operation, it is to revolutionize in their structure, their practice and their ideology the existing State apparatuses, suppressing some of them, creating new ones, thus to produce a *transformation in the forms of the division of labour* between the repressive, political and ideological apparatuses, to *revolutionize their methods of work* and the *bourgeois ideology* which governs their practical activity, and to *construct new relations between these apparatuses and the masses* on the basis of a new, *proletarian* ideology, in order to prepare the 'withering away of the State', *i.e.*, its replacement by organizations of the masses.

This necessity is related to the Marxist theory of the State. For Marx, the State apparatuses are not neutral instruments but, in a strong sense, the *organic* repressive and ideological apparatuses of a class: the ruling class. In order to guarantee the domination of the working class and its allies, and to prepare for the long-term 'withering away' of the State, *you cannot avoid attacking the class character of the existing State apparatuses.* That means 'smashing' the State. Otherwise the new ruling class will be defeated by its own victory, or be forced to mark time and get bogged down in its own conquests, thus abandoning any serious idea of completing the transition to communism.

If you want examples of States which were not 'smashed', which are not in the process of 'withering away', then you only have to look among the socialist countries, and you will see the consequences. The Soviet leaders declare: here the withering away of the State takes place through its reinforcement!

It is true that this is a difficult, even a very difficult problem, that it merits concrete historical investigation and profound theoretical analysis. But it is a *real* and *unavoidable problem* whose existence is indicated by a *necessary element* of the dictatorship of the proletariat. And it is undeniably one of the positive sides of the 22nd Congress that it forced us to think about this problem.

But it is also a fact that, in abandoning the concept of the dictatorship of the proletariat in a headlong and indiscriminate manner – *i.e.* in abandoning the simple and clear idea that the proletariat and its allies must *smash, i.e. revolutionize* the bourgeois State machine in order to 'make itself the ruling class' (*The Communist Manifesto*), that they must attack the very substance of the bourgeois State which they have inherited – the 22nd Congress unfortunately deprived itself of the possibility of understanding the 'breaking up' and 'withering away' of the State except in the sugar-coated terms of the '*democratization of the State*', *as if the simple legal form of democracy in general could suffice not only to deal with and solve but even simply to pose correctly*

the enormous problems of the State and its apparatuses, which are
class problems and not problems of law.

Sixth initiative

Can we say that this initiative really is to be found in potential
form in the proceedings of the 22nd Congress, or in the fore-
seeable consequences of the logic of the Congress? In any case,
here we are concerned with an historical necessity of importance
to every Communist.

I am talking about the need for the Communists to take contradiction seriously: not only outside the Party but also inside the
Party. I must therefore say a few words about *democratic centralism.*

Georges Marchais has insisted on the will to change *in the
Party*. It is obvious that the new line of the 22nd Congress will
necessarily have repercussions on the internal life of the Party, on
the forms of expression of militants and their freedom of action,
thus on the present conception of democratic centralism.

It is not my job to predict future developments or to anticipate
decisions of the Party, its leadership and its militants. I should
just like to try to set out a few principles of a question which is not
at all simple.

What is the purpose of democratic centralism? It is a response
to the vital political necessity of creating unity of thought and
action in the Party, in order victoriously to counter the bourgeois
class struggle. The working class has at its disposal only its
revolutionary will and organization, sealed in the unity of thought
and action. The purpose of democratic centralism is to create this
theoretical and practical unity. Its mechanism is simple: decisions
are freely discussed and democratically adopted at each level of
the Party (branch, section, district, National Congress). Once
adopted by the Party Congress they become binding on every
militant as far as his political activity is concerned. But as long as
he accepts this discipline, he can keep his own opinion.

In principle, the matter is therefore quite clear, even obvious.
But in practice it is more complicated.

You only have to remember for example that delegates to a
National Congress, the highest organ of the Party, are elected by a
3-stage majority vote (branches → sections, sections → districts,
districts → National Congress), which does not even represent the

most progressive kind of 'formal' democracy, and which automatically eliminates *any difference of opinion* in the plenary ses-
sions of the Congress, regularly leading to unanimous decisions
without any 'real discussion'.

In the television interview in which he brought up the question
of the dictatorship of the proletariat,[6] Georges Marchais insisted
that the 22nd Congress would be 'lively', that a *'tremendous discussion'* would take place there. He was of course talking about the
National Congress itself, because everyone knows that the discussions which take place in the branches, sections and districts
are always lively. Now given the structure of the Party (its
'apparatus', which in fact controls the internal life of the organization), the habits acquired by this apparatus, and also by the
militants, together with this system of election by elimination,
Georges Marchais' wish was destined to remain a forlorn hope.
There was no 'free discussion' at the 22nd Congress, where the
speakers did no more than 'comment on' the draft document, and
the final vote was unanimous.

It is easy to criticize the present forms of democratic centralism
from a legal point of view. You might of course improve them,
from this point of view, which could be an elementary democratic measure.

But personally I should go further. For the question of democratic centralism cannot be reduced to a legal question: it is above
all a theoretical and political question.

We know that in the history of the labour movement the question of the forms of organization and internal representation has
been the subject of many initiatives and controversies. It was
Lenin who introduced the concept of democratic centralism as the
form of organization *par excellence* of the revolutionary (Bolshevik)
party. But already under Lenin the question was posed in terms
of three possibilities: factions, tendencies, and democratic
centralism, without factions or tendencies.

Lenin always opposed *factions*, which he claimed would split
the party up into autonomous organizations and finally destroy it.
But he did for a time support the idea of *tendencies*, even though
these could degenerate into factions: thus he was against factions
but for tendencies, which might provide a better picture of the
diversity of the working class, of its origins, and of the strata

[6] See the Dossier: Georges Marchais, 'Liberty and Socialism'.

making it up – a picture which might moreover help to reinforce the unity between the working class and allied social classes.

Should we accept this formula to be found in Lenin: factions no, tendencies yes? Should we adopt it today? I should personally incline to answer this delicate question in the negative. I think that, theoretically and practically, the establishment of stable tendencies, even in a party which is not bourgeois, but a proletarian, workers' party, tends to reproduce a *typically bourgeois form* of representation of opinions, and thus a bourgeois conception of political practice.

The political practice of a Communist Party is quite different.

In order to provide some idea of what is involved in this difficult question, I should say that such a party does not limit itself to registering and representing opinions, that its relations with the masses are much more profound, that it possesses a scientific theory which guides its conception of any matter and its practical activity. Opinions in the Party are thus subjected to the demands of a scientific theory, which cannot be reduced to a pure democracy of tendencies.

I would say, finally, that what defines the Party is not so much simply the class character of its membership or its scientific theory alone, but the *fusion* of these two things in the class struggle against the bourgeoisie in which it is engaged. Opinions in the Party are thus subjected to the conflicts of the class struggle, which impose demands that cannot be reduced to a pure democracy of tendencies.

Of course, in a living party there are always contradictions and thus, if you like, different points of view and tendencies expressing them. There can be no question of denying this reality, this aspect of the real life of the Party. But the *legal recognition and institutionalization of tendencies* does not seem to me to be the best way of resolving these contradictions or of making the best of this situation in a revolutionary workers' party.

That is why the slogan of the recognition of tendencies does not seem to me to be correct in principle, and in any case it would certainly be wrong in the present conditions, because it does not correspond to the new political practice of the vanguard party of the working class. This slogan actually only *reproduces in the Party one of the forms of bourgeois political practice*. It is no accident if the right to tendencies is so profoundly linked to the history of Social-Democracy.

But we must be careful! If we reject the recognition of tendencies in the Party, it is not so as to fall back into a *more primitive* form of political practice, to *restrict liberty*, or totally to destroy it, as Stalin did: it is in order to *move forward, towards more liberty*, in order to respond to the demands of the political practice of the vanguard of the working class and to the appeal of the 22nd Congress.

To turn to the question of present developments in the Party, it is clear that, following the Congress, new tasks are emerging: the task for example of creating new forms of unity, of communication, of the exchange of experiences, of discussion and debate. As soon as the Party opens itself up more widely to the outside world and introduces new forms of discussion, communication and unity with non-Communists, this same task will be posed more forcefully *inside the Party*. More information, a better press, greater freedom of expression, more discussions, more debates – in short, a more lively, freer and more daring party, released from the clumsy controls which have served their time.

In this framework, it is a political necessity to open a discussion on the present forms of democratic centralism in the Party, whose object would be to study and define the *new practical forms* which, while avoiding any risk of the development of factions and organized tendencies, would make possible a genuine discussion in the Party, wider and freer than has hitherto been the case, safe from arbitrary censorship, within the framework of the class struggle and Marxist theory.

If the Party poses and confronts this problem in Marxist terms, in the spirit of the 22nd Congress, it will make its contribution to the necessary changes, imposed by the present state of the class struggle, which must take place within the Party itself.

And it will become the Party of the 22nd Congress.

Postscript to the English Edition

by Etienne Balibar

This English edition of my book differs from the original French edition, published in July 1976, although my essay on *The Dictatorship of the Proletariat* remains the largest part.[1] We have however decided to add several new elements to the present edition, both in order to make access to the book easier for the English reader, who will probably not have directly followed the debates on the French Left, and also because the book will thus appear more clearly for what it is: a particular moment, necessarily incomplete and provisional, in a wider discussion which is itself only just getting under way.

I want first to thank Grahame Lock for having agreed to present the text to the English reader in introductory notes, which in themselves constitute a contribution to the discussion. It goes without saying that while writing my own essay I had in mind above all the discussion opened up in France, which is taking place within the Communist Party and around it, in the whole of

---

[1] In the French edition my text was followed by two dossiers. The first (extracts from the proceedings of the 22nd Congress of the French Communist Party), is reproduced here. The second is omitted for reasons of space. It contained a number of classic texts of Marx and Lenin, which set out the foundations of their theory of the State and of the dictatorship of the proletariat, as I have tried to reconstitute it and explain it here. I think it would be useful for the reader to refer to them on this occasion.

These texts, which can be easily found in English, are the following: Lenin, 'The State' (a lecture delivered at Sverdlov University, *Collected Works*, XXIX); Marx, 'The Proletariat as a Class' (from *The Communist Manifesto*, 1848, ch. I); Marx, 'Bourgeois and Proletarian Socialism' (from *The Class Struggles in France*, 1850, ch. III); Lenin, 'The Touchstone of Marxism' (from *The State and Revolution*, 1917, ch. II, *Collected Works*, XXV); Lenin, 'A Contribution to the History of Dictatorship' (1920; *Collected Works*, XXXI); Lenin, 'The Economic Basis of the Withering Away of the State' (from *The State and Revolution*, ch. V); Lenin, 'Communist Labour' (from *A Great Beginning; Collected Works*, XXIV).

the French Left, among workers and progressive intellectuals. However, this discussion, as well as the spectacular 'shift in position' carried out by the 22nd Congress of the French Communist Party, can be seen to be aspects (with their own particular characteristics) of a much wider process, which also concerns other, neighbouring countries, and which does not only concern Communist Parties. And above all, as Grahame Lock explains, and as the reader will I think himself conclude from the texts contained here, the *theoretical* problems raised in this book bring into question by degrees the whole previous history of the international labour movement, the way in which this history is still a factor contributing to the present orientations and contradictions of this movement, and the way in which it is exercizing its influence on the interpretation and use of Marxist and Leninist principles. That is why, taking account of course of the considerable differences between the political situations of the different countries (France, Great Britain, Italy, Spain . . . but also – why not? – the USA, and even the Soviet Union and other socialist countries), and taking account in addition of the different, independent organizational forms which the working class of each country has constructed, I can only agree with Grahame Lock that this discussion does not concern one country and one party alone. Moreover, it cannot be confined to exchanges of views or polemics between the leaderships of Communist and Socialist Parties, in which their official positions of the moment are expressed. It must, if it is to bear fruit, remove all the obstacles to its own development, and lead to that renovation of Marxism of which we are in such dire need; it must involve the 'rank and file' of these parties, their militants, their 'friends' in the masses, whose number will itself be increased by the very openness of the discussion, and finally all socialists.[2]

[2] Here I should like to introduce a very general hypothesis. This renovation of Marxism will certainly owe a lot to the discussions and theoretical work now taking place among Communists in the countries of 'Latin' Europe, where they have conquered an important political position, and also to the debates inspired in recent years by the anti-imperialist revolutions of the 'Third World'. More than once we have also insisted on the need for a Marxist analysis of the history of the socialist countries, of the nature of the social relations which have developed there following the revolution, and of the tendencies now exhibited there by the class struggle. But it is *no less crucial* to combine these analyses with the study of the evolution of those capitalist countries – especially the Anglo-Saxon countries – where Marxism *has not been able* historically to become the organic ideology of the labour movement (in

If the perspectives in which this book is situated, whether by design or by accident, really are so broad, it is easy to understand that we are anxious carefully to underline the circumstances in which it was written and *its limits*. It only constitutes a part of the dossier of the discussion now under way.

The draft document presented for discussion at the 22nd Congress of the French Communist Party – which contains no reference to the dictatorship of the proletariat, one way or the other – was adopted unanimously by the Congress, without any modifications.[3]

I am of course not the only one to have intervened in the pre-Congress discussion in favour of the dictatorship of the proletariat. Other contributors, either for similar reasons, or for other, more or less different reasons, also took this line in the discussion published in *L'Humanité* and *France Nouvelle*, not to speak of the verbal interventions made by comrades at various stages of the debate 'among the rank and file'. But I have not reproduced these contributions here, simply because I had and I have no right to 'enrol' these comrades in the service of the position which I am defending, and because it is not my task to make an inventory of the discussions around the Congress.

The reader will probably have got the impression that these discussions concerned only the dictatorship of the proletariat. This however was not the case, for the good reason that this question was not originally a factor in the debate; but it is true, as I have explained briefly in the introductory remarks to my essay, that as soon as it *was* introduced it became the centre of attention.

---

spite of the age of this movement and of the tradition and force of its struggles). Why this 'failure' of the historical fusion of the labour movement with revolutionary theory? What are its causes in the economic and social structure, in the historical form taken by the State apparatus and in particular by the framework of ideological State apparatuses? If this enormously 'uneven' development of revolutionary practice is an integral part of the vista of Marxism-Leninism of which we are the heirs, and if it has to be admitted that the theoretical solution of this problem is an integral aspect of the enrichments and discoveries which are needed in other countries too, then there is in my opinion no doubt that this solution must come *above all* from the original analyses of Marxists in England, America, etc., and must include their critical *point of view* on the forms taken up to now by Marxism and Leninism. I should like in this connexion to mention the very interesting recent work of Michel Aglietta, *Régulation et crises du capitalisme: l'expérience des Etats Unis,* Paris, Calmann Levy, 1976.

[3] This document was entitled 'Ce que veulent les communistes pour la France' (see above footnote 2 to Althusser's text).

It must be said that in the existing conditions, with the Party being theoretically unprepared, this preoccupation at the same time distracted attention from the *concrete analysis* of the French political situation and of its present difficulties.[4] That is one – and not the least – of the paradoxes of the 22nd Congress, because the principle of the dictatorship of the proletariat, however general and 'abstract' it may at first sight appear, is in fact closely linked to the *practical* questions of the class struggle and of the movement of the people. However, it must be admitted that this link is not immediately obvious to many comrades, who either view it as a 'question of principle', in the bad sense of the term, or as a simple question of words, of propaganda and tactics. This situation is certainly not restricted to France, and it must be seen as one of the consequences of the Stalin deviation inside the Communist Parties. Not only did it distort the concept of the dictatorship of the proletariat, not only did it embody this distortion in a practice which is disfiguring and undermining the revolutionary objectives of the proletariat (in the USSR and in other socialist countries), but it also progressively imprisoned this concept in a theoretical ghetto, cutting its links with theory and practice.

At the 21st Congress of the French Communist Party (October 1974), following the adoption of the Common Programme of government by the Left Parties (Communist Party, Socialist Party, Left Radicals) and following the 49% vote obtained by their joint candidate, François Mitterand, in the Presidential Election, a discussion opened up on the question of the best way to develop this movement of the people. In what sense was it provoked by the present economic crisis of capitalism? What obstacles, external and internal, were still hindering the transformation of this massive (yet multiform and even internally contradictory) social discontent into a vigorous, conscious and

[4] It is only fair to point out that another debate, just as unexpected, enlivened the preparation for the 22nd Congress: a debate on *morality*. Some comrades attacked what they considered to be the immorality of decadent bourgois society, others made a positive evaluation of the growing revolts against bourgeois moralism. Here too the impression may arise of a departure or even of a diversion with regard to the major political objectives of the Congress. And yet, *at root*, these problems were essential, for they touch on the family, education, and the role of 'class morality' in the functioning of the Party. . . . This double deflection towards an apparently 'too abstract' question on the one hand and towards a 'too specific' question on the other, very well illustrates the difficulty of grasping the object of concrete analysis and of granting it the proper recognition.

unified political movement? At this moment the question at issue
was *both* how to strengthen mass activity in order to improve the
recruitment, influence and organizational capacity of the revolutionary party, *and* how to reinforce its proletarian character. In
other words, many Communists saw that a change in the Party's
style of work was necessary if the working class itself was to be
able to play its full political role. They also realized that this was
the key to any sustained attack on bourgeois rule: the economic
crisis alone is not enough, nor is the union of the parties of the
Left, even if it is obviously indispensable. However, because of
the real difficulty of the problem and because of the heritage of the
Cold War period and of Stalinism, it proved extremely difficult
(as clearly shown by the sudden 'switches' which took place during
and immediately after the 21st Congress) for Communists to get
a clear understanding of these apparently unavoidable dilemmas:
'Mass party' or 'vanguard party'? 'Union of the Left' at the top,
between parties (with all the day-to-day compromises which it
involves) or 'Popular Union' at the base, extending beyond the
simple parliamentary and electoral framework? And how should
this Popular Union be conceived and realized: as the unity of the
(varyingly) exploited workers, of the producers, alone? Or as a
unity with fractions of the bourgeoisie itself, with an eye to more
or less long-term objectives? These are questions which, in the
opinion of many comrades, were calling urgently for a new effort
of discussion, with all the cards on the table, without dodging any
contradictions. For if, from this period onwards, the Party's political work has indeed been 'walking on two legs' – one being the
political alliance constituted by the Common Programme, the other
the effort of the Party to develop the movement of the people by
taking the lead in all its struggles – we nevertheless have to recognize that these two legs are having a lot of trouble keeping in pace:
one (the movement of the people) is lagging behind the other (the
alliance between parties), when it is not simply sacrificed to this
alliance. For the Party has not been able to find the way to develop
a *proletarian practice* of politics, it has not been able to detach itself
sufficiently clearly from the *bourgeois practice of politics*, in which,
paradoxically but inevitably, the Stalin deviation had helped to
tangle it up. And yet – as Georges Marchais himself indicated
when signing the agreement – without the movement of the people
and the Popular Union, without the fusion of the Communist

Party with this movement of the people, the Common Programme has no chance of success, and certainly no chance of producing the effects which the workers expect of it!

By suddenly exhuming the concept of the dictatorship of the proletariat, even if it was for the paradoxical reason of immediately consigning it to the archives of the labour movement, or even to its museum of errors, the 22nd Congress did in a sense give these problems *their real name*, for they are in fact problems of the class power of the working people, of the means to the establishment of this class power, and of the historical tendency in which it is situated. But this name remains for the moment much too abstract and too full of ambiguities.

However, this is perhaps not wholly true, and the proof would lie in the fact that the discussion, far from being closed by the Congress, actually really began from that moment – one of the signs, among others, that something is changing, profoundly, under the surface, in the political conditions reflected by the evolution of the Party. A contradictory evolution, of course, whose dominant aspect is for the moment not one which might tend to liberate the thought and practice of Communists from every form of dogmatism, sectarianism, or their apparent opposites, utopianism and what Althusser has called a certain form of 'democratic adventurism'.[5]

As I have already pointed out, and as Althusser explains more clearly in the speech reproduced above,[6] it would nevertheless be quite wrong to imagine that this temporarily dominant aspect is the only one, the one playing the *motive* role in the transformations now under way, when on the contrary it actually constitutes, in various forms, the expression of the *obstacles* standing in the way of these transformations. Indeed, to imagine such a thing would precisely be to adopt the *point of view of the bourgeoisie* on the labour movement and on the evolution of its organizations, the

[5] In the course of a public debate with Lucien Sève (as reported in the Press), organized in April 1976 at the 'Marxist Book Week' by the Communist Party publishing house.

[6] We should like to thank Althusser for having allowed us to reproduce in this English edition the text of the speech which he gave in December 1976 at the Sorbonne. It will allow the British reader to gain a better idea of the problems raised by the 22nd Congress and of the way in which the discussion is continuing. Each of us of course bears the responsibility for his own contribution, though we should stress the general orientation which is common to all of us.

point of view of a class which is throwing everything into the struggle to transform its desires into realities (and may even succeed in doing so in certain circumstances, for a certain period).

The reader of the above texts may have gained the impression that there exists a certain distance between on the one hand Grahame Lock's introduction and my own essay, and on the other hand Althusser's piece. A difference in 'tone', due to the different circumstances in which these texts were produced; and perhaps a visible contradiction on certain points. This should surprise only those who mistake a discussion which is just beginning for a completed enquiry, who mistake a collective effort of reflection for the manifesto of a 'school of thought', or even of a group pursuing a plan established in advance. Everyone, I think, will realize that this is not how matters stand.

Althusser's (publicly delivered) speech helps to clarify, even if in very general terms, the tendency underlying the 22nd Congress, a tendency which allows us to explain the surprises which the Congress held in store, the uncertainties which it sometimes hid beneath correspondingly more strongly affirmed 'certainties', and its paradoxical effects. These effects are expressed in the profound doubts troubling the militants of the Party. Sometimes they result in a paralysis of their activity at the very moment when the development of the economic crisis, together with the perspectives of an electoral victory of the Left, are daily bringing it new members, new forces. That is why Althusser's account, taking into consideration the concerns which the Congress itself effectively posed in all their urgency (like 'democratic centralism'), is centred on the *contradictions of the 22nd Congress*. The position which the Congress adopted on the dictatorship of the proletariat is *one of the terms* of the contradiction, one of the poles around which this contradiction is developing. The ('overdetermined', therefore complex) contradiction of the 22nd Congress cannot be reduced to this term alone. But it is true, for the reasons which I briefly indicated a moment ago, that you only have to analyze the conditions in which the dictatorship of the proletariat re-entered the French political scene and to relate these reasons to the theoretical implications of the Marxist and Leninist concept of the dictatorship of the proletariat, in order to see that the contradictions of the 22nd Congress find their reflection there in an especially pronounced form.

My own contribution to the discussion is directed essentially to the *theoretical concept* of the dictatorship of the proletariat, which I tried as far as possible to restore to its true definition in order to provide that indispensable reference point which the discussion was lacking. I did not sever this concept from the historical conditions under which it was constituted (Marx, Lenin) and of its deformation (Stalin), but I was forced to limit this analysis. Others, I hope, will take it further.[7]

On this point, as the reader will have noticed, there is no contradiction between our analyses. We all agree that the concept of the dictatorship of the proletariat really is a fundamental concept of historical materialism and constitutes an essential part of its analysis of capitalist society. It is an essential part of the analysis of the mode of exploitation on which this society is based (exploitation of wage labour), together with the tendential constitution of the *two classes* and *two alone* (to the cost of all others), *i.e.* proletariat and bourgeoisie, resulting from this mode of exploitation.[8]

It is an essential part of the Marxist analysis of *the State* as a class State, whose 'general social functions' are precisely nothing other than the whole of the mechanisms of reproduction of capitalist exploitation. That is why *the broadening of the analysis of the State* (which must not be confused with the so-called 'broadening of the concept of the State'), whose foundations were laid by Gramsci in particular, following Lenin himself, *actually only reinforces* the need for the dictatorship of the proletariat: for it means that the dictatorship of the bourgeoisie *cannot be reduced* to the repressive 'armour' of the army, police, and law courts, even when supplemented by propaganda, but *extends* to the whole set of ideological State apparatuses which, at the price of a permanent

---

[7] In the same spirit, I take the liberty of referring the reader to some complementary texts:
— L. Althusser, *Essays in Self-Criticism*, with an Introduction by Grahame Lock (NLB, 1976);
— D. Lecourt, *The Case of Lysenko*, with an Introduction by Louis Althusser (NLB, 1977).

[8] Which does not of course mean either that this process of constitution follows a linear course, nor that the classes always have an identical social position, nor again that the complexity of capitalist social formations can be *reduced* to the juxtaposition of the two classes whose antagonism determines their evolution. *Cf.* also 'Plus-value et classes sociales', in my *Cinq Etudes du matérialisme historique* (Maspero, Paris, 1974).

class struggle, ensures the material domination of the dominant ideology.[9] The concept of the dictatorship of the proletariat is an essential part of the argument that there can be no socialism and no destruction of the very foundations of exploitation in all its forms without the overthrow, in one way or another, of the State power of the bourgeoisie and the installation of the State power of the working people. This is something quite different from 'giving their fair place' to the workers *within* the existing State. And it is something quite different from 'strengthening the State of the whole people' on the backs of the workers.

Finally, this concept is an essential part of the argument that there can be no definitive liquidation of capitalism without the effective, constantly fortified and developed combination of (i) *the mass democracy of the working people* (something incompatible with the whole State apparatus of capitalism) with (ii) *revolutionary transformations in the mode of production* (therefore in property, but also beyond it, in the antagonistic forms of the social division of labour, in the industrial structure of production, in the forced consumption which it entails, whose recognition is itself forcibly imposed in the form of more or less unsatisfied 'needs', in the manner of the development of the productive forces themselves). In short, there can be no liquidation of capitalism without a progression towards *communism*, which is the organic unity of these two aspects, whatever the length and difficulty of this process of progression, which no-one today imagines to be the affair of a single day.

On this basis we are all in agreement that to talk about 'transcending' the dictatorship of the proletariat – as do certain comrades, pretending to understand by this term 'dictatorship' a simple localized and dated 'tactic' of the revolutionary movement – is in effect to suggest that this whole body of basic concepts and theoretical arguments, *i.e.* Marxism itself, must be 'transcended'

[9] It is often suggested that Gramsci, in talking about *hegemony* and not simply about *dictatorship*, thereby *attenuates* the Leninist conception of the power of the bourgeoisie by adding 'consent' to 'coercion' or violence. But Gramsci, on the basis of the dramatic experience of fascism, actually *strengthens* this conception. He says: class power is much more absolute than you think, because it is *not only* direct 'coercion', it is not only the surface 'armour'; it is also 'consent', *i.e.* the materially dominant ideology and the organization of the 'general functions' of society by the ruling class. The proletariat must therefore substitute its dictatorship and hegemony for those of the bourgeoisie *on this terrain too*. The whole question is to know how: and here the means and forms of bourgeois hegemony will not help . . .

... Of course, Marx's *Capital* is not Moses' Law, whose rejection would be blasphemy! But before proceeding to such a 'transcendence', *i.e.* in the event to a *replacement* of the Marxist theory of the class struggle, the labour movement would do well to make sure that it possesses *another* theoretical basis compatible with its political autonomy and its revolutionary perspectives ... Another class basis, of course.

That is, why, beyond all questions of *words* (which may have their importance, but which are not decisive in theoretical matters), we have rejected the idea of the 'transcendence' of the dictatorship of the proletariat put forward by certain French and other Communists, considering this idea worse than equivocal. Not only did this formulation in practice appear as a compromise formula designed to 'persuade' comrades who might otherwise have jibbed at this change in the terminology and theory of the revolutionary party by dressing it up in a 'dialectical' justification (and such justifications can unfortunately serve any purpose); even more important, far from setting in motion the indispensable process of developing and *rectifying* existing theoretical conceptions inside the International Communist Movement, far from setting in motion the indispensable process of the renewal of Marxism demanded by the new conditions of the struggle for socialism today, such a formulation can only hinder it. In particular, instead of contributing to clarifying the contradictions of the 22nd Congress and the practice underlying them, and therefore to resolving them, it can only help to mask and aggravate them.

This having been established, it remains true that the question at hand does not concern only the theoretical concept of the dictatorship of the proletariat – far from it – but also, as several participants in the discussion underlined, *the relation* between this concept and *what is customarily called the 'strategy'* of revolutionary struggles in a given historical period. A problem like that of 'class alliances', for instance, seems to be directly involved by this question. And on this point, the formulations proposed by Althusser's text would appear to contradict what I myself have argued and what Grahame Lock for his part is arguing. I do not want to evade this point.

Let us be very scrupulous. Which are the formulations of Althusser which might cause difficulty when compared with certain analyses in this book? Essentially two. Althusser writes: 'this last argument – the proletariat as the heart of a broad alliance – is in the tradition of Marx and Lenin. The 22nd Congress takes it up in the form of the idea of the "leading role of the working class" at the heart of the broad union of the people. There are no serious problems on this point.' And further on, distinguishing between the relatively 'contingent' elements and the 'necessary' elements in the dictatorship of the proletariat, he classifies the problems of peaceful transition and of class alliances among the contingent elements, and writes: 'As far as these two questions are concerned [. . .] the 22nd Congress did [. . .] *correct certain errors* to which some comrades might have fallen victim with regard to the seizure of power and to socialism, errors induced by the Stalin deviation. But precisely on these two questions, the 22nd Congress added nothing new: it only repeated arguments about things which Marx and Lenin themselves had claimed to be *possible* (peaceful transition) or politically *desirable* (broadest possible alliance around the working class).'

We must try to understand what this distinction implies. Certain communists, arguing for the 'transcendence' of the dictatorship of the proletariat, make use of an analogous distinction in the following way: on the one side they argue for a 'necessary' general definition of socialism (socialization of the means of production and political power of the working people), while on the other side they classify the dictatorship of the proletariat itself among the 'contingent' aspects linked to particular historical conditions which have now been superseded.[10] One might say: the way of posing the problem is at root the same in both cases, and the differences are only verbal, concerning the question of what is new and what is not . . . Is this not a little scholastic? I do not think so, and I believe that this becomes clear as soon as you have understood the immediate link between the dictatorship of the proletariat and the Marxist conception of the State and of the struggle for communism.

What has to be demonstrated is that the problem of the proletarian revolution is not *first of all* a problem of 'strategy'. The

---

[10] *Cf.* for example Lucien Sève's study 'Le XXIIe Congrès, développement léniniste de la stratégie de révolution pacifique', in *Cahiers du communisme,* June 1976: an English translation was published by *Marxism Today* in May 1977.

revolution does indeed need a strategy for the seizure and exercise
of power, a strategy adapted to the historical conditions of the
moment, therefore founded on a concrete analysis of these conditions and of their transformation. That is undeniable. But such
an analysis can precisely only be made if it takes into account *the
historical tendencies* of the development of capitalist relations of
production, of the State dictatorship of the bourgeoisie, and the
specific forms of the historical *counter-tendency*, the tendency
to the dictatorship of the proletariat, in each new period. Every
true revolutionary 'strategy' therefore implies a *theory* of these
tendencies, and the development of this theory. This for example
is what Lenin provides when he develops the theory of imperialism, thus rectifying certain points in Marx's theory, certain
aspects of Marx's own idea of the development of the 'tendencies'
of capitalist society. On this basis, the characteristics of imperialism (those which Lenin was able to recognize at the beginning of
the imperialist epoch) are incorporated into the analysis of
capitalism, becoming the basis of a concrete analysis of the forms
of the dictatorship of the bourgeoisie, therefore of the conditions
and of the forms of the proletarian revolution.[11] The construction
of a strategy cannot be 'logically deduced' from a general historical
tendency, as if this tendency had to follow an immutable and
linear course, a predictable line of progression. Nor can it represent
an empirical adaptation to (apparent) 'differences' between one
country and another, between one epoch and another: on the
contrary, all such differences and changes must be analyzed as
(new, unforeseen but necessary) *forms of the historical tendency* if
their real importance is to be understood. Worst of all is the
temptation which often arises to *justify after the event* a strategic
change by *constructing the theory* from which it might have been
deduced (for example, in many of its aspects the 'theory of State
Monopoly Capitalism' is quite simply the transposition into
abstract economic terms of the conditions which one would have
to imagine fulfilled in order to 'justify' a strategy of peaceful

[11] We could go even further and suggest that they might become the basis of an
analysis of the *deviations* of the revolution and of the dictatorship of the proletariat.
If, as I have suggested, socialism and capitalism do not constitute two closed and
isolated 'worlds', but two aspects of a single system of contradictions, then the
internal obstacles to socialism, the deviant and regressive tendencies within it, are
not to be explained simply by reference to 'capitalist relations' in general but
necessarily to their present *imperialist form*.

transition to socialism, in order to 'justify' a strategic alliance between the working class, the petty bourgeoisie, the non-monopoly bourgeoisie, etc . . .).

It is quite easy to understand that the Stalinian degeneration of Marxism, which reduced the analysis of capitalism to a mechanistic prophecy of its 'final crisis', reducing the political conception of socialism to a form of technocratism armed with instruments of repression and propaganda, provoked revolutionaries and Communists to look for 'strategic alternatives', to try and find in Gramsci or beyond him political alternatives to the Stalinian form of 'Leninism', to replace the ideology of the 'frontal attack' on the bourgeoisie by that of the 'war of positions'. However, as long as you remain content to *juxtapose* one strategy to another, one 'model of socialism' to another, opposing them term for term, epoch for epoch, *without bothering* to construct the necessary theory and to make the necessary concrete analysis, every strategy must remain profoundly stamped with *utopianism*. Paradoxically at first sight, the reference to the concepts of the dictatorship of the proletariat and of communism, therefore to difficult objectives and to a very long-term tendency, has a profoundly *anti-utopian* significance, provided of course that this reference is made within the framework of an effective concrete analysis and theoretical development. If this reference is lacking, the revolutionary strategy becomes once again a form of the *construction of models*. *Models of the seizure of power*: first of all alliances, then victorious elections, then reforms in the economic and social structures, etc. . . . , with in passing the 'neutralization' of the class enemy and of foreign imperialism, etc. . . . *Economic models*: more or less extensive nationalizations, more or less rigorous planning, more or less autonomous management of enterprises, industrial priorities, improvement of the conditions of life of the working people, etc. *Models of the State*: the 'formal', purely legal type of democracy, limited by economic pressure groups, is contrasted with the 'real' democracy of the working people, each type of democracy having its own institutions; centralization is replaced with decentralization; the separation between the élites in power and the passive mass of the population is replaced by the active participation of the masses, etc. . . . *This is where utopianism and reformism meet*: both think in terms of models of the State whose merits and possibilities of implementation have to be weighed up

... Marxism, on the other hand, by placing the dictatorship of the proletariat and communism at the centre of its theoretical apparatus, destroys every idea of a model, therefore every form of strategic empiricism. On the one hand it forbids us to confuse the announcement of a political or economic programme with the prediction of events to come (as if these events had to follow a plan), for every programme is transformed and finally destroyed by the national and international class struggle in which it is situated. On the other hand it shows that the only strategy which can, at least in part, succeed is a strategy which right from the beginning takes account of the final objective: not the construction of a new model of the State, however different from the existing State, but the abolition of classes and of every State. That is also why only such a strategy allows us to understand and genuinely to rectify the previous deviations of revolutionary practice (and let us add: also future deviations) instead of simply holding them 'at a distance' and *relativizing* them in space and time as 'out-of-date strategies'.

Let us now return to the question of class alliances. As a real problem, requiring a concrete analysis, it is entirely open, and there can be no question of solving it in two words. In fact, this problem is posed in specific terms *in each epoch and in each social formation* in the history of capitalism. That is why there can also be no question of identifying the dictatorship of the proletariat in general with *such-and-such* a form of class alliance, for example with that form of alliance which made possible the Revolution of October 1917 and the installation of the dictatorship of the proletariat in Russia, and whose progressive break-up explains, at least in part, the subsequent aggravation of the class struggle and its Stalinian deviation. What we must say is, on the contrary, that in the writings of Marx and Lenin themselves the problem of the dictatorship of the proletariat is *never separated* from the problem of class alliances, for the concrete *conditions* of the realization of the one are also the conditions of the realization of the other. Thus, to borrow Althusser's provisional terminology, what seems at first to be linked in a purely 'contingent' manner to the *concept* of the dictatorship of the proletariat is shown in practice to be indissociably linked to it, in constantly new forms, which are but the 'realization' of this concept itself. Now this realization of the concept itself is in no way 'contingent': it is on the contrary just as necessary as the historical tendency of the class struggle.

Let us make this point in another way. It is perfectly absurd to *oppose* the dictatorship of the proletariat to the idea of class alliances, to reject the dictatorship of the proletariat on the grounds of the limits and failures of the class alliance of the Russian revolution. But it is indispensable to work out the *new forms* of the dictatorship of the proletariat which go together with the *new forms* of class alliance that have become possible and necessary in a capitalist country like France today (and in Britain too, I suppose). In this respect, Leninist practice can do no more than indicate the existence of an open problem. For not only is the concrete configuration of classes no longer the same, but you could even ask whether the term 'class alliance' has exactly the same sense now.

From a Marxist point of view, as we have already pointed out, the capitalist mode of production reproduces tendentially only *two classes*, bourgeoisie and proletariat. In the Russian social formation of the beginning of the century, the capitalist mode of production was *already* absolutely dominant, which means that the question of revolution was *already* posed as bourgeois dictatorship *or* proletarian dictatorship, bourgeois democracy *or* proletarian democracy. However, capitalist development was very far from having suppressed every trace of other modes of production, even though it was transforming them profoundly from the inside. This is what made the 'alliance of the working class and peasantry' the fundamental problem. The peasantry, internally affected by capitalist antagonisms, tendentially divided between distinct fractions, some of which were in course of proletarianization, the others developing into an agrarian capitalist class, nevertheless formed *a class* with its own specific historical interests, its own ideology and its own political forces, whose *autonomous position* became the principal stake of the class struggle at certain moments. The same is not true of a social formation like France today, in which the capitalist mode of production is not only dominant, but *the only* true mode of production. It would be absolutely wrong, however, to represent the social structure of such a country as a simpler, more 'homogeneous' structure. In spite of Marx's formula, which refers in the *Communist Manifesto* to the 'simplification of class antagonisms' resulting from capitalism, we have to admit that the history of social formations like capitalist France today is not producing a *less complex* class structure; it is simply a question of *another type* of complexity. The question of 'class alliances', as it is now once again posed, is precisely the political index of this new type of complexity.

I will give just two proofs of this argument, which would have to be backed up by a lengthy analysis.

In present-day capitalist France, *agricultural production* is now entirely under the domination of the capitalist mode of production, even with respect to what are called 'family farms', being entirely integrated into the whole process of capitalist production and circulation of commodities, 'squeezed' between the market in industrial products which the trusts are now imposing at monopoly prices, and the market in agricultural products controlled by the State within the framework of international competition. Even leaving aside the absolute drop in the active population in the countryside, this form of capitalist agricultural production cannot any more provide the basis of an independent social class. However, contrary to the imagination of the 'Marxist' evolutionism of the Second International (Kautsky), which has remained profoundly influential for a very long time, such a development in no way leads to the absorption of the peasantry within a single proletarian class, to its pure and simple fusion with the working class. What hinders this process is first of all the functional, decisive role which, in the case of France, the peasantry has played[12] in the reproduction of the State dictatorship of the French bourgeoisie. The existence and the policies of the bourgeois State, in France, are perpetuating the division between the working class and peasantry, *in opposition to* all tendencies to the proletarianization of agricultural labour. But that is not all: even if one could forget about this factor, it would nevertheless not be possible to place the process of proletarianization of agricultural labour *on the same basis* as that of the working class. This is because of the material (even 'natural') constraints of the agricultural labour process, which affect both the process of its operations (the cultivation of crops, the breeding of animals) and the reproduction of labour power (its 'qualification', its maintenance). The

---

[12] And is still playing – witness the way in which, in May 1968, the Pompidou government made use of it in order to split the front of its enemies.

complete 'industrialization' of agriculture, in this respect, is a myth. And the merging of agricultural and industrial labour power on a single labour market, in present conditions, is an impossibility. Thus, from the point of view of the socialist revolution, even if the problem of the 'alliance of the working class and peasantry' does not have the same importance nor the same content as in Lenin's time, it nevertheless remains a decisive problem whose exploration is vital.

The problem is posed in an even more decisive manner with regard to what is normally called the 'petty bourgeoisie', as when an 'old' petty bourgeoisie (artisans, small shopkeepers, small business men, liberal professions) is sometimes distinguished from a 'new' petty bourgeoisie (managers, technicians of the State apparatus and of private enterprise). Without attempting to justify my argument in detail, I will point out here what seems to me to be the more correct starting point: that *the 'petty bourgeoisie' does not exist as a class*. What is normally referred to under this umbrella term is precisely the complexity of social stratifications created by the development of capitalism. The fact is that the tendency to proletarianization develops in an *uneven* manner: with historical 'delays' which, sometimes for very long periods, prevent entire masses of wage-earners from being subjected to the same conditions of life, of work and of 'negotiation' of their labour power which the most exploited workers and employees experience. Delays which are followed by brutal leaps forward in the process of proletarianization, when for example entire sectors of office or laboratory workers, etc., are hit by mechanization and the extension of the division of labour. What is therefore being referred to by this inadequate concept is *the internal contradictions* of the process of proletarianization, which is not a process of the slow growth of a uniform mass of interchangeable workers, but a process which ceaselessly *recreates* groups which are unequal, and whose immediate interests are more or less deeply divided. I will go even further: what is normally called by the name 'petty bourgeoisie' is in fact *the internal division of the proletariat* and the *internal division of the bourgeoisie*, whose effects extend to *the whole* of these two classes, leading to the fact that they never constitute two absolutely distinct sociological groups, without any overlap or interactions, and that they *seem* to give birth to an intermediate 'third class'. I say 'seem', not in order to deny that different social groups occupy, from the economic and political points of view, an unstable position in the *no man's land* of class antagonism, more or less comfortably suspended 'between' proletarianization and capitalist bourgeoisification. I say it in order to deny that here we are talking about an independent class: in fact, its exact limits are indeterminate, and its specific interests non-existent, for they only represent a combination, changing with the conjuncture, of the contradictory interests *already* present in each class.

But the object of revolutionary politics is precisely *the present moment* of a given historical conjuncture. Thus, the denial of the existence of an independent petty-bourgeois class in no way implies the denial of the existence of a specific problem of 'class alliances', on the grounds that, in the very end, all these secondary stratifications and contradictions must disappear. For this very end will never arrive, and has no historical reality. What is however true is that to pose the problem in these theoretical terms necessarily has political consequences.

Schematically, to admit the existence of an intermediate *class* (of a more or less extensive kind: sometimes the whole of the 'non-monopolist bourgeoisie' is included here) is to open the way to a conception of class alliances in terms of *compromises*, or even in terms of an 'historic' *contract, i.e.* finally, in *legal* terms. The problem, in this perspective, becomes a problem of knowing what concessions the proletariat and the 'petty bourgeoisie' will each have to make to the other, what particular interests they will have to sacrifice in order to reach an agreement, and how this agreement will be 'guaranteed'. Thus the problem would be to determine whether this agreement is to be made between 'equal' partners (equal in rights and duties) or between 'unequal' partners (and therefore whether such an agreement is viable).[13]

---

[13] In the version which is dominant in France, that of the theory of State Monopoly Capitalism, the problem is resolved in the following way: tendentially, the partners are *already* allied on the economic level, and on an equal basis, for all are equally exploited by big monopoly capital. Their interests, in the face of the monopolists, are *spontaneously converging*. It remains therefore to 'translate' this convergence onto the *political* level: it becomes precisely a question of a contract between political parties, democratically sealed and guaranteed by its democratic character. But something thereby becomes quite unintelligible, something which Communists, in the light of their experience, ought not to be prepared to ignore: 'the leading role of the working class', which, as they very well know, is the decisive force in revolutionary struggles. We might even say that it is this contradiction

To reject the myth of the petty bourgeoisie as a third, independent class is therefore to reject the legal form which this argument about class alliances implicitly or explicitly takes. It is to propose another formulation, which may appear surprising if you extract it from its concrete historical context: that the class alliances which the proletariat needs are class alliances *with fractions of the bourgeoisie itself*, fractions which would turn against their class. It is therefore to imply that these alliances are in no way spontaneous, that they in no way result from a simple 'convergence' of interests, for they can only arise *from the destruction of the system of class alliances of the bourgeoisie*, which extends to within the proletariat itself, providing the bourgeoisie with its mass base through economic and political constraint, through the exploitation of divergent corporate interests, and through ideological domination. It is therefore to imply that the fundamental condition of this process, and in part also its result, is the *class unity of the proletariat* itself, which can never be spontaneously created.

As soon as you raise the problem of class alliances in the conditions of an *imperialist* social formation like France, then the internal divisions of the two antagonistic classes, together with the role played by the State in the reproduction of these divisions, become the main aspect of the problem. Lenin and other theoreticians of imperialism already showed something important: that imperialism reproduces the divisions within the proletariat and aggravates them. The proof today would be the existence of enormously important phenomena like the 'national' division between 'French' and 'immigrant' workers (there were nearly four million of these latter, counting their families, in 1974), which in large part redraws the division between skilled and unskilled workers, which becomes tendentially the main basis of the 'industrial reserve army' of capital, and which, without a dogged struggle, may succeed in implanting racism within the working class itself. Another example would be the way in which the 'family' division between men and women operates, a division which is not simply a form of inequality in employment and wages, but an internal division running through the whole working class,

---

which opens the way to the accusation of duplicity, to the accusation constantly made against the Communists that they want to maintain an underhand domination of the working class over its allies, or even the domination of their own party, behind the mask of a freely agreed compromise.

rooted in the bourgeois form of the family, in the role of the domestic labour of women, a form of super-exploited labour which the 'mass consumption' introduced by imperialism has not suppressed but perpetuated. For this mass consumption is a forced consumption of commodities of which the woman is the slave in the home, and the man the slave at work, because of the 'needs' which it creates. Another proof would be the division in the trade unions, which is an enormously important phenomenon of French social history, never really overcome, any more than its political divisions have been overcome (Gaullism constantly exploited these divisions). None of these phenomena, which demand a concrete analysis, can be reduced to simple ideological effects. To the extent that they concern the conditions of the *reproduction of labour power* and the *forms of organization* (whether trade-union or political) of the proletariat, they bring directly into question the function of the State in an imperialist social formation.[14]

Too many Marxists, it seems to me, remain imprisoned in a bourgeois sociological framework with regard to the question of the imperialist State. What holds their attention is exclusively, or almost exclusively, the relation *between the ruling class and 'its' State*. They ask: what are the internal divisions (national, international) within the bourgeoisie? Which fractions of the bourgeoisie 'dominate' or 'control' the State? How does the State guarantee the relative unity of the ruling class or, inversely, how does it run into a 'crisis' when these internal divisions grow deeper? In posing the problem in these terms, they think that they are being faithful to the Marxist argument according to which every State is a class State. In fact, they are distorting and misunderstanding this argument. If the terms of the problem are limited to the State on the one side and the ruling class and its different fractions on the other, the essential term disappears: *the internal relation of the State to the proletariat* (therefore to exploitation, and to the reproduction of the conditions of exploitation) no longer plays any role. But this is precisely the fundamental aspect, the aspect from which one must begin if one is to understand the role of the State and the particular forms of its historical trans-

---

[14] On this point some very useful indications can be found in Suzanne de Brunhoff's book *Etat et Capital*, Paris, Maspero, 1976.

232

formation. The function which the State fulfils in ensuring (or failing to ensure) the unity of the ruling class cannot be understood unless you analyze it on the basis of the relation of this State *to the exploited class*. In other words, the State of the ruling class cannot be understood from the point of view of the ruling class, it can only be understood from the point of view of the exploited class. From this point of view, *the basic function of the State is to hinder the class unity of the proletariat,* a function which is also the basis of its contradictions, both within its purely repressive apparatuses and in its ideological apparatuses. That is why you cannot seize on the contradictions of the ruling class and break up its historical system of class alliances, undermining its mass base, without attacking the existing State, in whatever form the existing relation of forces makes possible. You cannot create the class unity of the proletariat or the unity of all working people around it *within* the existing bourgeois State; you can only create this unity in a battle *against* the existing State, against its historical forms, in a pro-tracted trade-union, political and ideological class struggle.

As soon as you stop thinking about the class unity of the prole-tariat as an already existing or given fact, and class alliances as contracts or compromises, the true, materialist relation between the two problems comes to light. You no longer risk *substituting* one problem (alliances) for the other (class unity), as every reformist type of politics tends to do. History shows that, under these conditions, *neither the one problem nor the other* can be resolved, not to speak of those circumstances in which the illusion of an alliance around a divided working class quite simply *takes its revenge* on this working class by leading to the restoration of an open and even more powerful bourgeois dictatorship.[15] It is only

[15] It is of course not enough to *will* the class unity of the proletariat in order to bring it about. That is why the historical analysis of the internal obstacles which this class unity runs up against (an analysis which must include the critical examina-tion by the revolutionary party of the errors which it was not able to overcome in the past) is indispensable. It was not possible to bring about the class unity of the French proletariat either after the Popular Front (1936), or after the Resistance and Liberation (1945–47), or in 1958, or after May–June 1968 (the greatest workers' general strike in French and even European history!). Thus the masses of the people, instead of continuously playing the decisive role on the political scene and over-turning the political landscape in a revolutionary manner, have remained an inter-mittent supporting force, in spite of their revolutionary power. Thus the class alliances around the proletariat have not been forged, in spite of the 'convergence of struggles' (as in 1968), or have finally broken (as in 1938 and in the 1950s, after the

on the basis outlined above that you can really pose the question of the concrete unity of these two problems, which is at the same time the main theoretical question and the main political question.

These few remarks will, I hope, suffice to show that this question is wide open, and that it cannot be solved simply by being formulated. In any case we have never claimed to be able to offer solutions, even less ready-made recipes; we have only tried to clarify the terms of the discussion.

.

---

anti-fascist unity). Thus the alliances between the political parties of the Left have repeatedly shattered. Thus the French bourgeoisie, though shaken by internal crises which have sometimes appeared to be mortal (from Vichy to the colonial wars, and to the 'construction of Europe'), has always succeeded in reconstituting its unity and once again broadening its mass base. This whole history is still, it seems to me, awaiting a satisfactory explanation.

Index

Aglietta, Michel, 214n
Althusser, Louis, 132, 193–211, 217, 218, 221–2, 225
April Theses (Lenin; in *Pravda*), 126
Argentina, 9
Armed Forces Movement, Portugal, 82
Aron, Raymond, 36, 37n

Balibar, Etienne, 8, 11, 19, 33, 168–74, 175, 177, 178, 179, 180–1, 212–33
Bernstein, Eduard, 127, 178
Besse, Guy, 175–81
Blum, Léon, 89
Britain, 12, 31, 32, 33, 94, 213
British Communist Party, 9, 10, 13, 14
Brunhoff, Suzanne de, 231n
Bukharin, Nikolai, 7

Capital, 133, 141, 221
Cavada, J.-M., 163
CBI, Britain, 94
Chile, 9, 82, 99, 101 & n, 160, 172, 187
China, 99, 111, 161, 194
Chirac, Jacques, 195
CNPF, France, 94
Cold War, 137, 197, 216
Common Market, 172
Common Programme (of French Communist Party), 176, 177, 182, 190, 196, 205, 215–17
Communist League Central Committee (Marx to, 1859), 83
Communist Manifesto, 17, 62, 76, 79, 83, 89, 141, 142, 202, 207, 226
Conference of Communist Parties of Capitalist Europe (1974), 187
Critique of the Gotha Programme (Marx), 62, 141
Cuba, Cuban Revolution, 111, 161, 171, 180, 194

Cunhal, Alvaro, 37n
Czechoslovakia, invasion of, 42, 197

Dialectical and Historical Materialism (Stalin), 54
The Dictatorship of the Proletariat (Kautsky), 13

Economics and Politics in the Era of the Dictatorship of the Proletariat (Lenin), 139
Elleinstein, Jean, 42n, 46n, 112, 131n
Engels, Friedrich, 17, 51, 52, 58, 61, 66, 73, 76, 122, 177, 185

France, French, 12, 31, 72, 85, 115, 213, 226, 227, 230; civil service, 95, 96–8; CNPF, 94; Liberation (1945–7), 82, 232n; Paris Commune, 17, 58, 101, 103, 114, 118, 136; police, 100; Popular Front Government (1936), 82, 116, 179, 192, 232n; Resistance, 116, 232n; Revolution, 127
France-Inter (French radio), Marchais interview on (18.1.76), 165–7
France Nouvelle, 168, 200, 214
Franco, General Francisco, 100, 184, 198
French Communist Party: 21st Congress (1974), 215
French Communist Party: 22nd Congress (1976), 8, 28, 34–6, 38–49, 55–7, 74, 134n, 154, 212–13, 214, 215 & n, 217, 218, 222; extracts from pre-Congress debate and proceedings, 157–92; historical significance of (Althusser), 193–211

French Socialist Party, 166, 215; Tours Congress (1920), 201

French Television, Antenne 2, Marchais interview on (7.1.76), 161–4, 168

French Union of Communist Students: Sorbonne Philosophy Branch debate, Althusser's contribution to, 193–211

Germany, 159; Social Democrats, 92, 142; *see also* West Germany

Giscard d'Estaing, Valéry, 36 &n, 67n, 166, 195

Gottwald, Klement, 37n

Gramsci, Antonio, 20, 133, 220n, 224

Greece, 101, 159, 186

Guy, Christian, 162, 163

Haddad, Georges, 159–60

Hincker, François, 74–5

Hitler, Adolf, 184, 198, 199

L'Humanité, 97, 214; Balibar, 'On the Dictatorship of the proletariat' (22.1.76), 168–74; Besse's reply to Balibar (23.1.76), 175–81; Haddad, 'On the question of the dictatorship of the proletariat' (7.1.76), 159–60; Marchais's Report to 22nd Congress, extract from (5.2.76), 182–92; Marchais, on 'Liberty and socialism' (8.1.76), 161–4; Marchais, on 'Ten Questions, ten answers, to convince the listener' (20.1.76), 165–7

The Impending Catastrophe and How to Combat It (Lenin), 150

Iran, 9

Italy, 8, 12, 99, 159, 172, 213

Japan, 8, 12

Kant, Immanuel, 48

Kautsky, Karl, 13, 14n, 15, 16, 17, 18, 66n, 68, 89, 114, 140, 227

Kievsky, P., 103

Krupskaya-Lenin, Nadezhda, 7

Lecourt, Dominique, 100n

'Left-Wing' Communism – an Infantile Disorder (Lenin), 88, 139, 148

Lenin, V. I., 7, 10–28 *passim*, 30, 33, 43, 44, 51, 52, 53, 55n, 58–63, 64, 65, 66, 68, 70–1, 73, 77, 79, 88–90,

91–2, 95, 98–123 *passim*, 124, 125, 126–34, 135, 138, 139, 140, 142, 143–53, 155, 168, 169, 176, 179, 185, 191, 192, 193, 198, 203, 204, 206, 209–10, 219, 222, 223, 225, 228, 230

Letters from Afar (Lenin), 88

Linhart, Robert, 11, 130n

Luxemburg, Rosa, 114

Marchais, Georges, 34, 35n, 37n, 42, 134n, 161–7, 168, 175, 182–92, 197, 199, 202, 208, 209, 216

Marx, Karl, 7, 9, 17, 23, 25–6, 43, 48–9, 51, 52, 53, 58, 59, 60, 61, 62, 64, 66, 73–4, 76–7, 78, 79, 83, 88, 89, 92, 94, 99, 110, 114, 121, 122, 127, 135, 140, 141–3, 149, 155, 168, 169n, 177, 185, 191, 192, 198, 203, 204, 205, 206, 207, 219, 221, 222, 223, 225, 226

Mitterand, François, 166, 215

Le Monde, 97, 101n

Mussolini, Benito, 184, 198, 199

National Administration School (ENA), France, 97

New Economic Policy (NEP), 119, 131–2, 139, 145

On Co-operation (Lenin), 130

Paris Commune, 17, 58, 101, 103, 114, 118, 136

Plekhanov, G. V., 89, 140

Poniatowski, Michel, 96

Popular Union, France, 216

Popular Unity Alliance, Chile, 82, 101n, 187

Portugal, 8, 9n, 82, 101, 159, 172, 173, 186, 187

Problems on Leninism (Stalin), 130n

The Proletarian Revolution and the Renegade Kautsky (Lenin), 13, 14n, 16, 66

Rochet, Waldeck, 177

Rousseau, Jean-Jacques, 21

Russian Revolution (October 1917), 10, 11, 15, 51, 55n, 56–7, 59, 64, 65, 82, 104–5, 106, 111, 112, 113, 117–18, 125, 126, 129, 148, 186, 194, 225

Saint-Simon, Comte de, 74
Scottish Workers' Council, Glasgow, 106
Second International, 132, 227
Sève, Lucien, 217n, 222n
Sino-Soviet split, 194
Soares, Mario, 187
South Africa, 197
South Korea, 9
Soviet Communist Party: 20th Congress, 180
Soviet Constitution (1936), 49–57, 99
Soviet Union: Civil War, 120, 132; Five Year Plans, 148; New Economic Policy, 119, 131–2, 139, 145; Sino-Soviet split, 194; *see also* Russian Revolution
Spain, 8, 12, 31, 100, 101, 159, 186, 213
The Spiral (film), 101n
Stalin, Joseph, 25–6, 27, 29, 43, 49–55, 56, 57, 99, 108, 130n, 134n, 142, 144, 148, 198, 199, 203, 215, 216, 219
The State and Revolution (Lenin), 7, 18, 103, 104, 125, 132, 168

'The State – Some Problems' (Woddis; in *Marxism Today*), 14–15

Thorez, Maurice, 177
'To the Rural Poor' (Lenin), 66
Tours Congress of the French Socialist Party (1920), 201
Trotsky, Leon, 120

Union of the French People, 160, 163, 176, 181, 199–201
Union of the Left, French, 163, 216

Vandervelde, Emile, 16–17, 73, 74
Vietnam, Vietnamese revolution, 111, 171, 180

West Germany, 9n, 95–6, 109; *see also* Germany
Woddis, Jack, 14–16, 17–18, 19, 20, 21–2
'Workers' and Peasants' Inspections', 120
'Workers' Opposition', 120

Printed in the United States
by Baker & Taylor Publisher Services